"New Atheist polemic has backfired in surprising ways. Far from undermining informed Christian belief, Richard Dawkins and his allies have in fact inspired fresh forms of apologetics. A stream of first-class publications has shown belief in God to be far more coherent than even many believers realize. Lucid as well as exhilarating and wide-ranging, *Coming to Faith Through Dawkins* stands in this line. Highly recommended."

—Rupert Shortt, Von Hügel Institute, University of Cambridge, and author of *God Is No Thing*

"As this fascinating compilation of personal stories shows, Dawkins's strong opposition to Christianity can spur people on to critically examine their deepest beliefs and even to radically change them. Although the writers come to completely different conclusions on the Christian faith from Dawkins, they all agree with him that what you believe really matters, and that robust no-holds-barred intellectual inquiry is the best way to make progress in our thinking. We should be thankful to Richard Dawkins for inspiring this set of interesting thinkers."

—Ard Louis, Professor of Theoretical Physics, University of Oxford

"This is a truly fascinating book. Many people, including nonbelievers like me, have found Dawkins's strident atheism upsetting to the point of offensive. I would never have thought—as *Coming to Faith Through Dawkins* shows in wonderful detail—that, for some, Dawkins's rantings were the spur to Christian faith. One can be forgiven for feeling a strong element of schadenfreude."

—Michael Ruse, Professor of Philosophy Emeritus, University of Guelph, Ontario

"Difficult to put down once started, these essays wrestle with the inadequacies of scientism, growing up with communism, life in a world of rampant secularism, and shallow thinking. They identify illogicality, arrogance, and pseudocertainty in New Atheist thinking, not least in *The God Delusion*. . . . Here is a rich diversity that comes from the humanities, science, drama, and business; from website development, writing, and art; from countries both north and south of the equator. They speak of today's followers of Jesus."

—Sir Brian Heap CBE FRS, formerly Master, St Edmund's College, Cambridge; Vice President and Foreign Secretary, The Royal Society, London; and President, European Academies' Science Advisory Council, Leopoldina Academy of Sciences, Germany

"This is a novel book: real-life stories of people who have actually come to faith, not in spite of but *through* Richard Dawkins. It must be his own worst nightmare!"

—William Lane Craig, Houston Christian University

"An unexpected and wonderful book that I highly recommend. It provides the 'intellectual conversion stories' of twelve people from different walks of life, from scientists to artists. Each of them was at some point in their life driven to atheism, or reassured in it, as they were impressed by the New Atheism of Dawkins, Hitchens, and similar strong atheist proponents. Yet each of them converted to Christianity at a later stage of life, as they became disappointed by the intellectual persuasiveness of New Atheism and conversely discovered that the appeal of the gospel of Jesus was compelling to them. In reading these life stories, I was struck by the honesty and personal and intellectual integrity of these authors, who, each in their own right, did not stick with an apathetic attitude but pursued a search for truth with a willingness to follow the evidence wherever it would lead, a road that—much to their own surprise—led them from atheism to Christian faith. These moving personal stories signal the general disillusionment about New Atheism, which appears to have faded, and at the same time provide a strong testimony for the intellectual and life-changing power of the gospel of Jesus Christ *anno* 2023."

—Dr. Cees Dekker, biophysicist; author of various books on science and religion; Distinguished University Professor at TU Delft, The Netherlands; and Royal Academy Professor of the Royal Netherlands Academy of Arts and Sciences

"These essays recount the intellectual journeys of people who were initially attracted to what was called the New Atheism of authors like Richard Dawkins, but which today might more descriptively be called antitheism. A common thread through each of the essays is a gradual realization that, beyond the antitheists' facile rhetoric, their arguments are shallow and often inconsistent, relying on implausible scientism and knocking down easy straw-man misrepresentations of theism, not the long intellectual tradition of classic Christianity. Even more, though, than by the thoughtful retelling of intellectual journeys, my heart was greatly touched and warmed by the personal and deeply human stories in which they are embedded, showing how the gospel is good news for life as well as mind."

—Ian Hutchinson, Professor of Nuclear Science and Engineering, Massachusetts Institute of Technology, and author of the book *Can a Scientist Believe in Miracles?*

"The New Atheist case against religion has led some to abandon faith, but others, as these spiritual autobiographies illustrate, to discover or recover faith—a faith that respects reason and evidence and that lies between dogmatic fundamentalism and purposeless scientism. Is there a science-respecting faith alternative that makes sense of the universe, gives meaning to life, mandates morality, and offers supportive connections and hope in the face of adversity and death? Read this book and decide."

—David G. Myers, Hope College, and author of *A Friendly Letter to Skeptics and Atheists*

"*Coming to Faith Through Dawkins* contains twelve accounts of people who were forced to acknowledge that reality is much larger than materialism lets on. This group of hardheaded scholars was committed to the New Atheist agenda but realized its woeful inadequacies when they became disconcerted by the larger spiritual reality. They tell of the pivotal role of Jesus Christ in their awakenings. I commend this book to my fellow academics and technocrats as a window beyond the present reductionism that puts us in danger of neglecting that much larger reality, and I encourage my students to read about these scholars who learned to look beyond their preconceptions and be inspired to embrace the Christ who delivers life to the full."

—Bill Peirson, Adjunct Professor and Master at New College, University of New South Wales

COMING TO FAITH

THROUGH DAWKINS

12 ESSAYS ON THE PATHWAY FROM NEW ATHEISM TO CHRISTIANITY

Denis Alexander and Alister McGrath

EDITORS

KREGEL
PUBLICATIONS

Cataloging-in-Publication Data is available from the Library of Congress.

ISBN 978-0-8254-4822-5, print
ISBN 978-0-8254-7123-0, epub
ISBN 978-0-8254-7122-3, Kindle

Printed in the United States of America
23 24 25 26 27 28 29 30 31 32 / 5 4 3 2 1

Contents

CONTENTS

Preface

THE TITLE OF THIS COLLECTION of twelve essays may require some
explanation. Both editors, who have been involved in the academic
field of science and religion for many decades, were somewhat surprised when we started meeting people who told us that their path-
way to Christian faith began with, or was highly influenced by, the
so-called New Atheists. Richard Dawkins was at the top of the list
of those mentioned, but the late Christopher Hitchens also played an
important role.

This unexpected fact made us wonder whether there might be
more people with this kind of story. A little bit of networking and
browsing the web soon gave the answer: there were plenty. The personal narratives gathered here are diverse, written by those coming
from very different backgrounds, from five different countries, but
united in describing how the New Atheists played important roles
in their pathways to committed Christian faith. None of our authors
saw the contributions provided by the other authors until the book's
publication.

We can speak for all twelve of these authors in highlighting the
fact that in no way should this book be seen as presenting any kind
of personal attack on Richard Dawkins. Indeed, it is very much the
opposite. Several authors wish to take the opportunity to thank him

for playing such an important role in their search for truth. And as a popular writer on evolutionary biology, Professor Dawkins has authored books that are outstanding.

Life is full of surprises, and we wonder whether these accounts might act as a stimulus to many others to reflect upon their worldviews and take time to consider where they are leading.

—The editors

The Ambiguity of Richard Dawkins

ALISTER MCGRATH

ON SEPTEMBER 11, 2001, A series of coordinated suicide attacks were launched by Islamic terrorists against targets in the United States—events now invariably referred to simply as 9/11. The Dow Jones index slumped 7 percent when Wall Street reopened for business six days later. The "war against terror" became a dominant theme of the presidency of George W. Bush. Public anxiety about the deadly consequences of religious fanaticism reached new levels. Richard Dawkins had been arguing for years that religion was irrational and dangerous, without making much headway. Suddenly his arguments seemed both attractive and culturally plausible to many in Western culture. Someone or something had to be blamed for 9/11. Islamic religious fanaticism was an obvious possibility. In the white heat of anger against this outrage, *Islamic religious fanaticism* was simplified—first to *religious fanaticism* and then simply to *religion.*

Dawkins played a central role in changing the cultural mood within Western liberal circles. Four days after the attack Dawkins wrote, "To fill a world with religion, or religions of the Abrahamic kind, is like littering the streets with loaded guns. Do not be surprised if they are used."[1] Dawkins's words suggest that the events of 9/11 revealed religion to be dangerous because it is irrational; when it fails to win arguments, it resorts to terror instead. While some regarded these comments as ridiculously simplistic, others saw Dawkins as a bold thinker willing to tell the overdue truth. Religion is dangerous. It is not to be respected but to be feared—and, wherever possible, neutralized. It is a time bomb waiting to explode; a loaded gun, just waiting to kill people. The tragic events of 9/11 turned out to be the intellectual and moral launchpad for what is now generally known as the New Atheism, with Dawkins as its central figure.

It might therefore seem strange to suggest that this same Richard Dawkins, regularly cited as the "world's most famous atheist" during the heyday of the New Atheism, might have caused some to rediscover religious faith and others to embrace it for the first time. So how might Dawkins have helped some find their way to faith? It is a fascinating question, with multiple aspects. While the contributors to this volume each tell their own story, it is helpful to reflect on the context of this development. In what follows, I shall note five elements of the growing disillusionment about the New Atheism that appear to be part of a shifting cultural mood, suspicious of slick certainties, aware of the need to live with a degree of uncertainty, and open to reconsidering religious belief.

First, Dawkins's public attacks on religion, particularly Christianity, seem to have generated a surge of interest in exploring religious faith. As the sociologist Tina Beattie remarked shortly after the publication of Dawkins's *The God Delusion*, it seemed that Dawkins had reawakened public interest in God "more effectively than any preacher could have done."[2] This was certainly my experience. Before 2006, my own public lectures on the relation of science and faith attracted audiences in the low hundreds; for a period of more than five years afterward, the audience size increased dramatically, often forcing lecture organizers to turn people away. The tone of the question-and-answer sessions after those lectures also changed. Before *The God Delusion*, the questions were often academic or technical. What did I think about Albert Einstein's approach to science and religion? Was Dawkins's idea of the "selfish gene" helpful in illuminating the idea of original sin? From 2006 onward, questions became much more personal and existential, as audiences wanted to know how they could hold together science and religious belief.[3] Dissatisfied with what seemed to them Dawkins's simplistic dismissal of faith, they wanted to go deeper. Many of those asking weightier questions were clearly sympathetic toward Dawkins yet were suspicious of his aggressive rhetoric, which they suspected might mask intellectual shallowness and evidential precariousness.

Second, many of Dawkins's critics since the publication of *The God Delusion* have been leading atheist philosophers who were alarmed at the damage they thought his shrill and superficial engagement with life's deepest questions was doing to the intellectual reputation of atheism. The British public philosopher John Gray, for example, ridiculed the banality, superficiality, and shallowness of Dawkins and his circle, who offered a "tedious re-run of a Victorian squabble between science and religion."[4] Philosophically, this amounted to little more than an outdated positivism; culturally, it disingenuously ignored how such forms of "evangelical atheism" spawned violence and brutality (Gray highlights the violence of the French Revolution, the Soviet Union, and Mao's China). "Evangelical atheism is the faith that mass conversion to godlessness can transform the world. This is a fantasy. If the history of the past few centuries is any guide, a godless world would be as prone to savage conflicts as the world has always been."[5]

For Gray, the crude slogans of Dawkins and other New Atheists reduced atheism to a populist "media phenomenon," a "type of entertainment" that conducted its debates through sloganeering rather than serious argument.[6] For most philosophers, Dawkins's arguments lead only to agnosticism, not atheism, leaving Dawkins in the difficult position of being unable to prove his own core beliefs, despite demanding that his religious opponents should prove theirs. Dawkins thus uses intellectual criteria to judge his opponent's positions that he fails to apply to his own position. This epistemic asymmetry has left many potential fellow travelers feeling uneasy, wondering whether Dawkins was overlooking the vulnerability of his own position. Gray, recognizing the importance of this point, suggests that the discussion ought now to move on from a pointless discussion about whether God's existence can be disproved to the more significant exploration of why some people find that they have "no use" for God and are thus moved to search for "God-surrogates."[7]

Third, Dawkins's outlook on religion was deeply shaped by what now appears to have been an uncritical acceptance of the "warfare" model of the relation of science and religion, which dominated Western culture in the closing decade of the twentieth century, despite growing scholarly suspicions of its evidential foundation.[8] On the basis of his belief that there exists a total dichotomy between science and religion, Dawkins argues that a proper scientist simply cannot be religious. If science and religion are at war, then a scientist with religious beliefs is either a traitor or an appeaser.[9] To his critics, Dawkins seems unwilling to reflect critically about his own belief system, apparently believing it to be self-evidently correct—a position often associated with religious fundamentalism. Since the 1990s, however, the historical basis of the "warfare" model has been dismantled within the academic community and shown to be a social construction serving the needs of certain cultural power groups, thus leaving the New Atheists on the wrong side of intellectual history.[10] This point is particularly important, in that some were drawn to Dawkins because they felt his approach represented the future; they are now coming to realize it might instead represent a retreat into the socially constructed "certainties" of a bygone past.

Fourth, the New Atheism's certainties, though initially appealing to many, were soon deconstructed. This point was picked up by Gary Wolf, the journalist who coined the term "New Atheism" in 2006 to designate the messianic atheism of Dawkins and his colleagues Daniel Dennett and Sam Harris and to highlight the rhetorically aggressive means whereby they asserted their beliefs. Wolf was struck by the trenchant certainties of these leading proponents of atheism, noting that many people found these asserted certainties to be arrogant and improbable, amounting to a significant intellectual overreach on their part. "People see a contradiction in its tone of certainty. Contemptuous of the faith of others, its proponents never doubt their own belief. They are fundamentalists."[11]

Fifth, the New Atheism began to show the same habits of thought and behavior that Dawkins had presented as characteristic of religious people and institutions. For P. Z. Myers, a biologist at the University of Minnesota, it was a serious error of judgment to allow Dawkins and Christopher Hitchens to assume a leadership role within the movement. How, he asked, did that happen? Within a year, a "cult of personality" had emerged in which Dawkins and Hitchens were "turned into oracles whose dicta should not be questioned, and dissent would lead to being ostracized."[12] Had atheism, many wondered, morphed into a new religious movement, with its infallible prophets and authoritative texts—above all Dawkins and his *God Delusion*? Perhaps it was no surprise that the movement fragmented into "a shambles of alt-right memes and dishonest hucksters mangling science to promote racism, sexism, and bloody regressive politics."[13]

Today, the New Atheism, of which Dawkins was a leading representative, is generally regarded as having imploded, increasingly (though perhaps unfairly) seen as the crystallization of the cultural prejudices of old, white, Western males. Many of its former members, disenchanted by its arrogance, prejudice, and superficiality, have distanced themselves from the movement and its leaders.[14] The cultural mood began to shift, as many who had initially embraced the New Atheism found that it failed to deliver the secure knowledge they longed for or a sustainable vision of the "good life." The New Atheism may have presented itself as an antidote to religious delusions; its critics argue that it merely propagated a somewhat different delusion about the omnicompetence of reason and science. And, disillusioned by such spurious pseudocertainties, many began to look for better answers, wondering if there were alternatives that might be more credible, attractive, and satisfying. As the extent of Dawkins's personal and intellectual overreach became increasingly clear, some chose to look again at the alternatives.

In their own distinct ways, each of the contributors to this volume is a witness to this process of reconsideration and reevaluation—a process that Dawkins catalyzed, though not in the way he might have wanted. In this introduction, I have outlined a context that may be helpful in understanding each of the narratives of reconsideration and reflection gathered in this volume. But what really matters are these individual stories, which need to be heard and appreciated. We begin with the scientist Sy Garte, who tells the remarkable story of how his emerging Christian faith was invigorated rather than challenged by Dawkins's *God Delusion*.

Chapter 1

A New Christian Meets New Atheism

SY GARTE

Old and New Atheism

ON THE FIRST PAGE OF my recent book, *The Works of His Hands: A Scientist's Journey from Atheism to Faith*,[1] I describe the worldview of my family. My parents were not the least bit religious—they were Marxists, former members of the American Communist Party, and very militant atheists. My own long journey from that beginning to Christian faith is told in the book. The culmination of that journey happened to roughly coincide with the beginning of the New Atheist movement.

If we define atheism as the lack of belief in God, gods, or the supernatural, or even if we define atheism as the positive belief that gods do not and cannot exist, it appears that atheist philosophy is based on one simple, negative statement about reality. If things ended there, there would be little to nothing to discuss. My own original atheism, which was of the stronger version ("no gods exist"), was not something I spent any time thinking about, nor did I see it as an important part of my identity. I am pretty sure that was true for the majority of atheists I knew back then. The only time our atheism ever came up was if someone said something like "Pray with me" or "Do you believe in God?" For me, working in an academic scientific setting, this was a very rare occurrence.

This is probably still true for many nonbelievers today, but times have changed. New Atheism insists on taking atheism out of the closet and loudly proclaiming it to the world as an important and proud vision of reality. The slogan of the London "atheist bus campaign" ("There's probably no God. Now stop worrying and enjoy your life") is one of many examples of this new, in-your-face, public expression of atheism.[2]

The original "Four Horsemen" of New Atheism—Richard Dawkins, Christopher Hitchens, Sam Harris, and Daniel Dennett—made it popular to go far beyond politely declining an invitation to go to someone's church or to pray for a mutual friend. The public is exhorted to confront theists, demand rational evidence for their harmful and foolish nonsense, and proclaim the truth of atheism in the public square by publishing books, giving interviews, writing articles, and producing TV shows, films, videos—getting the word out by any and every method imaginable that gods are not real.

The original four have been joined by scientists like Lawrence Krauss, Jerry Coyne, Sean Carroll, and Peter Atkins; entertainers like Penn Jillette, Bill Maher, and Ricky Gervais; and YouTubers like Aron Ra, Seth Andrews, and a slew of others. There are now atheist conventions, atheist rallies, and many atheist organizations.

At the time when this new aggressive approach to confronting Christianity burst forth on public consciousness (around 2005–08), I was a new Christian, still quite private and quiet about the faith I had come to a year or two earlier.

Some Personal History

Before discussing how the emergence of New Atheism affected my newfound faith, I need to say a bit more about my original version of atheism. My youthful worldview was what would now be called progressive. It was based on three major pillars: science as the most important (but not necessarily the only) proven epistemology, history as the primary method to understand the nature of humanity, and a form of liberal moral ethics that stressed human dignity and equality, the inherent rights of humankind.

The value of science, history, and human dignity in understanding reality has remained the central core of my philosophical and emotional outlook to the present. But as a child, along with the importance of these three pillars, I was also learning atheistic and far-left narratives in each of these areas. I was taught that science had firmly ruled out anything supernatural or magical and that history had illuminated the evildoings of the church and religions in general. The books I was given made it clear that religious belief had been used by rulers and owners as a tool of oppression all over the world. The issue of human dignity and freedom was cast in stark relief by the plight of the American Negro (the term used back then), as well as the historic struggle for a decent life by working people everywhere.

The "facts" I had learned were clearly distorted by political and antireligious bias. When I later read the works of the New Atheists, their similarity to the legends I had absorbed as a youngster was uncanny—they were easily recognizable to me as the falsehoods I had been taught so long ago.

Science and Scientism

My father, a chemist, gave me an excellent introduction to science, especially the fundamental facts of physics and chemistry as well as the basic elements of scientific thinking. He included a dire warning against scientism—the idea that science and science alone can answer all questions. While that might seem odd coming from an atheist, it has been my experience that most scientists (as opposed to atheist fans of science) also reject the notion that the scientific method is the only way to understand anything of importance in our world.

As it happened, it was science, history, and liberal humanism that slowly and inexorably broke down the structural supports of my atheism and then of my agnosticism. The most important battering ram of the three was science. The more I learned about science, both in terms of methodology and the facts that research in many fields was discovering, the more I found my original deterministic and materialistic view weakening. I no longer felt that science buttressed pure atheism—it did not at all rule out the hand of some higher power. When science, a deeper study of history, and my new perspectives on human worth had left me open to hear and follow the Holy Spirit, I was blessed to be brought to a faith in Jesus Christ that was as surprising to me as it was glorious.

But it was also somewhat shaky. I did not know any other scientists who were Christians. I wondered if there were any, or if I was some strange, anomalous beast who would eventually go insane from all the contradictions and cognitive dissonance. It was around this time that the New Atheists burst on the scene. Harris's *The End of Faith*,[3] Dawkins's *The God Delusion*,[4] and Hitchens's *God Is Not Great*[5] were published in quick succession.

The God Delusion, especially, came as a tremendous blow since Richard Dawkins had been a hero of mine for decades. I thought of Dawkins as a brilliant exponent of biological science (I still do), and I was quite gratified when he mentioned me as the discoverer of a letter from Darwin to A. R. Wallace that showed that Darwin was in fact aware of particulate inheritance. Dawkins wrote about this letter in his foreword to a new student edition of *The Descent of Man*,[6] later reprinted as an essay in *A Devil's Chaplain*.[7]

I had found *The Ancestor's Tale*[8] to be a stunning magnum opus and was still deep in admiration of the mind of this man when out of the blue (at least for me) came *The God Delusion*. Later, I read

Alister McGrath and Joanna Collicutt McGrath's brilliant antidote, *The Dawkins Delusion*,[9] which put things right for me.

Of course, *The God Delusion* was not, strictly speaking, that much out of the blue. The very same book that included the discussion of Darwin's letter (*A Devil's Chaplain*) also contained essays full of Dawkins's awakening forceful antitheism. McGrath's response, *Dawkins' God*,[10] a rebuke of the unconvincing components of Dawkins's atheism, preceded *The God Delusion*. What disturbed me was not so much Dawkins's strident defense of atheism, which I had only recently left behind me, but the descent in the tone and content from the brilliance of his previous works to a style that came off the pages as snarling vitriol. It was hard to believe that the same person who had written *The Ancestor's Tale* also wrote *The God Delusion*.

Dawkins and Morality

Reading *The God Delusion*'s section on human morality was especially poignant for me. I started it with some trepidation that the brilliant mind of the writer would have an answer that would rock my still-tender faith, but I found the opposite to be true. It was a welcome surprise: if the most scientifically based book arguing against theism could not provide any better answer to why we see good and evil in the world, then I need not worry about other, potentially less weighty arguments. My faith, in fact, could grow stronger rather than weaker.

Dawkins's view, of course, is that morality (like just about everything else involving life) is simply a result of evolution.[11] He makes the case that humans do good things either as a tit-for-tat, "you scratch my back, I'll scratch yours" kind of bargaining (reciprocal altruism) or because evolution selected for people doing good things for their kin, who carry copies of some portion of their genes (kin altruism).

Dawkins then goes on to postulate what he calls "misfirings" of altruistic genes, by which altruistic behavior originally focused on relations and friends could be extended to all members of the species and even to other species.[12] This, the story goes, is why people are good. And, of course, the explanation for evil is much simpler: humans, like most mammals, do what they must to survive and help their offspring survive, even if it means being mean or cruel to others.

What is interesting about this solution is that, at least for some New Atheists, the morality that evolves this way is *objective*. Sam Harris, who holds to the same view on the evolution of human morality, frequently speaks of "moral facts" that are objectively true. He has claimed that certain practices, like stoning women for adultery or corporal punishment of children, are objectively bad based on the fact that—well, according to him—they *are* morally bad.[13] But millions of people in other cultures do not agree with him, which could make a very strong argument for *subjective* morality.[14]

Harris says that, ironically, he gets lots of agreement from theists, many of whom also hold to a version of objective morality that comes from God and is written in our hearts and in Scripture.[15] Of course, for Harris that is also an illusion, and the inevitable references to slavery and genocide soon follow.

But what really bothered me in Dawkins's explanation was not the question of objective versus subjective morality but the proposed mechanism: evolution. At that time, I had not done any professional research into evolutionary biology other than how it might relate to certain aspects of cancer progression, but I had read widely on evolution, and as a molecular biologist I certainly understood the theory and its fundamental mechanisms. The almost glib assertion that people had of course evolved to be good or bad due to natural selection, much as they had evolved to see colors or to walk upright, did not make a lot of scientific sense to me.

As Patrick Bateson says in his book *Behaviour, Development and Evolution*, "The common image of a genetic blueprint for behaviour fails because it is too static. . . . Strands of DNA do not, on their

22

own, make behaviour patterns or physical attributes."[16] Genes do not code directly for behaviors; they code for proteins. Some of these proteins are neurotransmitters, or they are part of the sensory apparatus or make up signaling pathways in brain cells. Highly complex interactions between many of these proteins can ultimately produce a combined phenotype that includes a new instinctual behavior. If that behavior (like caring for babies or appearing attractive to the opposite sex) results in some survival or reproductive advantage, evolution happens, and the genetic variant that produced the novel allele will spread through the population—but this happens over a long period of time.

And that is the other problem. Human beings are a "baby species," only about 200,000–300,000 years old. Since the dawn of *Homo sapiens*, there have only been a few known genetic variants that led to further evolution, and some of them are still not fixed in the human population (i.e., found in everyone). These include the ability of adults to tolerate dairy products[17] and the ability to consume alcohol without getting sick.[18] Milk tolerance has been slowly (from our human perspective) spreading among people for ten to twenty thousand years, but we all know people who are lactose intolerant, as we call what is in fact the original, or *wild type*, genetic form. Those of us who can tolerate milk as adults are the mutants.

So the question is, If human beings, while they were hunting and gathering, making various increasingly complex implements, and eventually growing food and domesticating animals—in other words, while being human rather than being chimps or other primates—had "evolved" genetic variants for being good to one another, exactly what genes are we talking about? Which proteins make us nice? And which alleles of that protein make us not so nice? How do those different alleles work? And how do they spread among the population to the point where every person on the planet knows (and has known throughout recorded history, at least) that there are good and bad behaviors, even if the definitions of what is good and bad differ with time and place?

Recent omnigenic models, which hold that many complex phenotypes could involve hundreds or thousands of different alleles, each with a tiny effect, raise other problems.[19] For morality to be determined by natural selection, which and how many of the multitudinous individual alleles responsible for an inherited moral genetic trait would need to be under strong selection? And can we really make the case that smiling at your neighbor or offering to carry her load would be under the same degree of genetic selection pressure as color vision, enjoying the taste of sugar, being attracted to healthy-appearing members of the opposite sex, or even being aggressive and selfish enough to grab the most desirable part of the hunt for one's own consumption?

Furthermore, enough studies have been done on a variety of behavioral traits to show that the genetic component of such phenotypes is roughly between 30 and 50 percent,[20] with cultural and other nongenetic sources making up most of the contribution to how people behave. Moral behavior is clearly among those.

Dawkins's purely evolutionary explanation simply does not fit with our scientific understanding of how biological evolution works. What we see here instead is another kind of evolution, namely, *cultural evolution*, a field in which Dawkins clearly took a strong interest when he coined the term *meme* to mean the cultural equivalent of a gene.[21] Memes include ideas, beliefs, moral codes, styles—all varieties of human thought. It is a brilliant concept but entirely different from biological evolution. New cultural memes about good and evil do spring up all the time, spread very quickly, and can become fixed in a population for some time, until a new meme is born and disseminated. But memes only behave like genes in a superficial sense; the mechanisms behind meme and gene activity and evolution are entirely different.

Here is why. Genes are specific sequences of nucleotides in DNA that are transcribed into a stretch of RNA, which is then translated by a system comprised of transfer RNA, several enzymes, and a machine called a ribosome to make proteins of a very specific amino acid sequence and structure to convey a very specific and highly functional catalytic activity on the protein to allow it to perform one of the thousands of essential chemical reactions that keep cells alive. Memes are . . . basically thoughts. The depths of reasons why these two things are so utterly different is impossible to fully illustrate here, but hopefully the point is made.

Dawkins and the Anthropic Principle

My skepticism about Dawkins's facile and ad hoc explanation for the scientific basis of human morality led me to wonder whether the book contained other dubious scientific statements. I found that indeed it did.

Perhaps the most difficult problem in biology that is also of major theological importance is the origin of life.[22] Dawkins begins his discussion of abiogenesis with an introduction to the anthropic principle—the argument that it is pointless to wonder about how it happened, against great odds, that our planet (or universe) is friendly to life; if it were not, we would not be here to wonder about it.[23] He invokes the anthropic principle as the alternative to theism, or design, for both the origin of life and the fine-tuning of cosmological constants, and he expresses surprise that theists do not see it that way. I must admit I am one of those theists—I do not think the anthropic principle is in any way relevant to the existence of God.

When I read *The God Delusion*, I already understood that the earth was very special, and Dawkins helpfully lays out some of the unusual properties of our home planet that make it fit for life to start and prosper. Among other things, he mentions our location within the temperature zone for liquid water, the nearly circular orbit that ensures a stable climate, and the presence of Jupiter, whose gravitational pull protects us from asteroids. He also admits that the origin of life was an extremely improbable event (one in a billion, he proposes for the sake of argument), but he stresses that it only had to happen once.[24]

He then reminds us that the number of planets in the universe is about a billion billion;[25] therefore, a probability of one in a billion would in fact guarantee life on a billion planets. His conclusion is that, given the large number of planets, the probability of life arising from chemistry is essentially certain; and, again, the anthropic principle tells us why it happened on ours: we are here because our planet was one of the life-friendly ones. Similarly, at the cosmological level, we are observing that every physical constant of our universe is exactly what it needs to be (within a very narrow range) to allow stars and planets to form, thus making life possible—because if they were not, we would not be here to observe anything.

But it seemed to me that the anthropic principle does not actually address either abiogenesis or cosmology at all. It simply states that we are sure to observe anything about our universe that allows us to be here to observe it. But that truism says nothing about why the universe has the constants it has—unless it is one of an enormous number of universes, all with different values of the constants. The extremely rare event of a universe getting just the right values of constants is only likely to occur at least once if there are billions and billions of other universes that are quite different. If this is the only universe, then the probability of its occurrence, despite the value of it for human beings, is effectively zero.[26] Indeed, the "strong" version of the anthropic principle, as defined in the book *The Anthropic Cosmological Principle* by John Barrow and Frank Tipler, says that "the Universe must have those properties which allow life to develop within it at some stage in its history."[27] The word *must* suggests that there is a natural law that requires observers such as humans to exist.

This is not at all what Dawkins means by the anthropic principle, since it raises the question, Why must it, if not because the universe was specifically created to allow for human beings?

When it came to the origin of life on our planet, I found the statistical argument somewhat stronger, since it is known that the number of planets is huge, while the number that could support life is unknown but likely greater than one. But, again, I was surprised that Dawkins the biologist includes none of the chemical and biochemical difficulties that are known to exist when trying to understand the emergence of biology from chemistry. There is not enough space to list these here, but the origin of life clearly remains a shrouded mystery, outside the purview of what we know about biological evolution, as Darwin himself makes clear in *On the Origin of Species*.[28]

All in all, the scientific arguments in *The God Delusion* left me more convinced that my recent embrace of Christianity was not in any way threatened by maintaining my lifelong scientific worldview. Dawkins—and certainly Harris and Dennett—did not have anything to say that would lead me to stumble in my faith in Christ on scientific grounds. This discovery came as a great relief and resulted in a buttressing of my faith that has remained with me ever since.

Historical Distortions

As good Marxists, my parents instilled in me a love and deep understanding of historical thinking. Learning how to read and interpret historical works and how to think about their meaning in contemporary terms was an important part of my childhood.

From my reading of communist and left-wing sources (such as books by American communist Howard Fast), I had learned truths that had been deliberately covered up or distorted by the American public educational system of the 1950s and 1960s. These included ugly facts about slavery and the Reconstruction period in the post–Civil War South. Even in the comparatively liberal New York City public school system, we had textbooks telling us that many slave owners were good to their slaves, who were happy and better off than they would have been on their own, and that after the Civil War, the Northerners who went south to help the newly freed slaves (the "carpetbaggers") were evil troublemakers and opportunists rather than an early version of civil rights workers. After reading *Freedom Road*[29] (by Fast) and other "subversive" literature, I came to understand that what we learn about history is quite dependent on who is writing it.

It was not long before I began applying the same skepticism to the communist versions of historical truth I had been taught. I learned about Soviet crimes against humanity—Stalin's reign of terror, the Katyn massacre, the crushing of the Hungarian Uprising—and as I got older, I realized they could not *all* be Western propaganda. The watershed moment came when, as a college student in 1968, I heard my mother obediently defending the Soviet invasion of Czechoslovakia. I understood then that historical distortion was a critical aspect of communist doctrine and always had been.

There was another distortion of history that I was blissfully unaware of as a young man. What I had learned about the history of Christianity, from its origins to its influence in Europe and elsewhere, was entirely negative. It was another couple of decades before I found out that, just like the glories of communism, many accounts of the horrors of Christianity not only had been exaggerated but were in fact simply untrue. I began looking into this history while I was still an agnostic, thinking about religion in general and wondering about how new movements like Christianity came to exist.

Modern History and Dawkins

While Dawkins does not delve into Christian history much in *The God Delusion*, one section caused me to raise my eyebrows. Among my historical interests, the Second World War has long been a favorite. Reading Dawkins's discussion of Stalin and Hitler raised alarm bells. As a young man, I had read *The Morning of the Magicians*,[30] which includes an account of Hitler's occult interests. British historian Nicholas Goodrick-Clarke's 1985 book *The Occult Roots of Nazism*[31] provides an in-depth study of the same. Yet the fact that Hitler, along with his close friend and mentor Alfred Rosenberg, were obsessed with Nordic polytheism, esoteric "border science," astrology, mythical supermen, and the like is entirely missing from Dawkins's narrative. While the text does include hints that Hitler's supposed Christianity was a front to avoid public and church disapproval, there is no mention of his true "religious" beliefs.

Even worse than this omission is the discussion about Stalin, who Dawkins admits was indeed an atheist. But he then argues that Stalin's crimes were not committed in the name of atheism. This may be true in the sense that there are always complex power struggles and political calculations behind any targeting of specific groups for persecution and genocide. (For the same reason, of course, antitheist claims that Christianity or religion in general is to be blamed for most wars, slavery, and all the evil in the world are historically flawed.) From my own background and early training, though, I knew that Stalin and many of his communist followers did in fact hate religion, and especially Christianity, passionately.

While the Soviet state never outright outlawed religion but, rather, alternated between degrees of actively suppressing and infiltrating or controlling religious institutions according to political interests and pragmatic considerations, its official worldview, taught in schools and upheld in all areas of culture, was scientific atheism. It is therefore hard to separate the slaughter of thousands of Russian Orthodox priests, the closure of countless churches, and the harassment of worshippers throughout the Soviet Empire from the idea of atheism. Catholic priests and nuns were routinely murdered as "enemies of the people" by the Stalinist faction of the Republican alliance during the Spanish Civil War. Stalin vowed to destroy religion, and if it were possible to do so, he would have succeeded. After World War II, the same policy was carried out to varying degrees in Eastern Europe, where being religious was a major expression of rebellion against Soviet tyranny for many decades.

In general, the New Atheist overviews of historical trends and perspectives rang a familiar bell from my Stalinist upbringing. They smacked of a great deal of hyperbole, exaggeration, and possible distortion. I decided to investigate some of these historical arguments. I already knew that the pre-Christian tribes of Europe—the Saxons, Danes, Visigoths, and others—were not merciful, compassionate devotees of reason and high moral standing. Whether their eventual conversions to Christ made them better people could be debated, but there is no evidence that it made them worse.

New Atheist Version of European History

When I began reading discussions of earlier European history in Sam Harris's book *The End of Faith* and in *God Is Not Great* by Christopher Hitchens, I quickly realized that I needed to go back to more neutral sources to check their accuracy. What I found completely confirmed my suspicions that the New Atheists were not giving an accurate account of what happened in the past.

Fortunately, I had a set of Will and Ariel Durant's classic multivolume work *The Story of Civilization*.[32] While the Durants were not Christians, they were actual historians. I remember that when I first read their volume on *The Age of Faith*[33] (covering the Middle Ages) in my strong atheist twenties, I was taken aback and annoyed at sections of the book that seemed to extol the more positive aspects of the Christian domination of Europe. While I did not doubt that the church had indeed done a few good things (like starting universities and hospitals, or encouraging art and scholarship), at the time I did not pay much attention to this part of the book since I had already learned the "terrible truth" about the evils of Christianity (the Crusades, the Inquisition, the religious wars) from my Soviet-published sources.

As I looked back now, it was clear that the Durants's treatment of the role of Christianity in European history differed considerably from the New Atheists' interpretations. These atheists were telling me that the majority of wars and human death and suffering could be attributed to the Christian religion, and that freedom of thought, liberal ideology, and the application of reason and logic were the sworn enemies of popes and priests. "The history of Christianity is principally a story of mankind's misery and ignorance rather than of its requited love of God," writes Sam Harris.[34] While there is no question that mankind has endured centuries of misery and ignorance, blaming Christianity for all of it looked like historical nonsense to me.

In the same vein, Dawkins writes in *The God Delusion* that "religious wars really are fought in the name of religion, and they have been horribly frequent in history."[35] He contrasts this with his "proof" that atheism cannot lead to war since "why would anyone go to war for the sake of an absence of belief?"[36] Of course, he is technically correct in that atheism per se has not led to any major wars, but, as we saw above, that completely sidesteps the fact that atheistic regimes have indulged in a great deal of murderous escapades, including warfare.

As I reread my trusted sources, it did not take long for me to put to rest the claim that religion (including but not limited to Christianity) was the source of most of the casualties from war and other forms of mass oppression in world history. There have indeed been religious wars, blood spilled between rival Christian groups and between different religions, but the fact is that about ten times more deaths have been caused by nonreligious warfare. I discuss the details in my first book of how Christianity might be said to account for roughly

5 percent of human death from war and related strife, but the main takeaway is that people fight wars, and religion is a minor reason for actual violence.

Part of the conclusion I eventually came to was that, contrary to what I was hearing from the adherents of New Atheism, Christianity has been a major force for peace in the world. This was especially true during those terrible years in Europe when warlords filled the governance gap left by the collapse of the Roman order with centuries of constant terror and destruction. During that truly dark period, it was the church, the monasteries, the clergy, and the faithful who provided the only havens of peace, security, learning, and eventually scholarship in a hostile and violent world. As the warlords slowly morphed into a Europe-wide extended family of avaricious kings and landowning aristocracy, the church was (initially, at least) a respite for people oppressed in every possible way.

Christianity and Science According to the New Atheists

Another common claim made against the church is that it has been the unrelenting and all-powerful historical enemy of science and reason, while heroic rebels like Galileo risked their lives to bring the light of truth to a population struggling under the weight of superstition and ignorance. I had absorbed much of this kind of historical propaganda in childhood. English translations of Soviet children's books had filled my young mind with the wondrous achievements of Stalin's support for science that brought the benefits of technology to the common people. But with time, and after learning about Comrade Stalin's own blood-stained history, I could see at least some of the distortions in these accounts. Looking into the actual historical record allowed me to assess the myths about Christianity's anti-science horrors in the same way.

I learned from Ted Davis's columns on the BioLogos website that the Galileo affair was far more complicated than the popular version has it.[37] The church was divided on the issue, with many powerful clerics taking the side of Galileo and heliocentrism. The 2010 book *Galileo Goes to Jail and Other Myths about Science and Religion* by Ronald Numbers dispels the myths that Galileo was tortured and imprisoned and that Giordano Bruno was killed for his scientific beliefs.[38]

Historicity of Early Christianity

I knew next to nothing about the history of the first century AD in the Roman province of Palestine, but most of what I read about it from New Atheists and their followers rang hollow to my historically trained mind. I found the idea that Jesus Christ never existed absurd even before looking into all the evidence, because when I read the Gospels, they struck me as reports of actual events. The resurrection, of course, seemed like a mystery, but there was one historical fact that could not be denied and needed an explanation: the explosive growth of Christianity in the years before, during, and after the Jewish War and the fall of Jerusalem. I wondered about all those churches that Paul wrote to and visited in the 50s and 60s, only a few decades after Jesus's death. How did they come to be established so quickly in so many parts of the empire if something quite extraordinary had not taken place? The New Atheist explanations I have seen, ranging from the idea that Paul made it all up to Peter somehow spreading his own hopeful hallucinations to every place around the known world, have always struck me as historically untenable. Later, after reading books by Gary Habermas and Mike Licona, Lee Strobel, and others,[39] I came to judge the New Atheists' historical arguments against the scriptural version of the origin of Christianity so weak as to be useless. As a new Christian, I found I could embrace the resurrection of Jesus without any hesitation. And, of course, if Jesus truly rose from the dead, there is not much else to discuss.

In summary, I did not find a convincing historical argument against belief in Christ or in support of the warfare model of the science-faith relationship in any of the writings of current or earlier atheists. As with the New Atheists' arguments from science, this resulted in a further strengthening of my new faith in God.

Human Dignity: Civil Rights and Justice

At the summer camp I attended as a child, we sang songs like "Swing Low, Sweet Chariot," "This Little Light of Mine," "We Shall Overcome," and "Go Tell It on the Mountain." It might be surprising that such overtly Christian songs were sung at a "commie camp," but there *was* an explanation that we learned for why most of the Negro spirituals we were taught included references to God or Jesus. Black people had been so oppressed, we were told, that they got fooled into becoming Christians, and some of them just did not know any better and were not ready to give it up, at least for now. The blatant underlying racism of this notion was not discussed at the time.

During my childhood and adolescence, I found the contradiction between being in favor of civil rights (good) and being a Christian (bad) troubling. I was confused, but I never accepted the explanation of Black people being easily fooled and just too ignorant to understand the truth of atheism. I had no answer for this dilemma.

I later found that Christopher Hitchens had come up with his own view that civil rights leaders like Martin Luther King Jr. were "nominal" rather than "real Christians."[40] I was struck by the absurdity of this answer to what is clearly a perplexing question for atheists. Hitchens apparently was as stumped as I had been.

I have always considered myself to be a humanist, in the strict sense of the word: I am in favor of human beings, and I think they are great. A true humanist, the way I understand it, is someone who believes that human beings are truly special, and that tribalism, nationalism, racism, and so on are morally wrong. I have always held such an understanding of humanism to be true—what changed when

I became a Christian was my awareness of the source of such feelings and convictions.

It turns out that while union strikes and picket lines for racial and economic justice incorporate these values, their source is not Karl Marx, Lenin, or any other communist ideologue but (as I was surprised to find out) none other than Jesus Christ. It was not the Greek philosophers who declared there is no difference between Greek or Jew, slave or free, male or female: it was Saint Paul. It was not the senate of the Roman Empire that declared that love between all people was the central commandment; it was Jesus Christ. And it was not because the Black preachers and ministers who began, sustained, and carried through the American Civil Rights Movement were, you know, not that bright, that they sang songs about God and were fervent Christians. It was because Christianity turned out to be the best way to live and breathe those ideals I had learned as a child.

Human Spirituality

Is there a spiritual dimension of reality in people? Some time ago, you could be an atheist and answer yes. But the New Atheists not only deny the existence of God—they also deny that there is anything spiritual in human existence. Along with their attacks on religion, militant New Atheist philosophers have embraced an extreme form of materialism. In his book *Consciousness Explained*, Daniel Dennett proposes that human consciousness itself is basically a myth.[41] According to him and his colleagues in the New Atheist movement, we are deceived by the neural networks of our brains, which evolved for other purposes, into thinking we are conscious beings with a clearly felt sense of self, when in fact we are not. The concept of free will has also come under attack; Harris even wrote a book about it.[42]

I would never have agreed with the view that human consciousness and free will are an illusion even when I was still an atheist. I find this view scientifically untenable. Dennett's approach reminds me of the early behaviorists, who decided to ignore higher mental talents and insights to the point of denying that they were worth studying. Denying the existence of a phenomenon because it does not seem amenable to current scientific analysis is the height of folly for true science.

Along with spirituality, human consciousness, and any sense of higher purpose, some people would throw out—in the name of "science"—the reality of *anything* that makes human beings special. According to this view, we are not at all much different from other animals, who can do almost everything we can do (some of it better). And, after all, our planet is a tiny, insignificant speck in a remote region of a ho-hum galaxy, making us humans small and insignificant as well. I could never quite follow that logic, but the idea that humans are not that special is one of those insane myths that sometimes sweep through a culture, against all obvious evidence and logic. Love, humor, art, music, science, creativity, spirituality, and other uniquely human attributes are denigrated as being "merely" artifacts of natural selection. I fail to understand why the fact that we evolved should be used as an argument against the idea that our transcendent qualities have real importance.

Antitheism

An important feature of New Atheism is that it goes beyond disbelief in gods to an all-out attack on religion as a useless or even evil force in human society. When Sam Harris writes in *The End of Faith*, "Religion, being the mere maintenance of dogma, is one area of discourse that does not admit of progress,"[43] he calls for a movement of resistance and a more aggressive stance against religion. The followers of New Atheism, rather than considering the value of this absurd view of religion, joined the "holy war" against the concept of *the holy*.

When I revealed on social media that I was a working scientist of strong Christian faith, I was called a fool, a liar, a fraud, and much worse. The sheer rage and uncontrolled hatred that my existence as a scientist of Christian faith provoked among the online followers of this new God-free moral philosophy is illustrated by the following recent example of a reply tweeted to me:

> [profanity] You diluted [profanity]. Your ignorance is only magnified by your beliefs in a feckless god. You and your ilk make me sick. I hate you. [more profanity]

I answered the woman who wrote this by telling her that I did not feel in the least bit diluted but in fact had come to feel quite concentrated in my love of Christ. I wonder how many Christians she convinced to give up their ignorant beliefs and join her in the thoughtful, well-reasoned, and morally upright practices of her version of the New Atheism.

When, after becoming a Christian, I learned that it was not necessary for me to immediately denounce evolution as a plot of the devil or reject any part of my long-held scientific worldview, I was quite relieved. But I also came to understand that, due to my acceptance of evolution, I was considered by both atheists and some Christians to be a "moderate Christian." I thought that being in that camp would allow me to be able to dialog effectively with more conservative, fundamentalist Christians as well as with atheist scientists, since I shared so many viewpoints with each group. I even made a comment or two on Jerry Coyne's blog, *Why Evolution Is True*.

How naive I was! One of Coyne's followers let me know that "moderate Christians," including those who accept evolution, are actually the worst kind of enemy, for while they have learned "the truth," they continue to indulge and support the great lie of theism. It turned out that this attitude was a common New Atheist trope, and that making common cause to promote good scientific education was harder than I thought. Never mind the powerful contribution that

Catholic Ken Miller made to the outcome of the Dover trial;[44] forget the fact that a Christian named Francis Collins was soon to become director of the National Institutes of Health, the US's medical research agency. In fact, Harris and others wrote scathing editorials against President Obama's choice of Collins.[45] No, it was clear that for many New Atheists, no quarter could be given to Christians who actually agreed with the scientific points the atheists were supposedly championing.

Harris writes in *The End of Faith* that "religious moderates are, in large part, responsible for the religious conflict in our world, because their beliefs provide the context in which scriptural literalism and religious violence can never be adequately opposed,"[46] whatever that means. He sees nothing good in any Christian, at any time in history. While he admits that Luther stood up to the established church, he then reminds us that he became a bigot and a supporter of tyranny. Even Saint Francis of Assisi is attacked: Harris quotes Bertrand Russell, who writes that the net result of the saint's life, through the Franciscan order he founded, was "to facilitate the persecution of all who excelled in moral earnestness or freedom of thought."[47] It appears that some New Atheists hate religion more than they love science and reason.

New Atheist Claims

The arguments of the New Atheists utterly failed to weaken my new-found Christian faith since I found nothing in any of them either convincing or even very coherent. I rejected the claims that religion exists to explain the natural world and that methodological naturalism is the one and only valid epistemology. Arguments against the existence of free will, human consciousness, and human exceptionalism made no sense to me, even when I was an atheist, and looked even less rational now that I was a Christian. I found the scientific backing for such arguments weak, as I did the idea that evolution can be used to explain all human characteristics. I knew that the claim of the immense historical evil of Christianity and religion in general was simply false.

I found the application of strict reductionism to deny the reality of purpose or meaning in the universe or in human lives not only terribly gloomy but contrary to ordinary experience and a throwback to long-discredited philosophical viewpoints. I also saw many fallacies and much confusion about what science is and is not; for example, claims that the resurrection is scientifically impossible since people do not rise from the dead ignore that Jesus was not simply a "person" and that his resurrection was a miracle, which by definition is outside of common experience or current scientific investigation. Some New Atheist claims were contradictory in an almost entertaining way, such as the notion that religion is dogmatic and rigid, unlike science (ask any scientist if there is any dogma in their field!), and the similarly common complaint about the large number of denominations disagreeing with each other and all claiming to be the "true" one. Clearly, a dogmatically unchanging Christianity cannot also continually undergo fracture into many sects.

Of course, not all New Atheists hold the same views on everything. There are political and social rifts within the "organized" atheist movement that have resulted in bitter feuds and disputes, including the cancellation of atheist conferences, hostility between prominent atheists, and a dawning suspicion that atheists may have little in common to talk about other than the stupidity of believers—a topic that can eventually get old.

I would argue that attempts to forge a philosophical consensus of what kind of ideas should replace belief in God have so far failed. Science is not a philosophical position but a method to find natural truths. One can use this method (originally formulated by people who were believers) no matter what one's religious or philosophical beliefs are, which is why, as Elaine Ecklund so clearly describes in her book

Science vs. Religion: What Scientists Really Think, scientists (including many Nobel Prize laureates) are not all atheists but are also Christians, Muslims, Jews, Hindus, and more.[48] And most Christians accept evolution and mainstream science.[49] Atheists cannot claim science as their specific and exclusive domain of knowledge or worldview.

The same goes for liberal political activity and social justice. Yes, some Christians endorsed slavery at one time, but both the abolitionist and civil rights movements were led by Christians. When it comes to the social and political issues of the present, Christians and atheists alike can be found on the conservative as well as the progressive side.

Conclusion

If it makes no sense to conflate atheism with science or with social justice, what should be the positive content of modern atheistic philosophy? If all that is left is the original core belief that there are no gods, there is not much to have a movement about. If atheists are unable to come up with some sort of positive message (other than "stop worrying"), it could spell the eventual demise of the New Atheist movement. I predict that within a few years, someone will coin a new phrase: "New Atheism is dead; God, not so much."

Reading the original books of the New Atheists and engaging with other New Atheist content since the movement's origins fifteen years ago has not changed what I believe, but it does make me feel that if I had not already crossed the threshold to belief in Jesus Christ, I would have done so in response to the empty rhetoric, poor science, mythological history, and wrongheaded view of human worth and spirituality that they espouse. As it was, since I had already embraced the faith, the New Atheist onslaught strengthened and confirmed all the reasons I had rejected a hopeless, barren, atheistic worldview and came to walk in the light of my Savior.

Chapter 2

Wrestling with Life's Biggest Questions

SARAH IRVING-STONEBRAKER

HOW DOES A HISTORIAN, WHO defined herself as an atheist and for whom questions of reliable evidence are the touchstone of her profession, come to faith in Jesus Christ? My story unsettles a number of popular but misguided assumptions about people who convert from atheism to Christianity, not least because I came to faith at a high point of my life when, far from needing a "crutch," I had everything I'd always wanted. Moreover, far from being led blind into faith, my conversion to Christianity emerged from an explicit engagement with atheist philosophy.

I am a historian of ideas, with a particular focus on the British colonial world, as well as the intersection of the histories of science, empire, and Christianity. In my midtwenties, as I began my academic career at the universities of Cambridge and Oxford, I embarked upon a serious quest to understand whether the atheism to which I had always subscribed was true. I was also compelled to investigate whether my atheism could sustain my ethical beliefs, not least my conviction of the innate equality of all human beings. This involved exploring the work of the self-styled New Atheists, including Richard Dawkins, as well as the philosophy of Peter Singer, whose utilitarian ethics are founded on his atheism. There were three chief issues that engaged me: first, the foundational role of Christianity in the origins of modern science; second, the issue of human value; and finally, the question of whether life has any ultimate meaning. These are by no means small subjects, and I do not pretend to be able to cover them comprehensively in what follows. Rather, my intention is to give you a vignette—a window of entry, as it were—into how an atheist historian, grappling with some of the most profound questions in life, realized that the God revealed in the Bible is real, that he loves us, and that Jesus Christ is his Son who died for you and for me so that we may have a relationship with God.

I grew up in Sydney, Australia, in a loving, non-Christian home, with parents who loved each other and their children dearly. My family took seriously the engagement with truth and ideas; my father was a renowned scholar of Australian labor history and professor of government at the University of Sydney. Family mealtimes were often a forum for discussing history, politics, and issues of social justice. The rhythms of university life punctuated my childhood; my brother and I loved spending some of the summer school holidays going on the train to "the Uni" with our father. We researched school projects at the university's Fisher Library and had the privilege of feeling grown up when our father took us for lunches at the student union. The Victorian Gothic sandstone quadrangle of the University of Sydney symbolized the world of learning and ideas. To me, the world was a wondrous and complex place, and the human mind must grapple with our existence in all its fraught complexity. My parents always encouraged me to learn and to pursue the truth.

When I was eight, my family traveled to England and to America while my father took up sabbatical appointments, including at the

University of Texas at Austin. While we were in England, we spent time at Darwin College, Cambridge. The trip was formative; I saw the remains of medieval castles and towns old enough to be in the Domesday Book of William the Conqueror. From that moment, the past captured my imagination. Just before my ninth birthday, I decided that when I grew up, I wanted to study history at Cambridge. This ambition gave me a very firm sense of who I was and what my life was all about. I knew it would take considerable drive to get from Australia to study at Cambridge. This no doubt helped shape the appeal of atheism, which I first began to explore as a teenager. I believed that I did not need a god to tell me who I was or how to make sense of the world. I knew what my life was all about. Surely Christianity was just a crutch. I didn't need it.

Christianity and the Origins of Modern Science

Bright, curious, and driven, I received a world-class education, nourished by loving parents, great schooling, and the world's galleries, museums, and libraries. My ambition to study at Cambridge motivated me to study hard. I took multiple prizes as an undergraduate at the University of Sydney and finished with the University Medal and a Commonwealth Scholarship to undertake my doctorate in history at the University of Cambridge. My childhood dream was coming true. I arrived at the University of Cambridge, as a student at King's College, just before my twenty-third birthday. Years earlier, as tourists from the other side of the world, my brother and I had posed for a photograph in front of Bodley's Court, a stately stone building on the River Cam. Directly behind us in the photo was the room that, almost fifteen years later, would become my bedroom.

I began work on my doctoral dissertation on the relationship between seventeenth-century natural philosophy and the origins of the British Empire. This involved studying the work of some of the founders of what we now call modern science, including Robert Boyle, one of the forefathers of modern chemistry; Robert Hooke, who did pioneering work on the microscope; and their colleagues who developed the experimental method. Reading the work of these natural philosophers, however, began to unsettle an assumption I had about Christianity. I believed that Christianity and science were fundamentally in conflict. As I was reading the work of Robert Boyle, however, it became obvious to me that such a statement would have made no sense to Boyle. To my bemusement, Boyle seemed preoccupied with questions of Christian faith and reason. I was struck by his attitude toward studying nature. He believed he was engaging in a study of God's creation, understanding the complexity and order endowed to it by God. In a work that delved into the question of whether natural objects have "final causes," or purposes, Boyle quotes Psalm 8 and then proceeds to explore its significance for his systematic study of nature: "Thou has made him, a little lower than the Angels, and hast crown'd him with Glory and Honour. Thou mad'st him to have dominion over the works of thine hands, and hast put all things under his Feet."[1]

But what did this vision of man as created in God's image, crowned with glory and having a position of authority over the rest of the creation, have to do with the study of nature? Boyle was very interested in the question of why mankind ought to study the natural world, and it was a topic he discusses in multiple works: "[God] makes most of the Creatures of the world visible to us, pay homage to him [man], and in some manner or degree do him service: God's liberality at once bestowing on him all those Creatures by endowing him with a Reason enabling him to make use of them; so that even those Creatures which he is not able to subdue by his Power, he is able to make serviceable to him by his Knowledge."[2]

For Boyle, it was the natural philosopher's task to study nature in order to reap its fruitfulness and to fulfill God's ordinance that humanity take responsibility for the creation, to make it useful to improve the conditions of human life. At first I dismissed Boyle's frequent references to the Bible and to figures like Adam and Eve as intellectual window dressing. But it became increasingly obvious that Boyle's entire epistemology—that is, his understanding of knowledge, its character, methodologies, and purposes—was shaped by his Christian faith. One of Boyle's chief interests was how to develop a method of establishing reliable and verifiable knowledge about the natural world. How do we minimize the error that arises from human fallibility? Can we rely upon our senses to gain knowledge of nature, and if we can, to what extent and under what conditions?

These were questions that also concerned Boyle's colleague and laboratory assistant Robert Hooke. Hooke's work *Micrographia* (1665) is one of the most important pioneering works on the microscope and the methodology of experiment to which instruments like the microscope are central. In his introduction, Hooke turns straight to the Bible. He believes that, in the garden of Eden, before Adam and Even rebelled against God in an episode known as the "fall" from grace, these two original humans possessed perfect senses and a perfect knowledge of nature. This interpretation of Genesis was commonplace among Protestants in the seventeenth century. Adam's ability to give names to all the creatures, described in Genesis 2, reveals his state of perfect knowledge of and authority over the creation. Through the fall, however, when Adam and Eve rebelled against God, disobeying his command, not only did they lose their dominion over the creation, but their once-perfect senses were damaged by the effects of sin. Our vision, for example, is now merely a poor reckoning of the perfect sight Adam and Eve had before they turned away from God. In fact, precisely this idea is the driving force behind the creation of scientific instruments. Here is an excerpt from Hooke's introduction: "By the addition of such artificial Instruments and methods, there may be, in some manner, a reparation made for the mischiefs, and imperfection, mankind has drawn upon itself . . . resulting from a corruption, innate and born with him."[3]

The epistemology and methodology of the experiment, it turned out, were in fact made possible by a Christian view of knowledge. The historian Peter Harrison has shown this in great depth. It was actually a *distrust* of human sensory and cognitive capabilities—rooted in the idea of original sin—that was vital for the foundation of the modern scientific experimental method. In fact, according to Harrison, the experimental method "arose out of a renewed awareness that the attainment of knowledge was not a natural, easy process, but rather one that called for the imposition of external constraints: rigorous testing of knowledge claims, repeated experiments, communal witnessing, the gradual accumulation of 'histories,' the use of artificial instruments to amplify the dim powers of the senses, and the corporate rather than individual production of knowledge."[4]

Reading Boyle and Hooke unsettled me. As an atheist, I had assumed that science and religion were incompatible. Indeed, this was an idea I had absorbed from reading Richard Dawkins, who had assumed the incompatibility of science with religion because, to his mind, both are effectively attempting to understand the world but with opposing methods and presuppositions: "It is a tedious cliché (and, unlike many clichés, it isn't even true) that science concerns itself with *how* questions, but only theology is equipped to answer *why* questions." He continues later that "if science cannot answer some ultimate question, what makes anybody think that religion can?"[5] In Dawkins's eyes, there is a conflict between science and Christianity. Indeed, in *River Out of Eden* Dawkins claims that "science shares with religion the claim that it answers deep questions about origins, the nature of life and the cosmos."[6]

But my doctoral studies of Hooke, Boyle, and their friends gave me pause for thought. Here were some of the most important founders of modern science, and yet they believed in the God of the Bible. Far from a conflict between Christianity and the foundations of modern science, the experimental scientific method was actually premised on a Christian worldview that involved the sinful fallibility of human cognition and senses, the order of the natural world, and the necessity of pursuing the study of nature as a duty to improve the conditions of human life and remedy the effects of sin. I began to realize that one of my major assumptions about Christianity, shaped in no small part by the New Atheism, was just plain wrong.

Human Value

Toward the end of my doctoral studies at Cambridge, I was elected to a Junior Research Fellowship at the University of Oxford. Full of enthusiasm for the years of scholarship that lay ahead, I embarked upon my Junior Research Fellowship at Wolfson College, one of the few Oxford colleges without a chapel. The college was built upon the site of the laboratory of J. S. Haldane and his children, son J. B. S. Haldane and daughter Naomi Mitchison. These two siblings conducted pioneering work in genetic experiments and were keen atheists.

A few months into my fellowship, my friends and I learned that one of the most famous atheist philosophers, Peter Singer, was visiting Oxford to give a series of lectures. Singer held a professorship at Princeton University. The lectures were on the subject of human value and ethics and provided a foretaste of his subsequent book, *The Life You Can Save*. Singer was thoughtful and calm, droll yet quick-witted, and I remember feeling proud to hear his Australian accent in the lecture hall at Oxford. He had an impressive intellectual honesty. With logical consistency, Singer pursued the implications of atheism for ethics, even when they led to uncomfortable positions. Indeed, I left Singer's lectures with a profound intellectual vertigo. I was compelled to confront one of my most deeply held beliefs.

I had always believed in the innate equality of all people: black or white, able-bodied or disabled, sick or healthy, young or old. I assumed this was something that all reasonable people agreed upon and that it was entirely consistent with my atheism. One of Singer's foundational claims, however, is that the innate preciousness and equal value of human beings is a Christian myth. Moreover, the sanctity of human life is a principle that "cannot rationally be defended" precisely because it depends upon Christian underpinnings.[7] In reality, Singer argues, humans are nothing more than a higher form of primate, and this has enormous ethical consequences. As he explains it, "The belief that mere membership in our species, irrespective of other characteristics, makes a great difference to the wrongness of killing a being is a legacy of religious doctrines."[8]

Indeed, let us consider the atheist worldview for a moment. If there is no God who created humanity with purpose and love, the ultimate reality of human life is biological. There is no basis for believing that human lives are inherently precious and valuable. Nor can the atheist hold that every human life is of *equal* worth. These claims about the inherent and equal value of human beings are totally inconsistent with observations of the natural world. Nature exhibits a cruel hierarchy of humanity's talents and capacities: physical, intellectual, moral, aesthetic, and so forth. Some people possess brilliant intelligence while others are profoundly intellectually disabled and can never so much as support themselves. Some humans suffer from cancer and die young, while others live beyond the age of one hundred. The biological reality of human life is hierarchical, not egalitarian. Indeed, as Dawkins puts it so memorably in *River Out of Eden*, "The universe we observe has precisely the properties we should expect if there is, at bottom, no design, no purpose, no evil and no good, nothing but blind, pitiless indifference."[9] If this biological reality is ultimate—which is the case if there is no God—then it is absurd, and entirely inconsistent with atheism, to suddenly believe that the life of the weakest human is as valuable as the life of the fittest and strongest. What a delusion!

Singer is not the first philosopher to recognize this. The nineteenth-century German philosopher Friedrich Nietzsche recognized that if

God is dead, then an ethics based upon the idea that all human beings are created in the image of God and are therefore equally precious has accompanied God to the grave. Collateral damage, indeed. If God does not exist and the sanctity of human life is a Judeo-Christian fiction, then we are left with two options when we confront the issue of human value and human rights. The first, which Singer takes as his project, is to invent a concept of "personhood." Personhood revolves around a set of capacities that, when possessed by an individual human animal, means that individual can be considered a "person" and accorded certain rights. For Singer these capacities center upon consciousness, rationality, and the capacity to experience suffering and complex emotions. But not all human beings can be considered "persons." If somebody lacks these capacities, through illness or disability for example, then his or her life ought not be accorded the same rights as those of others. Singer is well known for arguing that parents should have the right to kill their newborn babies if those babies are severely disabled. In his 1985 book *Should the Baby Live?*, Singer and his colleague Helga Kuhse suggest that "when the parents will be the ones who must care for a severely handicapped infant, it is the parents who should have the right to decide whether the infant lives or dies."[10]

Singer's belief that not all human beings are of equal moral worth alarmed me, but soon I began to question why I was alarmed. As Singer had explained, this position follows necessarily from an atheist view of human life. So on what basis could I disagree, other than simple emotivism? Just because I feel something is wrong does not make it wrong. Another aspect of the logical consistency of Singer's ethics with atheism was that I could not think of these arguments as held only by an extremist fringe of atheist philosophers. Far from it. Singer sits in the company of philosophers who hold positions at prestigious universities, including the bioethicists Francesca Minerva and Alberto Giubilini, who argue in the *Journal of Medical Ethics* that killing a newborn infant could be ethically permissible in all the circumstances where abortion would be, including when the "well-being of the family is at risk."[11]

The second option available to us when we grapple with the idea of human rights and value is to simply posit that the intrinsic value of all human beings is just a premise that needs to be agreed upon before any conversation can take place. Put another way, this is the idea that all reasonable and sensible people agree that all people are valuable and entitled to the same basic rights, and that is all there is to it. I must admit, until attending Singer's lectures, this was my position, which I had thought was unremarkable and not up for serious debate. But reading the work of Singer and his colleagues made me realize the naivete of my position, which is simply an ungrounded assertion. The fact that Singer took a very different position made laughable my defense that all reasonable people agree that my premise is a self-evident truth. All reasonable people simply do not agree. The equality of all human beings is *not* a self-evident truth, as Singer and other world-class secular philosophers are more than happy to remind us.

Moreover, this secular humanist value of mine could not even be defended historically. It does not take much knowledge of history to see that many cultures have decided that it was right—in their eyes—to devalue the lives of those they deemed weaker or undesirable. In Hitler's Nazi Germany, the nation determined that it was *right* to turn in to the authorities Jewish people and people with disabilities so that they could be put into concentration camps and gassed to death. So even in Europe, in my grandparents' generation, a country gassed to death millions of people because it was considered right as far as their culture was concerned at the time. So much for the idea that all reasonable people agree that every human being is of equal worth. This key tenet of secular humanism turned out to be not only philosophically flimsy but also historically naive and dangerously foolish.

What did the other atheists have to say about all this? Surely some of the New Atheists would have a compelling response. As I read, it was soon clear that Richard Dawkins makes strangely contradictory statements about human value. Sometimes, such as in *River Out of Eden*, he argues that there are no objective moral values because the universe is an accident.[12] Because there are no objective moral values, nor inherent value to human life—or anything else, for that matter—Dawkins would concur with Singer that there is no reason for believing that all human beings are inherently and equally valuable. And yet, at other times, such as in an interview with *Skeptic* magazine, Dawkins makes statements that indicate that he thinks life is somehow valuable and worth living well. In that interview, Dawkins comments, "What I want to guard against is people therefore getting nihilistic in their personal lives. I do not see any reason for that at all. You can have a very happy and fulfilled personal life even if you think that the universe at large is a tale told by an idiot."[13]

The interview in *Skeptic* pressed Dawkins a little on this point, asking him how, in the absence of religion, atheists should develop their moral compass and their ideas of how to live well.

Skeptic: Well, if we don't accept religion as a reasonable guide to "what is" or even a reasonable guide to "what ought to be," does evolution give us such a guide? Can we turn to evolution to answer not what is, but what ought to be?

Dawkins: I'd rather not do that. I think Julian Huxley was the last person who attempted to. In my opinion, a society run along "evolutionary" lines would not be a very nice society in which to live. But further, there's no logical reason why we should try to derive our normative standards from evolution. It's perfectly consistent to say this is the way it is—natural selection is out there and it is a very unpleasant process. Nature is red in tooth and claw. But I don't want to live in that kind of a world. I want to change the world in which I live in such a way that natural selection no longer applies.

But if natural selection is the ultimate reality, then Dawkins's desire to live contrary to what he believes is the blind and pitiless indifference of the universe does not make sense. If there are no objective moral values, and all life is ultimately valueless and pointless in a cosmically accidental universe, on what basis can Dawkins suddenly say we ought to live according to an entirely different principle? He has made statements about not wanting to live in the kind of world that is based upon evolutionary ethics, as well as various moralizing comments about what he calls the "child abuse" of teaching children about hell.[14] But if there are no objective moral principles, why is he moralizing? Half the time Dawkins is arguing that objective morality does not exist, and yet the other half of the time he is adamant about moral principles!

Dawkins's failure to present a consistent position on the issues of ethics and morality made me realize that I could not rely upon his arguments. Instead, I had to confront these issues for myself. I had always thought I was a good person. I had always believed that there were ways one ought to behave toward others and that the equal and precious value of all human beings was a profound moral truth. But now I had to wrestle with these questions deeply, honestly, and personally. If I believed the atheist position that the biological reality of the strong conquering the weak was the ultimate truth of nature and the universe, then why should I suddenly become unselfish and help the weak and vulnerable? That would fly in the face of everything I believed to be true! The key word here is *should*. I might *want* to be unselfish and argue that society ought to care for the marginalized and weak. Moral *feelings* are one thing, but moral *obligations* are quite another matter.

I might choose to live what I saw as an ethical life, but I would have to recognize that my ethics were merely an invention to appease myself, inconsistent with the principles of atheism, in which human life was nothing more than matter in motion and survival of the fittest was the natural world's governing truth.

Would not such a life lack integrity? If I believed that there was no God, and consequently no objective morality or inherent value to human life, then surely I ought to have the integrity to actually live in accordance with my belief. To invent an ethic of care for the marginalized and weak would actually deny my atheist naturalism; it would be a blatant slap in the face—to both my atheism and my integrity. As I thought this through, I had an awkward sinking feeling. Care for the marginalized and the equality of all human life—principles to which I clung so dearly—did not stem from atheism at all. They were actually (I cringed) Judeo-Christian principles. I later learned that the prophet Isaiah summed it up perfectly: "Learn to do right; seek justice. Defend the oppressed. Take up the cause of the fatherless; plead the case of the widow" (Isaiah 1:17 NIV). Atheism, it turned out, was incompatible with my most cherished moral principles, not least of which was the precious, and equal, value of human life. My heart sank. Atheism had failed me.

The Question of Meaning

But atheism was also failing me in another, more personal, way. To my mind, because God didn't exist, I was free to create the meaning and significance of my life. I was in my midtwenties, and that is how I had been living, relishing one success after another. I had everything I had always wanted; the last thing I needed was a crutch. At twenty-seven, I had fulfilled my childhood dream of earning a PhD from Cambridge University as well as a fellowship at Oxford University. I had published an award-winning first book. I was having a great time with my friends at Oxford. Life was great. But here's the strange thing: no matter how much I achieved, it was never enough. Every hurdle of achievement just revealed the next rung of the ladder to be climbed.

One gray Oxford winter's day, I found myself alone in the Wolfson library. I noticed that my usual desk in the college library was in front of the theology section. With an uncomfortable reluctance, and curious about where the origin of these ideas about care for the marginalized and love came from, I opened a book of sermons. I was curious, but I expected to read some pious, self-righteous vagaries. But the sermons I read were genuinely intellectually robust. They pointed me to a number of biblical verses that presented a very different account of human life and human value. One was Psalm 139:13: "It was you who formed my internal organs, fashioning me within my mother's womb" (ISV). There was another verse in Genesis I had heard before but never properly thought about: "Let us make mankind in our image, in our likeness" (Gen. 1:26 NIV). The most arresting verse, though, was from the New Testament book of Galatians. I had never come across this before. "There is neither Jew nor Gentile, neither slave nor free, nor is there male and female, for you are all one in Christ Jesus" (Gal. 3:28 NIV).

There was a stark contrast between atheism and these glimpses of a biblical view of human life. Those who were weak and those who were strong, able-bodied and disabled, black and white, male and female, God created all these people *in his image*. I remembered, from my studies of the abolition of slavery, the phrase "Am I not a man and a brother?" emblazoned underneath a distressing image of a black man, wrists in shackles. This was the iconic image of the great abolitionist movement that abolished the transatlantic slave trade in the British Empire. If God created all humanity in his image, then all people were inherently and equally precious. What a beautiful idea. But could it be true?

It was not long, however, before my mind turned to the historical and present reality of human life, with its suffering, brokenness, and despair, its exploitation and superficial frivolity, the endless striving, not least my own. How does one make sense of that? I knew little of the idea of sin, but to be honest, I was arrogant enough to have mentally rolled my eyes at this concept. Surely sin was an idea levied by the self-righteous moralizers to condemn others, to stop people from being who they wanted to be. Surely the Enlightenment had liberated us from all that. But if the Bible's doctrine about human life was robust and compelling, perhaps I had been wrong to dismiss sin and there was more to it. I promised myself I would explore further and not be narrow-minded. Meanwhile, I had been successful in applying for academic jobs. I was appointed to an assistant professorship at Florida State University, ironically in the religion department because of my scholarship in the field of the historical relationship between science and Christianity.

I immigrated to the United States, to Tallahassee. One of my new friends gave me a copy of C. S. Lewis's *Mere Christianity*. I was struck by how reasonable Lewis's arguments were, and that book chipped away at some of my narrow-mindedness. Eventually, I opened a Bible and decided to read the story of Jacob from the book of Genesis. I read that Jacob had "wrestled" with God. The idea of wrestling with God seemed to be an apt description of my own grappling with the idea of God, with doubt and faith. As I read, I found myself identifying with Jacob in some ways; he was ambitious, hardworking, and determined. He knew what he wanted in life, and he was driven to pursue the life he wanted for himself.

Jacob pursued the good things in life as if they could bring him fulfillment. But there was always more to be attained, and even Jacob's means of attaining what he wanted brought him all kinds of trouble. One night, he finds himself wrestling with a man. The man, it turns out, is God himself. God lets Jacob pin him down, and Jacob demands, "I will not let you go unless you bless me" (Gen. 32:26).

But Jacob had never actually wanted God. He had only ever wanted God's blessings. He had used God as a means to an end—negotiating, bargaining, to get what he wanted in life. And yet, all the blessings of a bountiful family, much wealth, and his brother's birthright were never enough.

Reading about Jacob made me realize that I too had never wanted God. Suddenly, I had another perspective on sin. Sin isn't best understood as a system of prohibitions. Rather, it is a state of the heart that does not want God. Like Jacob, I had turned my own success into the thing I lived for, the thing that gave me my self-worth and meaning in life. Intellectual achievement is by no means a bad thing, but I had turned it into my ultimate life pursuit, relying on it for my ultimate fulfillment. But it could not bear that burden. Little wonder I kept needing more and more success. Not long after, I read this passage in the book of Ecclesiastes, in the Old Testament.

> And whatever my eyes desired I did not keep from them. I kept my heart from no pleasure, for my heart found pleasure in all my toil, and this was my reward for all my toil. Then I considered all that my hands had done and the toil I had expended in doing it, and behold, all was vanity and a striving after wind, and there was nothing to be gained under the sun. (Eccl. 2:10–11)

This was the truest description of a world without God, and indeed my own heart, that I had ever read. In an atheist worldview, this meaning I created for myself was all I had, because human lives have no ultimate meaning, value, or purpose. In the absence of God, we were not created with a purpose in mind. And yet, if I am nothing more than my biology, then the ultimate meaninglessness of life ought not trouble me. But it did. And of course, across cultures and civilizations and throughout history, humanity has grappled with questions of meaning in life. This problem of meaning was what truly laid bare the poverty of atheism. But here, in the profoundly apt description of Ecclesiastes, was a better explanation of my condition. I was living a life turned away from God, the ground of all meaning. Little wonder I felt like I was chasing the wind, even when, like the author of Ecclesiastes, "my heart found pleasure in all my toil."

Jacob, too, delighted in all his work. What became of him? Jacob, after all, had lived a life rejecting God. He deserved to be turned away from God, the giver of life. He deserved death. But how did God respond that night when they wrestled? God showed Jacob mercy; he spared Jacob, letting him off with a wound. He crippled his hip such that Jacob walked with a limp for the rest of his life. When he awoke at dawn, Jacob realized it was God with whom he had wrestled. And suddenly, he saw that what he really needed was not another good gift from God, because it would never be enough. Jacob grasped that what he really wanted and needed was the ground of all good, God himself.

But where was God's wrath? Jacob had resisted God all his life, only desiring his blessings—the things God could give him—but not wanting God himself. Yet God spared him. Sometime later, I learned that the full story of Jacob is a metastory, which is fulfilled in the New Testament. After wrestling with Jacob, God changes Jacob's name to Israel. Jesus is called the *"true* Israel." God allowed Jacob to prevail in his wrestling so that he could show him mercy and not destroy him. What a gift! Jacob, the completely undeserving, the one who had arrogantly swindled and rejected God and manipulated others, who had pursued his own ambition to the hurt of others. Jacob, a liar and a crook. Yet God rescued him.

But why? God's mercy to Jacob/Israel did not make sense to me until I understood the rest of the story. In the New Testament, the cost of God's mercy was paid by the *true* Israel. At Calvary, the true Israel, Jesus Christ, stood in Jacob's place. God himself was nailed to a tree so that he could take the wrath that Jacob deserved—that we all deserved—for rejecting him. That wrath, meted out to Jesus, was death. So Jacob (now Israel) was blessed, but only because Jesus, the true Israel, took the curse that Jacob deserved. God blesses those who deserve to be cursed because on the cross God cursed Jesus, the true and sinless Israel, who deserved a blessing.

I reflected upon my own struggle with finding my meaning and satisfaction in my life's work and how it could never bear the burden of giving my life ultimate meaning. Only Jesus, who is God himself, can bear the weight of giving my life ultimate meaning. This is because Jesus is life itself: "I am the way and the truth and the life. No one comes to the Father except through me" (John 14:6 NIV). Jesus bore the burden of my sin on the cross. Over the next few months, I began to attend church and continued reading the Bible. I spent a lot of time in reflection. I came to the conclusion that atheism could not provide adequate answers to the big questions; it could not make sense of what I saw as a historian and what I experienced of the human predicament of living in a world that does not satisfy our deepest longings.

The more I learned about God's love for us in Jesus, the more I found myself overwhelmed. I realized that God had always known me, always loved me, and that he wanted me to stop running after everything else in life except him. I had lived a life rejecting God, arrogantly ridiculing and poking fun at the very idea of God. And yet, God showed me grace. But he gave me this grace at the horrific cost of taking the punishment that my sin deserved onto himself, in Jesus. While there is so much more to this story, I decided that the Bible's explanations of who God is, who we are, and what life is about were true. I wanted to follow the God who made me, loves me, and died for me. So one night I knelt in my closet in my apartment. In prayer, I admitted I'd lived a life of turning away from God, and I asked Jesus to become my Savior. This was not because God would enable me to avoid suffering or disappointment or so I would achieve all my dreams, but rather because God himself *is* life. And life with him is life with abundance: "I came that they may have life and have it abundantly" (John 10:10).

Becoming a Christian is not something one does in order to attain a better or easier life. God does not promise us health or wealth or to minimize our suffering. On the contrary, the Bible describes how Jesus himself was "a man of sorrows" (Isa. 53:3) and how he endured suffering in his own earthly life before the ultimate suffering on the cross. In fact, one of the ways that God has strengthened his relationship with me is through my own experience of suffering. A few years ago, my husband and I went through a very difficult time, in which I lost four of our babies through miscarriage. Through our tears, we kept returning to what Jesus says in John's Gospel: "I have said these things to you, that in me you may have peace. In the world you will have tribulation. But take heart; I have overcome the world" (John 16:33). Jesus's words gave me a hope that I never had as an atheist. In the dark moments, before I knew God, all I had was despair. But now that I was a Christian, I knew the God who loved me. I knew that my suffering was not ultimate, because at the end of time God will remake the heavens and the earth. Jesus himself "'will wipe every tear from their eyes. There will be no more death' or mourning or crying or pain, for the old order of things has passed away" (Rev. 21:4 NIV). Even in the midst of suffering, Jesus is the source of abundant and eternal life.

Chapter 3

From Dawkins to Christ via William Lane Craig

PETER BYROM

The God of Theater

I WAS RAISED IN A Christian home, but whatever "faith" I had at the time did not survive when I moved out. I was eager to become a great actor and do life my own way. The company of fellow drama students, artists, and theatergoers was what gave me meaning and where I felt I truly belonged. The ideas of God and religious belief gradually faded into irrelevance until I could no longer identify with them. We drama students were the sophisticated and daring ones who could handle the gray areas of life, studying the intricacies of the human condition and the animalistic tendencies inside us all. Religious people, by contrast, were those simplistic, backward folks who saw everything in black and white, believed the world was only six thousand years old, and got easily offended.

It was 2005. I had settled into university life and was reveling in the company I kept and the activities available. I was finally setting my own course and forging my own destiny, and I was immortal (at least that's how I felt).

The Death of Apathy

Approaching the beginning of my third year, however, I was forced to reopen "the God question" in a way that I never anticipated. It involved two of my very best friends, who went in radically different directions at roughly the same time.

The first friend, who had no religious background at all, became a Christian. He'd been drawn into a circle of Christian students, attended their church's "Alpha" course, and then, suddenly, he believed! This was seriously inconvenient. I'd effectively erased all traces of God and Christianity from my life, and then he had to go and "get saved."

If this were the only thing that had happened, then I might have been able to move on. But what happened next, with my second friend, destroyed any hope of being able to do so.

My second friend had carried some Christian convictions with him since teenage years, but then it all changed. I remember the moment vividly. It was a cold evening as we walked in a group along the outskirts of Canterbury (probably between pubs), and I heard him say, "You have got to read this new book called *The God Delusion* by Richard Dawkins—it's amazing!" My friend had seen the light.

While the conversion of my first friend from atheism to Christianity was pretty disturbing, it was the de-conversion of my second friend that had the bigger impact. As far as Christianity was concerned, I had "been there, done that" (and I certainly was in no hurry to revisit it). But the idea of looking into this thing called "atheism" properly, as a view, was something new and intriguing.

Furthermore, Richard Dawkins's approach to "the God question" seemed revolutionary. Even though I had no interest in anything God related, I had adopted a somewhat relativistic stance on the matter.

Religion wasn't for me, but if somebody else found it meaningful, then good for them.

But Dawkins had a different take on the matter: truth is at stake here. Either the claims of a religion are true, or they are false. Either there is a God, or there isn't one. And, most of all, it is possible objectively and scientifically to argue that people who believe in God are *wrong*. Not only that but, he claimed, religion—as well as being untrue—is intrinsically dangerous.

So, one (or both) of my friends had to be wrong.

On the one hand, if my atheist-turned-Christian friend was right, then this God of the Bible was "the one true God," and our acceptance or rejection of him would affect our eternal destinies.

On the other hand, if my Christian-turned-atheist friend was right, then both he and I had escaped the clutches of a "pernicious delusion,"[1] whereas my atheist-turned-Christian friend had fallen prey to it.

Or maybe there is a *non-Christian* god?

To put the icing on the cake, all three of us ended up living in the same flat as we approached the summer before our final year at university.

Only a miracle could have sustained my apathy.

Challenged by Dawkins

Upon reading *The God Delusion*, I was struck not only by the eloquence of Dawkins's writing but also by a number of challenges.

The biggest one, by far, was how Dawkins defined what it means to have faith. Faith, according to Dawkins, means believing in something *without any evidence*.[2] He contrasted this with the scientific virtues of pursuing truth and being open to changing your beliefs when presented with superior evidence.

What, then, is the evidence for God or the claims of religion? According to Dawkins, there isn't any.

Not only is there no good reason to believe in God, but there are many reasons to *reject* the existence of God. The appearance of design in the universe can be entirely accounted for by natural, evolutionary processes, whereas God is so improbable and useless as an explanation that it would be irrational to invoke him. We can find fulfillment in this life alone and marvel at the elegance of how the cosmos and life as we know it came to be, all on its own. Theism, and religion especially, teaches people to close their minds and to give up trying to understand the world.

While not settling every question, Dawkins's arguments were nevertheless very compelling, and the atheism it described felt extremely attractive. I'd "done" Christianity, so now perhaps it was time to nail my colors to the mast and become an atheist. Why would I want a cosmic authority over my life—especially when there isn't any evidence for one—when I'd only recently left my parents' authority?

I took Dawkins's principle of seeking the truth through basing your life on evidence and ran with it. Given that I did not want Christianity to be true or God to exist, I thought all I would need to do is ask, "Where is your evidence?" and no religious advocate would be able to give any.

Then I made the mistake of watching YouTube.

Reasonable Faith

Nowadays online video streaming has become part of everyday life, but back then there was something fresh and exciting about it. Being able to just type a search term and then binge on the results was a great way to relax or to procrastinate writing an essay.

So, I searched for Dawkins. I wanted to learn more about this "God debate" and to see how far I could push his demand for evidence, to make sure that this God stuff really was as weak as he said it was.

It looked extremely weak indeed. Religious people were getting an intellectual kicking.

I soon discovered that Dawkins was one of four contemporary atheist thinkers called the New Atheists (or sometimes the Four Horsemen, or even the Brights). Accompanying the evolutionary biologist Richard Dawkins was the philosopher Daniel Dennett, the neuroscientist Sam Harris, and my favorite of them all, the polemic journalist Christopher Hitchens. Video after video had them engaging in debate with cringeworthy, feeble religious people.

Watching obsessively, I stubbornly demanded to be shown the best evidence that God-fearing people had. If they couldn't produce the goods, then my attraction to atheism would be validated, and I could dismiss religion once and for all.

I wouldn't have used the language of answered prayer at this stage in my life (it certainly wasn't a prayer), but I got what I asked for.

One day I stumbled upon a YouTube clip of a well-turned-out young American with smooth dark hair and a neatly trimmed beard who instantly brought to mind the suave villain Hans Gruber, played by Alan Rickman in *Die Hard*. He was seated opposite a fellow whom I could only describe as a British version of Doc Brown (Christopher Lloyd) from *Back to the Future*. The atheist was somewhat overconfidently insisting that the Christian only believed in God because he was "desperate to believe" and that "science is omnipotent" and can "account for everything."[3]

The Christian then proceeded to calmly dismantle both of these assertions.

First, the atheist's dismissal of belief in God was genetic fallacy. This is where you make the illogical mistake of trying to disprove a view by attempting to show how the belief in it originated. Even if it were true that this Christian only believed in God because he was desperate and afraid of death (or, as folks like Dawkins also argue, "because you happen to have been born in a Christian country"[4]), it could still be the case that God exists.

Second, in response to the claim that "science can account for everything," the Christian proceeded to rattle off a list of five things that science cannot prove, yet belief in them is still entirely rational:[5]

1. Logical and mathematical truths (science presupposes them, so it would be arguing in a circle to use science to prove them).
2. Metaphysical truths (e.g., there are minds other than my own, or the external world is real, or the past wasn't created five minutes ago with the appearance of age).
3. Moral truths (science is *de*scriptive but not *pre*scriptive—e.g., science will tell you that if you want to kill your grandmother, you should put arsenic in her drink, but science cannot tell you whether it is right or wrong to try to kill her in the first place).
4. Aesthetic truths (the beautiful, like the good, also cannot be scientifically proven).
5. Science itself (not only is science permeated with unprovable assumptions, but the statement "you should only believe what can be scientifically proven" is itself not provable by science).

I discovered that the atheist was Peter Atkins, a professor of chemistry and a colleague of Dawkins from the University of Oxford, and the Christian was the philosopher and theologian Dr. William Lane Craig.

I looked up more about who this William Lane Craig was. He ran a ministry called Reasonable Faith and was involved in what I would soon learn is called Christian apologetics (the word has nothing to do with apologizing; rather, it comes from the Greek word *apologia*, which means to provide a reasoned defense). There were countless other recordings of Craig debating with atheists, and they appeared to be having a very hard time arguing against him.

Craig would present a cumulative case of philosophical arguments to defend the existence of God, followed by a historical argument for why this God has revealed himself to be the God of Christianity. I do not have the space to describe these points in detail, but they can easily be looked up on ReasonableFaith.org. Here, however, is a summary list of the arguments that I saw Craig typically defending:

1. The cosmological argument from contingency
   (God is the best explanation for why anything exists rather than nothing.)
2. The Kalam cosmological argument
   (God is the best explanation of the beginning of the universe.)
3. The teleological argument
   (God is the best explanation of the fine-tuning of the initial conditions of the universe for the development of intelligent life.)
4. The moral argument
   (God is the best explanation for objective moral values and duties in the world.)
5. The ontological argument
   (The very possibility of God's existence entails that God must exist.)
6. The resurrection argument
   ("God raised Jesus from the dead" is the best explanation of the historical facts surrounding the life, death, empty tomb, and postmortem appearances of Jesus of Nazareth, as well as the origin of the disciples' belief in his resurrection—which entails that God exists.)

As I watched Craig's debates and lectures, read his articles, and listened to his podcasts, I realized that I was being fed the equivalent of a bonus university module in critical thinking and analytic philosophy. It became apparent that the whole atheism versus theism debate was not a matter of science versus religion but philosophical view versus philosophical view. As Craig puts it, "Science can provide evidence in support of a premise in a philosophical argument leading to a conclusion that has theological significance."[6]

The weird thing was that, despite Dawkins's and his fellow New Atheists' insistence that atheism was the superior, rational view, it was this *Christian* academic who was leading the way in setting the example for how such logical argumentation ought to be conducted. Craig would present his arguments as ordered premises leading to a conclusion and then defend the truths of those premises. For example:

The Kalam Cosmological Argument[7]
1. If the universe began to exist, then the universe has a transcendent cause.
2. The universe began to exist.
3. Therefore, the universe has a transcendent cause.

The argument above is of the logical form *modus ponens*, which works in the following way:

1. $P \rightarrow Q$ (If P is true, then Q is true.)
2. P (P is true.)
3. $\therefore Q$ (Therefore, Q is true.)

This is a logically valid argument, which means that if premises 1 and 2 are true, then the conclusion (3) follows necessarily and inescapably. Given the validity of the logic in this argument, Craig would then need to share reasons and evidence for why those premises are more plausibly true than false (for example, he argues that the Big Bang supports premise 2).

What impressed me most was that, by laying out his arguments in this way, Craig was making them transparent and vulnerable. This approach does away with rhetoric and emotional manipulation. If you want to argue that he is wrong, then you need to identify the flaws in the arguments (which is precisely what Dawkins had been saying people ought to do with his own book!).

On that note, what was alarming was how Richard Dawkins's published work fared when held up against these standards of logic and argument. For example, according to Craig, Dawkins's central argument against the existence of God (from chapter 4 of *The God Delusion*, which Dawkins himself has called "devastating" and "un-rebuttable"[8]) was a logically *invalid* argument.

Dawkins's Summary of the Central Argument from *The God Delusion*[9]

1. One of the greatest challenges to the human intellect, over the centuries, has been to explain how the complex, improbable appearance of design in the universe arises.
2. The natural temptation is to attribute the appearance of design to actual design itself.
3. The temptation is a false one because the designer hypothesis immediately raises the larger problem of who designed the designer.
4. The most ingenious and powerful explanation so far discovered is Darwinian evolution by natural selection.
5. We don't yet have an equivalent explanation for physics.
6. We should not give up hope of a better explanation arising in physics, something as powerful as Darwinism is for biology.
7. Therefore, God almost certainly does not exist.

If we were also to represent this in symbolic logic, it would read:

1. P
2. Q
3. R
4. S
5. T
6. U
7. ∴ V

What Craig pointed out (indeed you might have noticed this at a glance) was that even if all the premises in Dawkins's argument were true, the conclusion "God almost certainly does not exist" still would not follow! It appears out of nowhere at the end of the argument, with no logical connection to any of the premises.

This made me wonder: What would happen if Richard Dawkins debated William Lane Craig?

Given Dawkins's exhortation for people to seek the truth and to be open to changing their views when presented with evidence and argument, surely this kind of rigorous academic critique and interaction would be exactly what Dawkins would be looking for?

It wasn't.

Debatable?

Dawkins had been approached by various organizations on several occasions and was resolute in refusing to debate—or engage in any way, including in print—with William Lane Craig. For example, I learned of an invitation sent to Dawkins in 2007, to which he replied, "I don't know who your William Craig is, but maybe you'd have better luck with an Archbishop or a Cardinal?" accompanied by the gibe, aimed at Craig, "That would look great on your CV, not so good on mine."[10]

This didn't make sense. Why would the world's leading apologist for atheism be so dismissive of the opportunity to engage with the world's leading Christian academic apologist?

I was aware that others had also criticized Dawkins and his fellow New Atheists for approaching the God question in a superficial manner, but it was only now that I started to appreciate why this accusation might legitimately be made. I listened to the recording of William Lane Craig's critique of Daniel Dennett from 2007 and was struck by the double standard in Dennett's response: while trying to defend his atheistic scenarios (including the logically incoherent claim that the universe caused itself), Dennett urged the audience to consider that "whatever the truth is, it's going to be jaw-droppingly implausible and counter-intuitive one way or another";[11] but when objecting to theism, he characterized it as such a "remarkably implausible conclusion" that the arguments for it *must* contain false premises *somewhere* (i.e., Dennett seemed open to evidence for anything *other than* God)![12]

Christopher Hitchens was the next New Atheist to engage with William Lane Craig, in April 2009,[13] and I noticed that he was unusually subdued when he did so. In the press conference before the debate, Hitchens generously described Craig as "very rigorous, very scholarly, very formidable."[14] By the time the debate came to closing statements, Hitchens yielded his time, giving Craig the last word. Despite coming to the debate with a plethora of complaints about the evils of religion, Hitchens had no arguments to offer to defend his claim that God does not exist (a view that, during the cross-examination, he even appeared to try to filibuster his way out of admitting that he held).

The atheist blogger Luke Muehlhauser of *Common Sense Atheism* didn't pull his punches when he reviewed the debate: "Hitchens was rambling and incoherent, with the occasional rhetorical jab. Frankly, Craig spanked Hitchens like a foolish child."[15]

As much as I loved Hitchens's personality, prose, and wit, I could see that he wasn't the substantive atheist I'd once thought. Indeed, while watching the debate unfold, I caught myself answering many of his objections due to how familiar I had become with Craig's work!

While my interest in apologetics was growing, graduation was looming. Instead of embracing the excitement of whatever came next, I had buckled under the anxiety of feeling ill-prepared for what lay ahead. University was not going to last forever. We were all going to disperse and move on. I was *not* immortal.

In an attempt to escape the pressure of my final university year, I'd bought into the atheistic assumptions of Dawkins and others: there is nothing that "comes next," and there is no reason why you are here. You just make the most of the life you have now and choose your own path. I took this macroview of the cosmos and boiled it down to the microlevel of how to spend my final year.

In that same year, the British Humanist Association had launched a widely publicized "atheist bus campaign," whereby buses all over London and various other cities carried advertising banners adorned with the slogan: "There's probably no God. Now stop worrying and enjoy your life."[16]

I didn't need prompting. I already felt like I wanted to just stop worrying and enjoy my life. For me, that meant taking refuge in the indulgence and hedonism readily available in the student world, as if it were never going to end. I was already a heavy drinker with a proclivity for throwing money away on eating out. On top of that, however, I added smoking and also wound up in a relationship that I should have had the courage to end after three weeks but instead remained in for three years. Beyond graduation I was directionless and did not chart my own course.

Against this backdrop, I threw myself into consuming as much apologetics and debate content as I could. It was the only thing keeping my mind alive, and it became relevant on a whole new existential level.

There was still one debate, above all others, that I was eager to see happen.

Confrontation

In November 2009, I discovered that there would be a debate in Berkshire over the motion "atheism is the new fundamentalism," featuring Richard Dawkins on the panel.[17] I immediately booked tickets—I was looking forward to this one!

While sitting in the audience, the thought kept creeping in, "Is this the one opportunity, during the audience Q&A, to ask Dawkins face-to-face about his refusal to debate William Lane Craig?" I kept dismissing the idea, however. It didn't seem relevant to the topic.

However, there was a moment during the Right Reverend Lord Richard Harries's opening speech that changed my mind. Harries listed what he considered to be four key characteristics of fundamentalism, the second of which was the following:

> [Fundamentalism] always picks on the weakest points in another person's argument. But is it not true that if you're really confident of your case, you face the opponent's strongest argument? You don't simply always focus on their weakest arguments. . . . It looks as though religious fundamentalism and atheistic fundamentalism need each other and feed on each other.[18]

That was the permission I needed.

When it came to the audience question-and-answer period, I took the roving microphone and asked Dawkins about his repeated refusals to debate William Lane Craig. He gave the following answer:

> I always said when invited to do debates that I would be happy to debate a bishop, a cardinal, a pope, an archbishop—indeed I have done both—but that I don't take on creationists and I don't take on people whose only claim to fame is that they are professional debaters. They've got to have something more than that. I'm busy![19]

While there were Dawkins fans in the audience who applauded his answer, I could not. It was unimpressive, to say the least. Dawkins had already debated people who were not clergy, and William Lane Craig was not a "creationist." Had Dawkins done any homework on him, he'd know that Craig sees no conflict between Christianity and evolution and that he affirms the 13.7-billion-year-old age of the universe (he would have to, given that the first of his two earned doctorates argues that the Big Bang supports the Kalam cosmological argument for God's existence).

As for dismissing Craig as a "professional debater," this was to ignore Craig's credentials as a professional philosopher. Consider the words of another atheist, philosopher Quentin Smith:

> A count of the articles in the philosophy journals shows that more articles have been published about Craig's defense of the Kalam argument than have been published about any other philosopher's contemporary formulation of an argument for God's existence.[20]

Several days after that debate, I noticed that somebody had captured a video clip of me asking Dawkins about debating Craig and had uploaded it to YouTube! The whole debate had been officially filmed and uploaded, but this person—whoever he or she was—had isolated my moment and posted it under the title "Richard Dawkins Says He Won't Debate William Lane Craig."[21] This short clip went viral. To date, it has exceeded 300,000 views.

Having become hooked into this whole issue by watching YouTube videos in the first place, I had now stepped into the YouTube arena myself and become part of the drama!

Disillusioned with Dawkins

As I continued to consume apologetics material, I came to appreciate even more how weak Dawkins's case for atheism was. In fact, the more I learned about how Dawkins mischaracterized belief in God, the more I came to understand what belief in God entailed.

Craig had already demonstrated that Dawkins's central atheistic argument from *The God Delusion*—intended to show that God almost certainly does not exist—was logically invalid, but it didn't stop there.

Craig, and others, explained how Dawkins's argument also contained false premises, meaning that it couldn't even be salvaged for more modest purposes, such as countering the teleological (design) argument for God's existence.

Dawkins tries to defend the most crucial premise (premise 3) of his central argument in the following way:

> The temptation [to attribute the appearance of design in the universe to actual design] is a false one because the designer hypothesis immediately raises the larger problem of who designed the designer. The whole problem we started out with was the problem of explaining statistical improbability. It is obviously no solution to postulate something even more improbable. We need a "crane," not a "skyhook"; for only a crane can do the business of working up gradually and plausibly from simplicity to otherwise improbable complexity.[22]

The first problem is the "who designed the designer?" objection. This is based on a principle that would, ironically, destroy science! Science progresses by establishing explanations one inquiry at a time (as Dawkins otherwise loves to remind us). However, this objection is of the form "you cannot recognize an explanation as the best unless you also have an explanation *of that explanation*," which would make it impossible to explain anything! For example, if this principle were taken seriously, we would have to reject theories such as Darwinian evolution by natural selection and the Big Bang because we do not yet have explanations for *those* explanations (i.e., if it is legitimate to raise "but who designed the designer?" as an objection, then we could likewise protest "but what evolved into the stuff that evolved?" or "but what banged the big banger?"). The absurdity of an infinite explanatory regress is not being caused by the design inference but by Dawkins's own faulty reasoning.[23]

Secondly, as Craig and others (including nontheists) also pointed out, Dawkins assumes that if the designer is God, then he must be more complex, and thereby more improbable, than the universe.[24] The problem here, however, is that Dawkins equivocates between two different kinds of "complexity."

When describing the appearance of design in the universe, Dawkins refers to *complexity of structure* (i.e., the intricacy of how all the discrete, physical component parts are arranged), but when objecting to God, he only ever cites *complexity of function* (i.e., what God must be capable of thinking and doing). For example:

> A God capable of continuously monitoring and controlling the individual status of every particle in the universe cannot be simple. His existence is going to need a mammoth explanation in its own right.[25]

Dawkins's confusion of complexity of structure with complexity of function undercuts his efforts to dismiss God as the designer. When one considers the arguments for theism (such as those defended by Craig), it becomes clear that the very concept of God is that he is an uncaused, beginningless, timeless, spaceless, immaterial, powerful, and personal being (unlike the created universe). Specifically, God is an unembodied mind.

Such a being would, ironically, perfectly satisfy Dawkins's demand for a "crane"-type explanation that "can do the business of working up gradually and plausibly from simplicity to otherwise improbable complexity."[26] This is because an unembodied mind is simple in the sense that it is not composed of any parts, whereas the universe is. Such a designer—while capable of having complex *ideas*—would therefore be simpler than even the universe's most primeval state. As the agnostic philosopher Sir Anthony Kenny explains:

> A thought or idea does not have the same complexity as its expression in a written design or blueprint would have. A thought does not have spatial or temporal parts in the way that the sentence that expresses it has. A thought is a unified whole and is not made up of a succession of parts in the way that a sentence is made up of successive words. Even in our mundane world, therefore, there is reason to doubt Dawkins' principle.[27]

Dawkins has leapt to the conclusion that because the entity to be explained consists of statistically improbable configurations of parts, the same must also be the case for its designer. More precisely, he has assumed that God would have to be a physically complex and contingent "creature" instead of a metaphysically necessary, eternal, *immaterial* being.[28] But if Dawkins had an argument for why unembodied minds cannot exist, or why only material beings can exist, then why didn't he use that instead? Dawkins's entire argument is question-begging: dependent upon the very materialistic worldview that he's supposed to be trying to substantiate.

Of all the critics who have pointed this out to Dawkins, it is perhaps the atheist philosopher Thomas Nagel's response that is most noteworthy:

> God, whatever he may be, is not a complex physical inhabitant of the natural world. The explanation of his existence as a chance concatenation of atoms is not a possibility for which we must find an alternative, because that is not what anybody means by God. If the God hypothesis makes sense at all, it offers a different kind of explanation from those of physical science: purpose or intention of a mind without a body,

capable nevertheless of creating and forming the entire physical world. The point of the hypothesis is to claim that not all
explanation is physical, and that there is a mental, purposive,
or intentional explanation more fundamental than the basic
laws of physics, because it explains even them.[29]

In summary, far from being "devastating," the central argument
of *The God Delusion* is not even an argument against God in the
first place. Dawkins has not so much as taken aim—let alone fired a
shot—at the transcendent divine mind postulated and argued for by
theists both over the centuries and in the present day. As Scott Hahn
and Benjamin Wiker observe, "At best [Dawkins] has shown that an
infinitely magnified Richard Dawkins cannot have been the cause of
the universe. Of that, we are already well aware."[30]

The Petty Christ

Not only was Dawkins presenting fallacious arguments against a
false concept of God, but he appeared to violate his own standards
for truth seeking when it came to the question of whether God has
revealed himself to us or takes any interest in human affairs.

As I studied William Lane Craig's arguments, I was drawn to
the question of why he defended Christianity in particular, rather
than just some generic theism. The more I explored this question, the
stronger the historical case for Christianity appeared to be. It all de-
pended upon the resurrection of Jesus ("If Christ has not been raised,
then our preaching is in vain and your faith is in vain," 1 Cor. 15:14).

Craig marshaled a powerful case for why the gospel accounts of
Jesus's fate can be regarded as historically credible with respect to
four main facts:[31]

1. After his crucifixion, Jesus of Nazareth was interred in a tomb by
   a member of the Jewish Sanhedrin named Joseph of Arimathea.

2. Jesus's tomb was then discovered to be empty by a group of his female followers on the Sunday morning following his crucifixion.
3. Thereafter, various individuals and groups experienced appearances of Jesus alive.
4. The earliest disciples came suddenly and sincerely to believe that God had raised Jesus from the dead despite their every predisposition to the contrary.

Craig established these facts by employing the standard tools of historical-critical studies. These facts require an explanation. Surprisingly, the disciples' own explanation, that God had raised Jesus from the dead, was appearing much stronger than the alternatives (especially given Craig's other arguments that, if successful, already establish that at least some kind of transcendent, monotheistic God exists and thereby makes miracles at least *possible*).

Watching an exchange between Dawkins and the Christian apologist John Lennox, however, I was disappointed to see how incurious, inconsistent, and unscholarly an attitude Dawkins took toward this question of Jesus's resurrection.[32] He repeatedly said, "I don't really care about it, because it's petty." Dawkins is well known for saying, "It doesn't matter whether you like something or not, what matters is what's true," yet here he placed his own personal dislike of the claim over and above the question of evidence. He went on to say, "Surely you can see that a God who is grand enough to make the universe is not going to give a tuppenny cuss about what you're thinking about and your sins and things like that."[33]

So Dawkins is somehow allowed to regard morality and justice, on this speck of dust called Planet Earth, as a matter of "great importance"[34] (his own words), but the God who designed and created the whole show, and who might therefore have one or two things to say about it himself . . . isn't? Wouldn't this possibility, of a God who *does care* about us, at least be worthy of proper exploration, instead of dismissing it simply because it doesn't fit one's own presuppositions?

By failing to engage on any substantive level, Dawkins had effectively handed Craig—and others such as Gary Habermas and N. T. Wright—the last word on the rational, historically evidenced grounds for believing in Jesus's resurrection.

The God of the Bible was appearing increasingly plausible as the best contender for the designer of the universe. Though outwardly I was calling myself an agnostic, by this point inwardly I'd grown persuaded by the strength of the arguments and evidence for God and, specifically, Christianity.

I was, nevertheless, keeping the issue at arm's length and treating it as something academic. My life and commitments weren't yet going to follow this evidence where it led. Despite the deep dissatisfaction it perpetuated, I was hanging in there with my aimless hedonism. That lifestyle would have to fall apart first. I didn't have intellectual objections anymore to God and Christianity. I was just entangled in a different life, like a monkey clenching its fist around the bait inside the monkey trap.

It was the concluding act of the "Craig versus Dawkins" saga that would push me over the edge.

The UK Tour

By 2011, I had switched allegiances. I felt let down by Dawkins, especially given that his published work had been so influential throughout the latter half of my university years. I was now invested in William Lane Craig's work, as well as that of many others who were giving strong rational grounds for their belief in God.

The New Atheists were struggling with William Lane Craig. Near the beginning of that year, Craig debated Sam Harris on the foundations of morality (in which Harris described Craig as "the one

Christian apologist who seems to have put the fear of God into many of my fellow atheists"![35]). The bizarre thing, however, was that after Craig gave a lengthy "knock-down"[36] refutation of Harris's moral theory, Harris's rebuttal gave no response to these criticisms. The irony was that, while Dawkins had persistently refused to debate with Craig, Sam Harris *had* shown up to debate . . . and then behaved as though it was Craig who hadn't shown up!

There had been a brief and unexpected encounter where Craig and Dawkins ended up interacting for a mere two minutes as part of a three-versus-three panel debate in Mexico the previous year (neither of them knew that the other was invited and, according to Craig, Dawkins had said upon meeting him, "I don't consider this to be a debate *with you*" before turning his back and walking away![37]). This was not the substantive exchange that I and others had been hoping for. Dawkins had yet to engage with Craig's criticisms of the arguments in his bestseller *The God Delusion*.

But the spotlight was about to fall back onto Dawkins's refusal to engage, one last time. William Lane Craig was coming to the United Kingdom for a speaking and debating tour, scheduled for October. Not only had Dawkins refused four separate invitations to debate him as part of this visit, but an atheist philosopher from Oxford—Dr. Daniel Came—had written the following to Dawkins: "The absence of a debate with the foremost apologist for Christian theism is a glaring omission on *your* CV and is of course apt to be interpreted as cowardice on your part." This letter made its way into an article on *The Telegraph Online*,[38] kicking the drama up a gear. Having declined to debate Craig in the Sheldonian Theatre, at the heart of Oxford University, Dawkins was informed that the invitation would remain open literally to the last minute in case he changed his mind. By this point, Dawkins was resorting to ad hominem attacks, such as calling Craig "a ponderous buffoon who brandishes impressive-sounding syllogisms from Logic 101 to bamboozle his faith-head audience."[39]

Around this time, I became involved in supporting and promoting Craig's upcoming tour, thanks to that viral clip of me confronting Dawkins. Two of the organizers—the presenter of the *Unbelievable?* apologetics podcast, Justin Brierley, and the former chair of the Universities and Colleges Christian Fellowship (UCCF), Dr. Peter May—had seen it, and we soon became friends and collaborators after establishing contact.

Then the idea hit us! Dawkins had been behind the launch of the British Humanist Association's "atheist bus campaign" back in 2009. We could turn this upside down, putting banners on Oxford buses that, instead of reading "There's probably no God. Now stop worrying and enjoy your life," read "There's probably no Dawkins. Now stop worrying and enjoy Oct. 25th at the Sheldonian Theatre" (i.e., expect a no-show from Dawkins and enjoy a substantial critique of *The God Delusion*).

Eventually, thirty of these buses were driving around Oxford and were featured on BBC local news. We were hearing feedback along the lines of "I don't really know what to make of these Christians, but you've got to admit they seem to be doing rather well on the humor!"

As I became more and more involved, it grew evident that the life I'd made for myself since university was finally going to come crashing down. I was barely supporting myself, and the relationship with my girlfriend came to an end. It was time to move out to God knows where, which meant, for the moment, sofa hopping as I prepared to follow the Reasonable Faith Tour.

It was a life-changing ten days, spanning London, Cambridge, Birmingham, Southampton, Manchester and, of course, the pivotal event in Oxford (where Craig was scheduled to deliver his critique of *The God Delusion*). It was a privilege to meet William Lane Craig and his wife, Jan, alongside the others who made the tour possible. It was filled with substantive and stimulating debates and talks, Craig being pitted against some of his toughest and most academically rigorous opponents.

When speaking with me, Jan was very curious as to where I was in my personal search. It seemed as though I was almost a Christian. Having told her that I hadn't committed yet, she said something to me that, I think, was the final nudge on my journey.

She said, "Peter, if you can't give everything to Jesus—everything in your life—don't do it. I've seen what it's like for people who only put one foot in and leave the other out. They'd be better off if they stayed atheists. This involves you handing everything over to him. If you can't, then don't do it."

This really made me pause. That's what this was about. It's not ultimately about the arguments but of coming to know God personally through his Son, Jesus Christ, and the sacrifice he made on that cross and his resurrection from the dead two thousand years ago. By receiving Jesus, a person is set free from past sin and given a new life of meaning and purpose: "For whoever would save his life will lose it, but whoever loses his life for my sake will find it" (Matt. 16:25).

I understood this and also that there was good historical evidence for the life of Jesus, the reliability of the Gospel accounts, and the fact that a divine miracle does not threaten the laws of nature (which God himself created in the first place!). The evidence was there, and I had every good reason to accept it.

With that stone in my shoe, on the third day of the tour—October 19, 2011—it really hit me: Pete, you're a Christian! You've believed this for a while, you've completely turned away from Dawkins and atheism and are supporting a Christian apologetics ministry. In fact, you're even *praying* for its success. Just get on with it!

I had come home. I knew that it was for real this time. There weren't any great lights like the apostle Paul saw on the road to Damascus. The only light was a flicker from my cigarette lighter, as I stood outside a bed and breakfast on a cold, rainy night in Cambridge wondering what to do next. But I knew that my journey, which started with one friend becoming a Christian and another becoming an atheist, had reached its destination. A new journey was about to begin.

Life After Dawkins

October 25 came—the date for Craig to deliver his critique of *The God Delusion*. There was a sense of anticipation in the air, but Dawkins failed to appear. Three Oxford scholars, however, did accept their invitations to respond to Dr. Craig. The event was chaired by atheist professor Peter Millican, who had debated Dr. Craig just a few evenings prior at the University of Birmingham.

Craig delivered his lecture to a full house. He outlined the arguments for God's existence and explained how poorly Dawkins had interacted with them, summarizing that "the objections raised by Richard Dawkins to these arguments are not even injurious, much less deadly."[40]

After the tour had wrapped up and goodbyes were said, it was time for me to pick up the loose ends of my life, and there were many! It was a big reset. In 2012, I was baptized, symbolizing how I, like all other Christians, would die in Christ and then rise in Christ.

The whole of William Lane Craig's UK tour had been filmed and is available on YouTube (where else!), and it's even been edited into a documentary called *The Case for Christian Theism*.[41]

As for Dawkins, he still has not responded to any of Craig's critiques of his arguments. The closest he ever came to doing so was four months after the tour, during a dialogue with Rowan Williams and Sir Anthony Kenny (also held in Oxford's Sheldonian Theatre, coincidentally). Kenny asked Dawkins to consider the comparison between an electric razor and a cutthroat razor: the electric razor is more complex in structure than a cutthroat razor, yet the cutthroat razor has more complex powers than the electric razor. The electric razor can only be used to shave a beard, whereas the cutthroat razor can shave a beard *and also* be used to cut a throat! This example pithily illustrated how Dawkins equivocates in his appeal to complexity in *The God Delusion* (showing that it is not necessarily the case that complex powers need to be accompanied by correspondingly complex structures).[42]

Dawkins's only response was incredulity. "I really don't see what you're saying, I mean, you cannot be serious!"[43] He later attacked Kenny in an online forum post, calling him a "meddling chairman who, to make matters worse, was a 'philosopher' with special training in obscurantism"[44] as well as claiming in his 2013 movie *The Unbelievers* that Kenny "completely ruined" the dialogue.[45] It has been unfortunate to witness how Dawkins seems to have found a new disdain for philosophy, in addition to theology, since William Lane Craig's tour of the United Kingdom. One hopes that his defenses may soften over time.

Fast-forward to today, and God has done so much that I cannot do his love justice. There was reconciling to be done with my parents, moving away to restart a career, giving up smoking, and ferociously battling anxiety that involved the help of a brilliant and insightful biblical counselor.[46] Today I live with my wife, Helen, and our two children, working to administrate and produce apologetics material of the kind that was so important for me on my own journey.

To be a Christian does not mean that you suddenly get better life circumstances. It is first and foremost about how you relate to God and how that changes your character. Even in the darkest struggles (in fact, especially in the darkest struggles), God's faithfulness has been shaping me and my family—every aspect, heart as well as mind. One of the biggest lessons I have learned, through studying the Bible and reflecting on myself, is how much of a perfectionist I am—prone to attaching my self-worth and identity to how well I can please others. This was the driving force behind my anxiety and likely why I embarked on that self-destructive trajectory toward the end of university. I now self-describe as a "recovering perfectionist." My fundamental outlook has changed, knowing that my security is in Jesus Christ, not my own accomplishments or performance.

This security is eternal (*real* immortality!), with the promise of a better world that does not simply lie dormant waiting for us on the other side of the grave. Rather, it starts *now* and means that we have the ultimate basis for working and striving toward that better world, because it all falls under God's redemptive project, in which we have the privilege of participating. It is this fact that it is God's project, not ours, which brings the hope, purpose, freedom, stability, and liberation we crave.

And if that sounds too good to be true, I encourage you, look into the evidence for it!

Thank You

Despite the criticism I have been directing at Dawkins throughout this story, I ultimately do need to thank him. Dawkins stirred up a massively important conversation that otherwise might have lain dormant. The arguments and challenges in *The God Delusion* have stress-tested how seriously people take their views on God, how well thought through such views are, and whether their proponents even believe them in the first place.

He wouldn't like me saying this, but Dawkins put me on the road to Christian faith (which is not belief without evidence but placing your trust in what the evidence shows you). He shook me out of my apathy and insisted that I follow the evidence where it led. The only twist was, the evidence took me where he (and I, initially) didn't want it to go, and it transpired that his atheism was not as airtight as he'd claimed.

Even Dawkins's persistent refusals to engage with William Lane Craig were a provocation and a catalyst for my own exploration of the arguments for God's existence, which poured fuel onto the fire of my curiosity. Dawkins helped me to take the God question seriously and to discover Christian apologetics, which ultimately brought me to know the living God himself.

This whole journey revived my thinking and revived my faith. It is no coincidence that those two things go together.

◆

"Do not be conformed to this world, but be transformed by the renewal of your mind, that by testing you may discern what is the will of God, what is good and acceptable and perfect" (Rom. 12:2).

Chapter 4

A Winding Path Through New Atheism to Faith

ANIKÓ ALBERT

Religion Through a Communist Lens

THE ONLY EVIDENCE OF THE first event on my faith journey is a small piece of paper, about three by five inches and easy to lose among the family photographs. Its color is a deep, burned sepia—one can't quite tell if it started out as white or some shade of office yellow. It attests that I was baptized at the age of six months at a Franciscan parish church named for the Heart of Jesus in western Hungary. My parents' names are followed by the abbreviation *r.k.*, Roman Catholic, but they were not practicing Catholics and did not attend the ceremony. I was staying with my paternal grandparents at the time, and this baptism was my grandmother's secret operation, with a visiting relative as coconspirator. I don't know if the priest raised any objections due to questionable parental consent, but if he did, I can picture the scene: my grandmother (who raised her younger siblings after their parents died) was not the timid kind. She would have made it clear that she was not leaving without her grandchild properly baptized.

Other than this act of resistance (which my parents would tell as

an amusing anecdote), my family's situation was probably fairly typical. Both of my parents, born in the early 1940s, had the beginnings
of a religious upbringing, but they stopped going to church as older
children. That would not be unusual anywhere in the world, but
Hungary had, of course, become part of the Soviet bloc, and while
church attendance was not outright banned even in the most hardline Stalinist years, it was certainly not encouraged. My grandparents
themselves stopped going, as far as I know—I spent quite a bit of time
with them in my younger years, and the idea of going to church on a
Sunday never came up. I grew up calling the relative my grandmother
had involved in her scheme "Godmother," but to my child's mind,
that was just her name—I had no idea what it meant. She also lived
far away, and if she ever had any plans of seeing to my Catholic education at some point, it never happened. There was also no repeat of
the clandestine baptism operation when my brother was born.

So I grew up in an agnostic family in what was a largely agnostic
country. I use the word *agnostic* because even though the Soviet-
controlled regime held materialist atheism to be the correct worldview, the regime was not engaged in an all-out war with religion. The
post-1956 Hungary of János Kádár was all about compromises and a
lighter touch: just as the relative affluence of "Goulash Communism"
kept people reasonably well-fed and content, churches could be kept
in line with a bit of freedom mixed with infiltrating and monitor-
ing. Religious practice rarely got people into trouble unless they were
Party members and held or aspired to important positions. In rural
areas, it was even more likely to be overlooked and seen as a quaint
folk tradition rather than a commitment to "counterrevolutionary"
reactionary ideology.

And that was, in fact, the impression of religion I had as a child:
that it was tradition, a thing that belonged to the past, where you
could find it in everything. It was this content that history, literature, and art were filled with, a set of stories, ideas, and images that

apparently everyone had shared at some point but now only a few people took seriously. It might surprise today's New Atheists—especially the Americans—how much a child educated in the public schools of an atheistic regime could learn about religion, but small countries with long histories tend to place a lot of value in their language, literature, and history.

During the communist years, a Marxist lens was supposed to be applied to everything, but it was often thin and left many things, including what people had believed in the past, clearly visible. We learned about the Bible as literature; we studied medieval poetry with Christian themes; we read historical novels in which everyone was a believer or at least spoke in religious terms—and often the most positive characters were shown as the true representatives of their faith and the most negative as hypocrites. Our history textbooks focused on material causes and social conflict, but we also learned about world religions and their effect on society. Field trips to historic places included churches and cathedrals, where we were taught not only about architectural styles but also about differences between denominations. My agnostic mother, a history and literature teacher, never passed an old church without trying to go inside to look—as a tourist, of course. (Part of her vacation wardrobe included a large shawl for sacred places that required covered shoulders regardless of the summer heat.) And there was all the art and music you had to know about to be an educated person, so much of it based on biblical themes. Our world was unquestionably secular, but religion echoed through it everywhere one went, both alien and strangely familiar, like a heritage language one understood imperfectly, at some very basic level, but did not speak.

This kind of secular exposure to the cultural marks of Christianity no doubt happens everywhere in Europe. But, like a lot of things, in communist Eastern Europe it came with additional twists and ironies. Atheism was the official, state-approved position, but people did not exactly hold state-approved positions in high regard. "The system," as we called the regime, was generally assumed to be wrong about everything. So, while atheism *had* become the dominant worldview, it was rarely held firmly and on principle. It was a default, cultural atheism, a mirror of the cultural Christianity that has become common in the Western world.

Curious About Religion

By the 1980s, one of the effects of all this was a growing curiosity about religion among young people. During my high school years, several kids I knew became religious, to the astonishment of their atheist parents. Some of them explored and returned to their family's heritage religion (the labels were still in common use); others found a home in a different denomination or a new religious movement. A few years later, my brother joined this wave when he started hanging out with friends from a Reformed church youth group and eventually got baptized there (our parents, unenthusiastic but supportive, were present for this one).

I was, however, merely an observer, stuck in the curiosity phase. I felt moved by Sienkiewicz's *Quo Vadis*, which inspired me to read the Gospels, but I didn't get much further—the rest of the Bible was an alien, scary land, safer to look up in an encyclopedia than to risk getting lost in. When the film version of *Jesus Christ Superstar* was released in Hungary (it was initially banned as religious propaganda), I watched it five or six times, following it to small theaters around Budapest. I also managed to get the soundtrack somewhere and, like many of my classmates, learned all the lyrics by heart (my generation probably picked up more English from album sleeves than from our government-issued English textbooks).

Through my college years, I continued circling around Jesus: there was that textual criticism elective about the differences between the portrayals of Christ in the four Gospels, and the Spanish linguistics thesis on dialect versus literary language in a Mexican novel that reimagines the Gospel of Luke through the life of a poor man called Jesucristo Gómez. But my interest remained intellectual, without a clear path to a spiritual commitment.

There were, of course, other things happening in my life, which soon took a sharp turn: I married a Jamaican student who was attending college in Hungary, and after we both graduated, I moved to Jamaica with him. When it came to religion, my new country could hardly be more different: suddenly I was surrounded by churchgoing Christians. Jamaica is often said to have the most churches per square mile of any country. Whether that popular claim is true or not, religion is certainly an important part of the culture and of people's everyday lives, a source of meaning and identity, especially for women. I found this out very quickly when, on one of my first walks in the neighborhood, a friendly older lady at a bus stop asked me where I was from, what my name was, and where I went to church, in quick succession. When I said that I didn't, she assumed it was because they didn't have my denomination in Jamaica. I explained that I was supposed to be Catholic, but I didn't grow up in the church, and I wasn't sure, and something about communism . . . I remember her looking sad, and I'm fairly sure she invited me to her church, though I don't remember what kind or what it was called.

I soon learned the term "lapsed Catholic" and started using it when needed, even though it was not quite accurate, since I had never been a practicing Catholic. It worked well at the school where I was teaching Spanish, a girls' high school founded and still run by Catholic Sisters, though now a part of the public-grant-aided system. Most of the students and teachers were not Catholic—Jamaica is a majority Protestant country—but they were Christian. The day started with devotions organized by the students: usually a song and a prayer. There was a duty roster, but volunteers were ready if needed. Some days the prayer was like a mini-service, with all the passion and cadences of the young girl's church tradition; on less inspired days the girls recited one of the psalms they knew by heart in lieu of prayer. The songs varied too, from talented renditions of Sandi Patty favorites to jumping around to "Father Abraham" (the latter frowned upon by the Sisters). As homeroom teacher I was supposed to supervise this, and it was a bit scary and magical at the same time—how did these children know all this? I felt the same way as I would a few years later, when my first son was born, and I found myself admiring all the women (and some of the same young girls at the school) who picked him up and held him in a such an easy, smooth, second-nature way. Coming from a small family on both sides, with few babies around when I was growing up, I didn't know how to do that. And since my mother was back in Hungary, I learned how to take care of babies much the same way I had been learning about religion: from books. (For what it's worth, the kids turned out fine.)

I was not all alone, of course. When I went back to work, my mother-in-law came to stay with us for a few months before we could find a day-care center. I also had friends at work, wonderful, warm-hearted Christian women who helped in every way they could. Looking back, I find it difficult to formulate where exactly I stood in terms of faith during this period. In some ways, I thought of myself as a Christian, though deep down, the faith was not there. My husband's family was Seventh-day Adventist, but he was not interested in religion. Since I was supposed to be Catholic, I started going to Mass some Sundays. I loved the music and the liturgy, but I didn't feel a strong connection and didn't know how to seek it. At times it felt like I was faking it. It didn't help that I was very busy with everything else in life: teaching, being a mother to young children, traveling to Hungary to visit my parents when we could. There was never enough time for anything, let alone figuring out life's greatest questions. In retrospect, there was clearly a push and pull going on; the closeness and warmth I felt in response to my Christian friends' witness, the beauty of their faith lived out in helping others, was at times undermined by the negative things I saw and connected to religion. There was the woman I had seen at church who asked at the neighborhood watch meeting if we could kill those thieves if we caught them. There was the intense, often violent homophobia, which, if not actively stoked, was then rarely condemned by churches. Not every Christian looked like Jesus. I liked the idea of Christianity, but I sometimes wondered why it didn't work better.

Making the Case for Atheism

Then, a year after the birth of our second child, we moved back to Hungary, only to move again after less than a year to California. The interlude in Hungary, short as it was, unfortunately deepened my doubts about faith. There was much more Christianity in the public sphere than when I had left, but a lot of it was not the kind I needed to see. A sadly familiar type of nationalism was back, conjured from the dark crevices of the past, and it was frequently masquerading, once again, in a Christian garb. Things seemed to be falling apart—the great unifying experience of the democratic transition had faded, and former friends found themselves on opposing sides, not talking to each other. There were many signs, including from the immigration office my husband had to deal with, that families like ours were not welcome. He took a job in the United States instead, and we arrived in the San Francisco Bay Area at the end of August 2001, in time for our older son to start first grade. Less than two weeks later, the event that would put him in a different generation from his younger brother happened: he remembers when the planes hit the towers and the subsequent weeks when he was afraid of our Sikh mailman, who wore a turban. Forget about Hungary—suddenly the rest of the world didn't seem to be doing that well either.

It was there, living as a new immigrant in war-on-terror America, that I gave up on Christianity altogether and became an atheist. I don't remember exactly how it happened. During the previous years, I would think that if I wasn't exactly a Christian, I was a Christian sympathizer—but now that sympathy was gone. I was upset with a lot of what I saw from self-declared Christians but also, I suspect, was upset about my own long history of seeking and not finding. Was there something wrong with me? If God was real, why did he call all these people but not me? Perhaps it was all false, I started thinking; perhaps none of it made sense. Once that idea formed, it wasn't hard to find lots of confirmation on the internet, where one "rationalist" website with lists of fallacies could point to ten others making fun of antiscience creationists, the sillier the better.

Since I was not able to work during this time, I read a lot. We didn't have a lot of money, and young children go through picture books fast, so we went to the library, and to my great surprise (I admit I had some negative preconceptions about the United States), it was amazing—every book you'd ever want and virtually no number limit! Isabel Allende and Richard Dawkins might not appear to have a lot in common, but they were among the authors whose entire collections I checked out and went through one by one, as I tend to do when I find a writer I like. I loved the way Dawkins wrote about science, how he mixed biology and poetic imagery to illustrate the unfolding of evolution, but during this period I also appreciated what were then only occasional and parenthetical comments critical of religion. Like the atheist blogs I had begun following, they were saying what I wanted to hear. I started thinking of myself as an atheist.

Around the same time, I saw an internet ad for a fiction contest, and I joined the site that was hosting it. Gather.com, launched mid-2005, was a brand-new online space, billed as a site for people interested in writing, culture, and discussions around shared topics (its investors included public radio and publishing companies). While, perhaps predictably, it eventually lost the race against the large social networks that currently dominate the scene, for about nine years it did fulfill part of its original mission and hosted groups of people from around the world who shared their writing and discussed their ideas with each other. It was in this space that I first identified as an agnostic/atheist. Many of the people I interacted with were probably as new to these discussions as I was. The New Atheist intellectuals' movement was just starting to take shape; the Four Horsemen had not yet been so named, and their 2006–07 publishing storm was yet to happen (Sam Harris's *The End of Faith* had already come out, but I wouldn't encounter it until later). We were excited to be a part of something—we pointed each other to our favorite smart websites, talked about blind watchmakers as we explained evolution to the less enlightened, made cool Flying Spaghetti Monster references, and followed P. Z. Myers into cephalopod fandom. We also despaired over fundamentalists' support for wars and denial of climate change. And, of course, we eagerly awaited the magnum opus, the definitive word from the top authority to be published. This was, I suppose, the peak of my atheist period. I didn't run to the bookstore to buy *The God Delusion* on the day it came out, but I did have it on pre-hold at the library.

Disillusioned by New Atheism

When I finally got *The God Delusion* in my hands (I was seventh in line, if I remember correctly), I read it in a couple of days . . . and I felt a little disappointed. It's not just that there wasn't anything really new in it—I figured, well, I've been clicking through all those blogs with the Scarlet A and Atomic Whirl logos, so of course it's all going to be familiar. But I thought it would be a delight to read, told in the rich evocative prose I had come to expect from Dawkins, and somehow it wasn't. I don't know if this was a real, measurable difference in style or merely my perception, but I felt, even while I agreed with most of what I was reading, that scientist Dawkins was joyful and creative and atheist Dawkins was angry and rigid, and I liked scientist Dawkins better.

There were also things I did not quite agree with. I had never thought the title was a good idea, but I figured it was meant to be provocative, perhaps the publisher's idea—Dawkins had stressed before that the word *all* in the BBC documentary *The Root of All Evil?* was not his choice. Surely, calling theism—a worldview shared in some form by the majority of humans for all of recorded history—a psychological disorder is similarly irrational. I was surprised to read Dawkins's defense of this term in his preface; it just repeated the mockery instead of attempting a serious argument and inserted a complaint about dishonesty by creationists in the middle. This tone was probably a good part of what did not click for me in the book.

In the same vein, I felt that calling the mainstream religious education of children "child abuse" was over the top—all parents, whether consciously or not, teach parts of their worldview to their children, along with their language and culture. I also knew, of course, about my peers brought up as atheists in Eastern Europe whose teenage rebellion took the shape of religious conversion. Then there was that anecdote about a newspaper story identifying the four-year-olds playing the three wise men in a school nativity play as a Sikh, a Muslim, and a Christian child, drawing Dawkins's ire. I could see his point, but those labels also represented cultures and their coming together in a country where the first two children were children of immigrants. That felt like a good thing to me, and an important thing, regardless of any criticism of those religions. And perhaps because my own immigrant children participated in the Bay Area Hungarian community's Christmas pageant, I did in fact find the idea charming and heartwarming.

I was also unconvinced by Dawkins's dismissal of "sophisticated theologians" as not representative of religion[1] and his assertion that "moderate, nice religious people . . . make the world safe for extremists."[2] Does that mean they should be condemned along with the terrorists who flew into the Twin Towers? If we are concerned about the harm done by the fanatics, wouldn't the "moderates" be our allies? In retrospect, I think what I wanted from atheism was a reassurance that religious claims were questionable and that it was okay to not believe, not an overarching narrative in which religion was a uniquely evil phenomenon. I enjoyed reading about bowerbirds and moths—at the time, I found the arguments about the evolution of religion and morality compelling—but I was not impressed by speculations about what was happening inside believers' heads today. This was especially true of Sam Harris's declarations about Muslims at a time when Islamophobia and anti-immigrant sentiment were on the rise in the West—and not only harming individual humans but threatening liberal democracy itself. Based on these concerns, I decided I was not terribly interested in reading Harris's *The End of Faith* or *Letter to a Christian Nation*.

I was even more unhappy with the position Christopher Hitchens took on the Iraq war and on (literally) fighting Islam. If I found the idea that all religion is bad (or that "religion poisons everything")[3] problematic, the claim that Islam was even more uniquely evil was an unmistakable red flag for me. After reading several excerpts from *God Is Not Great* posted in an online group by a very enthusiastic fan with a loose understanding of copyright law, I decided I wasn't interested in more. (I admit I also didn't think Hitchens's article "Why Women Aren't Funny"[4] was all that funny.) The other book that I read from the New Atheists' *anni mirabiles* was Daniel Dennett's *Breaking the Spell*. Here, as in *The God Delusion*, I found the evolutionary angles interesting, though at some point I began to wonder if having so many possible explanations was making the argument for the evolutionary origin of religion stronger or weaker. I appreciated that, for the most part, he was less certain than Hitchens and Dawkins that the world would *definitely* be better off without religion.

While I found a number of things that I didn't like in the Four Horsemen's books, articles, and the couple of debates I watched, it was in my interactions with online atheists that the first real cracks appeared. When I started participating in these discussions, I quickly got some recognition for my fact-checking skills, my knowledge of evolution (almost all learned from reading Dawkins), and my basic understanding of the logical arguments popular at the time. I was mostly interested in presenting atheism as an acceptable position and countering science denial. I also defended the idea that atheism was simply a lack of belief, not a set of beliefs much like a religion, as many of the believers we were arguing with claimed. Unfortunately, as I read some of the comments of my fellow atheists, I had to admit to myself that not only did they indicate a clear commitment to a set of beliefs, but also that many of those beliefs were simply wrong.

The most obvious of these were wild statements about history: religion is the cause of most wars and genocide; the Nazis were motivated by Christianity; the church has always been against education; Jesus never existed as a historical person but was a character copied from mystery religion. Many online atheists believed these things, some perhaps because they hadn't learned much history, others because they thought the mainstream history they had learned had been unduly influenced by Christians (or the New Atheists' *bête noire*, "our society's overweening respect for religion"[5]). But I knew that wasn't the case—*our* textbooks had been written by Marxists, after all, and they were very clear that wars were ultimately fought over control of resources, with religious or other justifications invented as needed.

As for Jesus mythicism, I had never heard of it until I ran into it on the internet. But when I tried to add nuance to some of these claims or indicate that they may not represent mainstream views, the response was often more of the same, with links to sources of questionable quality. There were endless threads about the harm religion does, and I soon noticed that otherwise smart people who prided themselves on their objectivity and rationalism simply assigned all the bad things (war, tribalism, slavery, misogyny) to religion, and all the good things (science, art, progress, civil rights) to secularism. It was, of course, a given that atrocities committed by people who subscribed to a religion were *obviously* caused by their religious beliefs, but atrocities committed by atheists were not, because atheism, by definition, could never inspire violent acts. This asymmetrical razor was applied, over and over again, to every data point pulled from anywhere in human history. When I mentioned that homosexuality was criminalized and punished with imprisonment by the atheistic Soviet regime, I was told this was clearly due to the persistence of Christian beliefs from the past, but religion got no credit for the clergymen who had led the American Civil Rights Movement.

More Cracks Appearing

Confirmation bias and attribution error were everywhere. The goalposts kept moving, but the underlying assumptions—religion is evil and religious people are deluded—remained. One day I saw on a friend's profile page a quote by Martin Luther King Jr. right next to a rant about how Christians are ignorant and hypocritical and should not try to influence national policy. My irony meter (a term we used a lot back then) exploded. Couldn't they see the contradiction? No, I was assured, Dr. King and those other ministers from the Southern Christian Leadership Conference weren't really religious; they just had to pretend for political reasons. While such absurdities were the rare extreme—the more typical atheist response would have been that good people do good things with or without religion—I realized that much of the discourse about Christianity by white American atheists completely erased the Black church.

Many of those I connected with were, of course, much more reasonable than the above examples reflect, but after some of these conversations it was hard to maintain the idea that atheists were by their very nature more rational than believers. Another thing that started to bother me was that some of the people who identified as secular humanists didn't sound like any kind of humanists at all. Perhaps I connect the term to its Renaissance beginnings in a way many Americans might not, but I felt that one couldn't be a humanist and consider a great part of humanity's cultural heritage worthless and the majority of one's fellow humans stupid. There was also an undercurrent of Western chauvinism that I was beginning to perceive, and I had hoped that we could defend human rights around the world without declaring entire cultures inferior. These crypto-racist themes have since broken to the surface and split the atheist movement into factions, one of which veers clearly toward the alt-right—I can't say that I saw that coming, but I was uncomfortable with these recurrent themes and wondered why allegedly liberal people would not see the problem with them. In retrospect, of course, the New Atheists' unquestioned sense of superiority and enthusiasm for taboo breaking stand out as predictable entry points for the racist and misogynist alt-right.

Science was, generally, a cleaner, safer area of discussion. Other than what I'd read about evolution, I knew little more than the typical humanities major, so I was there to listen. The atheists, naturally, claimed science in their corner, and there were a few Christians around who could be counted on to question evolution, climate change, or the efficacy of vaccines and thus needed to be enlightened. But the people who turned out to have the most knowledge on these matters were themselves Christians. Of course, it was not news to me that there were very smart Christians, and atheists who were less so (I had always thought the attempt to establish "bright" as the label for atheists was ridiculous and a little embarrassing). But it's one thing to know something and another to see it illustrated day after day. These Christians also pushed back against claims that science supported an atheistic universe. When it came to physics, I had very little idea of what was going on, and one of them reached out by email and pointed me to books for lay audiences where I could read up on quantum mechanics, relativity, and fine-tuning. I quickly realized that the rationalist-materialist ideas I had about the world were far from a solid scientific worldview—my understanding had been stuck in a deterministic, nineteenth-century positivist mode and needed a lot of updating.

As these cracks appeared in what I had previously considered to be my unmovable, perhaps psychologically determined naturalism, my email conversations with these caring (and very patient) Christians continued. I had many questions and objections—some simple, some more complicated. My obsession with theodicy would have driven most people to give up, but these individuals persisted. There were probably many breakthrough moments, but one I remember distinctly concerned the origin of morality. Yes, of course, humans have moral intuitions, I argued, but they can't come from God—they're full of bad stuff mixed in with the good: self-serving, tribalistic, violent instincts clearly shaped by evolution and causing much harm and suffering. Well, what about the moral standard that I'm using to make that judgment, a friend asked. Where does that come from?

Experiencing God

These conversations, as well as more books I was recommended —C. S. Lewis, of course, William James, N. T. Wright, and Francis Collins—started slowly pointing me toward "something more." One day, while walking under a row of old trees, I had one of those experiences that New Atheists like to mock (or shake their heads at in bafflement when it's told by someone whose intelligence and education they can't deny). I looked up through the branches and saw a shimmer, as if the world had shifted or a veil opened for a second. No, I did not become a Christian that moment—I felt something that I later recognized in John Wesley's description of his heart being "strangely warmed." I didn't quite know what to make of it. I was starting to think, at times, that it would be good to be a believer, but I was still fairly sure that I was just not wired that way. My Christian friends disagreed—one of them even declared that I was a "closet Christian" and started treating me that way.

Some of the atheist contingent had soured on me earlier, when I argued too much about history or epistemology, and around this time the others also concluded that something was up. I saw one explain to another on a thread that while I *used* to be the voice of reason, I was now "hanging out with theists" and could not be trusted. They were right. One day, walking on the beach, watching the gentle bay waves roll in and the sandpipers running around, the words just came to me, and I realized they were true: *I believe in God.*

I had also begun to visit churches on Sunday mornings, sitting in the back, telling myself I was there just to observe. I went back to one particular church several times, a Methodist church opposite the high school where my older son was then a freshman, a church whose building with its quirky mix of Renaissance and Mission Revival had been winking at me. I knew close to nothing about Methodism, but the online friend who called me a closet Christian was a Methodist, so I was curious and, I suppose, hoping to find good people. And, of course, I did, the kind of people who came over to talk to me before I could escape. After the second or third time, the pastor invited me to come in to talk to him. I explained my history, what I was confused about, and what I was still not sure I believed: how do I get from theism to the resurrected Jesus? He told me to stop worrying and trying to figure everything out. What had brought me there was faith; I needed to start living it, and Jesus would do the rest.

And he did. After all, he has been close to me all along, whispering to me across the divide all my life, wherever I was at the time. If God could create the universe from nothing, what inside that universe could he *not* do? And what story would be more beautiful than one in which the Creator chose to live, incarnate, among his creation and give his life for them? Faith and reason, far from the enemies the New Atheists *believe* them to be, held hands and led me to the communion table one Sunday. Not long after, I was in the choir. When I joined the church by profession of faith the following year, people were surprised that I wasn't already a member. A few years later, when my marriage fell apart, my church community was there, making sure I wasn't alone, holding my hand along the way. I was among friends, no longer on the outside looking in.

When I remarried, it was to another Christian—one of the friends I had met online. But that is another story. Many of us from the same e-community, including some of the atheists, are still friends—with some, we don't talk about religion; with others, we try. I feel I understand where some of the anger comes from, and I hope that I might one day be able to help someone along the way as I have been helped. But most importantly, I am grateful to all who played a role in my journey, in real life and online, in whatever way they had—even the New Atheists.

Chapter 5

Hearing God Through an Enchantment with Nature

ANDREW G. GOSLER

THE GREATER HONEYGUIDE (*Indicator indicator*) is an extraordinary bird. The largest and most widely distributed of nine *Indicator* species, found through much of sub-Saharan Africa, its evolution is something of a mystery. Superficially resembling a passerine,[1] detailed study of its anatomy and DNA demonstrates conclusively that it is more closely related to woodpeckers, barbets, and toucans (birds of the order of Piciformes). Nothing so remarkable about that; evolution often repeats effective patterns. But honeyguide species show several adaptations reflecting their dependence on honeybees (*Apis mellifera*) and in particular on beeswax. For example, modification of the gut allows them to digest beeswax, which is inedible to most birds.[2] A number of anatomical modifications, including thickened skin, also protect them from bee stings.[3] Yet the best evidence suggests that the honeybee only entered Africa about six million years ago and evolved into distinct African subspecies in the last three million years.[4] Considering the honeyguides' bee-related adaptations,

Short and Horne comment, "Thus there are intriguing questions and puzzles regarding the evolution of the honeyguides."[5]

But the intrigue goes far beyond simple questions about the speed and direction of evolutionary change, questions that challenge the neo-Darwinian model[6] of "descent with modification" championed by Richard Dawkins throughout his writing on evolution. The recent evolutionary history of honeybees in Africa suggests that the honeyguides might not be merely an evolutionary contemporary of *Homo*, as suggested by this time frame. Indeed they, and the greater honeyguide in particular, might be more than mere *witnesses* to the emergence some two to three hundred thousand years ago of "anatomically modern" humans (*Homo sapiens*) and culturally modern humans less than one hundred thousand years ago. Rather, through a mutually beneficial relationship, this bird may have participated subtly in our emergence as we participated in its evolution. Since the period in question saw one of the most rapid evolutionary changes of any animal apparent from fossil evidence, namely the increase in human brain size, we may in part owe to this bird, and to this cultural *co*-evolution, that most prized feature of our humanity: intelligence.[7]

The name *honeyguide* gives the clue to our relationship, for the greater honeyguide uniquely guides humans to the nests of wild bees. It appears to guide humans, rather than other animals,[8] as humans have mastered fire and use it to smoke out and subdue the bees, so that neither man nor bird is stung. While the human participant is more focused on the nutritional and medicinal benefits of the honey, the bird's interest is in access to the wax. Nevertheless, in most traditions the honey hunter leaves a piece of empty wax comb, sometimes containing larvae, as a token gift for the honeyguide, which the bird readily consumes.[9]

The unique relationship[10] that the honeyguide has with man is mediated through a complex inter- or multispecies culture. When the bird wishes to guide, it attracts attention to itself by using specific "chatter" calls. It then uses other calls and behaviors when guiding. People must learn these calls. Similarly, the birds learn specific calls or whistles given by people wishing to attract the bird's attention, sounds that differ from one people (such as the Boran of Kenya or the Yao of Mozambique) to another, and so are locally and culturally specific. The knowledge of which calls to give and how to read the honeyguide's behavior are part of the traditional ecological knowledge of the peoples: more specifically, of those individuals who specialize in gathering honey for the community. Ornithological and archaeological evidence suggests that these local cultures may have survived over thousands of years.

Much of what is known to science about the biology of this bird and the detailed anthropology—more specifically the ethno-ornithology—of this relationship is owed to Hussein Adan Isack, a Boran, who undertook a detailed study over many years to "test" scientifically whether the Boran honey hunters' claims were correct. His work culminated in a doctoral thesis at the University of Oxford in 1987 under the supervision of Dr. Richard Leakey.[11] Of course, the Boran honey hunters knew their claims were true; they had relied on this relationship for millennia and were not fools. So Hussein Isack's demonstration that these people were 67 percent more efficient at finding a bee's nest when guided by a honeyguide was a demonstration to a skeptical scientific community of the validity of traditional ecological knowledge, and indeed a demonstration to a wider post-industrial, postimperial, postcolonial world that the unique, ancient knowledge and wisdom of local people deserves to be heard. In other words, in a uniquely modest way, this study spoke truth to power.

Recognizing My Vocation

In the early months of my employment as a part-time field assistant in the Edward Grey Institute of Field Ornithology in Oxford, I was fortunate, indeed blessed, to hear Hussein Isack speak about his doctoral work. Something about it touched me deeply, not least the sense of a profound, spiritual sadness that—through the inexorable advance of that postindustrial, postimperial, and postcolonial world today represented by the global power of multinationals, modernization, and consumerism—this unique, fragile, and ancient relationship between bird and man was dying out. The knowledge was no longer being passed down from generation to generation, of either the humans or the birds, since the people increasingly bought honey or sugar from markets, and honeyguides in suburban areas no longer attempted to guide humans.

On these multiple fronts, from the challenges to conventional evolutionary theory to the nature of wisdom and the extinction of experience, the resonance that I felt with the story of the greater honeyguide was somehow symbolic of a deeper discomfort or disease that I felt about the world. The early Christians had the greatest respect for *phronesis*, a kind of "practical wisdom," which for me is characterized by the traditional ecological knowledge of the Boran and the stories they tell about why the greater honeyguide guides them. As with many traditional stories of oral cultures, these have a strong moral message, such as that one supports oneself only through the support of others.[12] This resonated with the core ethic of my own Jewish heritage, and as if to underline this sense that the traditional knowledge was built on a moral foundation of mutual dependence, I also learned that the Boran considered the relationship between human and honeyguide to be sacred and that it is a great sin to kill a honeyguide or a bee or to hunt honey during the bees' principal breeding season.

The decline and loss of such practical wisdom, resulting from creeping globalism, is a narrative resonant with the loss globally of knowledge of nature, the sacred, and of faith. Gradually I came to associate or identify my sense of dis-ease with the writings of Richard

Dawkins. For me, finding healing and making my peace with these realities were profoundly bound up with coming to faith, while (almost independently of faith) rejecting the atheist rhetoric that had come to pervade the literature of evolution after Dawkins. To be more specific, I became more sensitive to the association between the degradation of life on Earth, the extinction of species and cultures, and the lost awareness of the sacramental nature of life—the effects of which are plain to see pervading our own postimperialist cultures. Nowhere is this loss better illustrated than by the accumulation of garbage, even bodies, left by would-be adventurers on Mount Everest, the sacred mountain of the Sherpa people on whose hospitality and forbearance these visitors have relied for decades.[13] Furthermore, as a scientist, I came to reject Dawkins's strident, unquestioning belief (unwavering even in the face of contrary evidence) that only the peculiarly masculinist, neo-Darwinian framing of evolution could possibly yield adaptive change in living organisms over time.

This was the same neo-Darwinism that spawned eugenics and thence the Holocaust: a post-Darwinian legacy that left deep scars across my own family in the Netherlands from 1942 onward. For a young naturalist evolving a career path out of a love of nature in general, and birds in particular, I sensed a deep hurt in being told by a distinguished academic through the authority of a book that, while it's unfortunate if you find these truths distasteful, that's the way of the world, so grow up and deal with it. My later realization that Julian Huxley (grandson of "Darwin's Bulldog," Thomas Henry Huxley)—the author of *Evolution: The Modern Synthesis*,[14] which provided the framework for evolutionary biology for more than fifty years—had been a staunch advocate of eugenics merely served to underwrite my discomfort. In becoming a biologist, neo-Darwinism was the culture I was being invited into. The language of eugenics is the language of competition, which Darwin and Dawkins believed was the driver of evolution and speciation (the origin of species). Its political consequences are overtly racist. Replete with its belief in the supremacy of winners and the irrelevance of losers, eugenics is a repressive worldview that frames the Holocaust as the inevitable consequence of the selfishness and cruelty that its adherents believed underpinned all of life. But while these beliefs affirmed the assumptions of the better-off classes and therefore reflected the realities of life for many poor folk in the empires of the nineteenth century, they owed little to evidence-based science. With its scoffing rejection—based on the crudest of experiments—of Lamarckian evolutionary processes (contrary to Darwin himself who accepted them) and the assumption that adaptation could only result from directed selection operating on randomly generated genetic variation, the neo-Darwinian framing of evolution is profoundly flawed. Through science, we now know that these things are not true.[15]

On October 28, 2020, the University of Oxford conferred on me the title of Professor of Ethno-ornithology. Ethnobiology evolved out of an anthropological interest in the local and traditional knowledge of indigenous peoples and the survival of that knowledge, of the languages in which it is held, and in the plants, animals, and ecosystems of which it speaks. It has emerged as a discipline with a unique message to the world: biodiversity includes us, and conservation is a human rights issue. Resonant with my personal journey, conferment of the title of professor reflects an evolving career from pure ecology to ethnobiology; from unemployed graduate to employment within the Department of Zoology (University of Oxford), to a joint appointment with the School of Anthropology and Museum Ethnography, to a fellowship in Mansfield College as Director of Studies for Human Sciences; and from part-time field assistant to professor. It is a story deeply entwined with my journey *to* faith, and *in* faith, to identify the peace of Christ that is *shalom* with the peace that I always found in nature ("the peace of God, which surpasses all understanding," Phil. 4:7). I have come to recognize that having something to kick against can be a life-changing and creative process of finding truth, and for providing my kicking post I am ever grateful to Richard Dawkins.

Learning to See Holistically

Elsewhere I have written of the part played by Richard Dawkins's writings in my philosophical journey to faith. In summary, in 1981 I came to work in the department in Oxford where Richard Dawkins's teaching and writing had the most influence. While if pressed I'd have regarded myself as agnostic, a truer position was that the confusion of religious influences I experienced in childhood (liberal Jewish family, the Lord's Prayer at school) left me rejecting religion. Having read *The Selfish Gene*[16] as a student, I had already perceived its philosophical flaws (see below), but the drip-drip-drip of sneering atheism in Dawkins's books, with its implicit anti-Semitism (as I sensed it), had the reverse effect on me than that intended. I started to explore faith, and specifically Christianity, because I sensed a resonance between the teachings of Jesus and my own sense of environmental and social justice.[17]

Here, however, I want to explore more of the scientific underpinnings and the changing paradigms of evolutionary and ecological science that have affirmed me in my journey while also saying something of the mystical experiences of my faith journey that have challenged my assumptions about the nature of reality. Through this I hope to indicate that my journey to and in faith has been entirely consistent with my personal moral and scientific convictions. I wish also to challenge readers to recognize that the fundamental demand on our humanity to support and sustain life on our planet (for who is my neighbor?) is not a cultural veneer artificially constructed to defend us from our "selfish genes" but an expression of the moral imperative that is the very ground of life underwritten through mutual dependency.[18]

Ethno-ornithology held a key for me. It was while opening an evolution lecture by presenting an Australian Aboriginal story as an allegory for Darwin's model of speciation driven by competition that I discerned a new reading of Darwin's insight. The traditional story tells how Pelican and Emu once lived together. But they quarreled all the time over what to eat. So Pelican and Emu agreed they would go their separate ways and eat their favorite foods *and peace would be restored.* Pelican went to live in the lake and ate fish, and Emu stayed on the land and ate lizards. While biologists in following the reductionism of biology had always focused on the competition, the conflict, to underpin the worldview of its practitioners, they failed to perceive an alternative: that life's diversity reflects the working out of millions, if not billions, of years of conflict resolution. Speciation is the very act of peace building, and so the tree of life, represented symbolically in Judaism by the menorah and the seven days of creation, is truly rooted in the peace of God, the central day of rest, *shalom*, and *Shabbat*.

Since Darwin, a belief has been accepted within biology that exclusive and bitter self-interest underpins life. But note that since that "underpinning" cannot be the product of the systems or organisms themselves, these beliefs imply another place—the mind of God. In their rejection of God as revealed through Scripture, the New Atheists merely replace him with a theology of their own, and it isn't pretty. The enculturated science and eugenic sympathies of the neo-Darwinists led to the Dawkinsian argument that plants and animals exist purely to replicate and promote copies of their genes. Biologically one might as well argue that a man exists to make fingernails! As Noble[19] points out, this thesis lacks scientific evidence or credibility and represents the most dangerous example of *reductio ad absurdum*, but it is a belief that has utterly permeated evolutionary biology for more than forty years. Robbing all life of meaning or value, it denies all motivation for human concern for the welfare or indeed existence of others, let alone other species, other than that of pure self-interest. After Dawkins (following in the footsteps of J. B. S. Haldane, Julian

Huxley, and Bill Hamilton), no act of kindness could be perceived as other than a thinly veiled attempt to promote one's genes. In the eyes of the neo-Darwinists there can be no sainthood, for even Saint Francis, who lived and died in poverty in the service of Christ, got his reward in the fact that eight hundred years after his death, many revere his memory. Yet the fact that one can construct such perverse and corrosive arguments against virtue hardly stands as evidence for the theory of the selfish basis for existence. For one thing, why should we revere Francis's example if it were truly explained by a deeper, darker motivation? And for another, it hardly benefited his genes!

But what of biology? Interpreted through the prism of neo-Darwinism, every observation of nature could be seen to support the assumptions of nature's bitter self-interest. The classic "evidence" is found in kin selection, which argues that altruistic behaviors (kindnesses) are most commonly observed between kin, as expected if life existed to promote genes, since kin share (marginally!) more genes than nonkin. Much has been made, for example, of the fact that parent animals (and plants) invest in their offspring greatly in time, energy, and nutrients, with the neo-Darwinians arguing that of course they invest in their children because they carry their genes. But what if they didn't so invest? Well then, their children wouldn't thrive and ultimately their lineage would go extinct. Whether that matters or not is not the point at issue. Rather, it is that a simpler (more parsimonious) explanation than that of the "selfish gene" for why organisms care for their young is that we will not see living examples of organisms that went extinct because they failed to invest in their offspring. So caring appropriately (i.e., requirements differ for buttercups, bees, bats, and beggars) for your own offspring, as every good parent knows, is a necessary responsibility; and it is a necessary responsibility of *all* organisms, not in order to propagate their genes but simply because it is adaptive.

Similarly, much was made of birds that have "helpers" at the nest, since helpers tend to assist kin more often than expected at random. A classic study was that of the white-fronted bee-eater (*Merops bullockoides*) in Kenya. These birds nest together in colonies, excavating nest burrows, typically in a river cliff. Half of all breeding pairs have helpers, which genetic analysis indicates are typically offspring or grandchildren from a previous year.[20] When one looks more closely at the behavior of many bird species that have "helpers," the evidence that they are actually helping (i.e., that helped pairs fledge more chicks) becomes more equivocal—or at least in terms of young raised, their contribution is marginal. So, if they are not really helping, what are they doing? Birds such as the white-fronted bee-eater inhabit a harsh, arid environment in which learning how to raise young may be as important to future success as producing offspring. These birds tend to be relatively long lived (typically seven-plus years) so that serving an apprenticeship may be essential, and any student needs experienced tutors. For each bee-eater, the only individuals with proven knowledge and experience are its parents and grandparents: the bird itself is the living proof. So the answer to why they help kin may be they are learning how to raise young, and as they gain experience they may indeed become "helpers." I suggest rather that, although they may indeed become helpers, their contributions are "tolerated" by their parents and/or grandparents because education of the young is a necessary part of their adaptive, parental responsibility.

The Selfish Gene is rich in contradiction. Having argued for the genetic determinism of life, in the end Dawkins suggests that it doesn't have to be like this and that we can choose to defy the tyranny of our genes. As this undermines his own fundamental premise, one must ask Dawkins from where this profound desire for true altruism has come. Furthermore, while constructing a grand narrative that life has *no* purpose, *The Selfish Gene* argues that the purpose of life is to promote copies of genes (the replicators). Since no purpose can reside in the genetic material itself since it is mere chemistry, it can have neither motive nor goal of its own and so any "purpose" must be located elsewhere: the mind of God again?

So we are left with the fundamental question and the incapacity of science to answer the question: Does life have purpose or not? Similarly, if the purpose of life were for genes to promote copies of themselves, we must observe that they have been singularly unsuccessful since what has survived down the ages is not ancient, unaltered nucleic acid sequences but what works for the persistence of life: what is adaptive. And what is adaptive is contextual, "learned" behavior and immunity, and conditioned through the functional operation of the epigenome at least as much as the genome. Indeed, science demonstrates abundantly that the multidimensional wonder and complexity of life is far richer than the one-dimensional caricature of it offered by the neo-Darwinian model. What has emerged in the years since Richard Dawkins implored us to look at genes is the realization that inheritance is not merely genetic (but also cytological, epigenetic, and cultural), and that while living organisms may use a random process under certain conditions to evolve specific regions of the genome, much adaptive, nonrandom, genetic change is engineered by cells in response to their environment.[21] In other words, as Darwin himself believed, Lamarck was right, and selection isn't the whole answer. We might even say that if evolution proceeded by so simplistic a mechanism as the neo-Darwinian framework of random genetic mutation and natural or sexual selection, it would be so inefficient that life would have long since gone extinct, if indeed it would have ever started.

One of the great misdirections of history is a belief that an incompatibility between Christian faith and the scientific narrative of our evolutionary origins rests on the truth or otherwise of the book of Genesis. Rather, I want to suggest that any incompatibility lies not between Christian faith and the evolving history of life but with the neo-Darwinian framing of that history, with its focus on conflict rather than conflict resolution. The role of competition was clearly overplayed in the construction of a scientific evolutionary narrative, since while biogeography points to *allopatric* speciation (i.e., the divergence of geographically isolated populations), competition can only operate within populations (i.e., driving *sympatric* speciation). Furthermore, competition plays no part in driving allele-frequency change in some of the classic examples of evolution observed, such as the color-morph change of the peppered moth (*Biston betularia*) or the evolution of MRSA. While competition is surely one of many weak and subtle influences on local adaptation, it probably doesn't drive the origin of species.

It is clear to anyone with an open mind and eyes to see that Genesis 3 is a rich allegory of the evolution of *Homo sapiens* under the influence of both natural and sexual selection,[22] and that taken with Genesis 1 and 2, not to mention Genesis 4–9, it offers a timeless account linking our present environmental and extinction crisis to the human discernment of morality.[23] Here is true wisdom of great significance to our modern age. Yet sadly, the failure to read Genesis as the allegorical Word of God rather than literal, historical fact has reduced issues of real importance to "the Genesis argument" for or against faith, to simplistic notions of time and whether life originated on Earth 6,000 or 3.5 billion years ago, and of whether life is God's work or not. When I read such accounts, I recall Paul's first letter to the Corinthians, "When I was a child, I spoke like a child, I thought like a child" (1 Cor. 13:11). Growing up through the 1970s, with an increasing awareness of environmental issues, it seemed to me that the authors of Genesis had discerned a deeper wisdom about the human condition: that disconnection from our spiritual roots (Gen. 3) would ultimately lead to the destruction of our planetary home (Gen. 7).

When we ask questions of deep time, we speak as if we understand time. Yet time's passing is not the issue so much as what we understand of the present. I have found no satisfactory scientific explanation. Consider this: everything that exists, exists in the present. The past exists now only as our experienced memory, as the ripples of cause and effect of an infinity of past present moments on this present reality. The future exists now as potential, and in our hopes, fears, and intentions. So if everything that exists exists in the present, the present must be very special. How might I define the present? Since we are trapped in time, we experience and conceptualize the present as where the past meets the future. It is instantaneous. It has no "thickness," no existence, in time. Yet the past doesn't exist, because it is not the present; and the future doesn't exist, since it hasn't happened yet. So if the present, where everything that exists is, exists at the meeting of two nonexistent perceptions, the very mysticality of existence comes into sight.

While we experience time passing, the present point of existence is outside of time. If in this instantaneous present, this "still point," present eternal, there is no time, there also is no frequency, no color, no sound, only pure being, pure relationship—a connectedness of all things—perfect peace, perfect love. When Paul said that in God "we live and move and have our being" (Acts 17:28), was he in fact discerning that this present experience is God's consciousness? As we cannot look on the face of God (Exod. 33:20), so we cannot look on the present moment, for the moment we say *this* is the present, it has passed! Our experience of time's present and passing (as the gap through which the future pours into the past[24]) resonates with the biblical wisdom of God's immanence and transcendence. Furthermore, it offers the framework for the principal scientific method of hypothesis testing, since it is through our observations of the past (experience) that we make predictions (prophecy) of the future to construct models of the present. The present, where all existence has its being, is whole and indivisible—the epitome (and etymology) of holiness—and reductionist science only allows us to create models of it, by which we hope for insights into reality itself. We might refine our models, as indeed we are doing with evolutionary biology as we come to reject the neo-Darwinian model, but our refined model is always only that, a *model* of reality and not reality itself. In our journey to knowing, then, we are destined forever to dance around the truth, constructing ever-refined models of it but never apprehending it. To do that requires a spiritual engagement through the psyche: an engagement with our very being, our present moment in God's eternal present moment.

Accepting the possibility that the ground of all being, the "locus" of existence and consciousness, is the "mind" of God led me to reject the reductionist scientific agenda that underpinned *The Selfish Gene*. In essence, this agenda, which arises from a materialist philosophy, assumes that biology can be explained by chemistry, and chemistry by physics. If correct, understanding the properties of entities at one level of complexity should predict properties of entities of which they are constituents. Yet the failure of reductionism is easily demonstrated. For example, the properties of water, which is liquid at room temperature and uniquely important for life, cannot be predicted from the properties of its constituent elements, hydrogen and oxygen, both of which are gases at room temperature. Trapped within a mindset of cause and effect, scientists frame the creation of such novelty as "emergence," that is, the properties of water only emerge upon the 2:1 combination of hydrogen and oxygen. Yet if we understand reality as existing whole and indivisible within the present, neither emergence nor reductionism can fully satisfy our desire to apprehend the truth. Emergence abounds in creation from water and subatomic particles to Gaia through which life maintains the optimal conditions for life and its own persistence.[25] Ecologists now recognize that Gaian systems abound, coupling life to its physical setting. They balance the rate of photosynthesis with atmospheric CO_2 concentration; and through the creation of cloud condensation nuclei, by means of the release of volatile organic compounds by rainforest trees or dimethyl sulfide (DMS) by marine phytoplankton, they regulate atmospheric temperature and precipitation respectively (Rom. 8:28). As Richard Dawkins correctly observes,[26] Gaia cannot have evolved through a process of evolution by natural selection, but contra Dawkins, it is not because Gaia doesn't exist, but because Dawkins's framing of evolution, indeed of life, is inadequate (Mark 2:22). Yet in Gaia's existence we can apprehend a deeper wisdom behind the creation and sustaining of life, and it is the wisdom not of competition and conflict but of mutual dependence.[27]

As exemplified by the honeyguide and honey hunters, life at every scale, from subcellular organelles to the global biosphere, expresses a fundamental relationship of mutual interdependence. This essential wisdom of interdependence runs through every being—plant or animal—that has the breath of life. But to look upon the pains and sufferings of the world, and of our own lives, and to recognize and believe this deep truth about life rather than to hold to a belief in the selfishness of genes requires a willingness to see differently, irrespective of what our culturally constructed assumptions demand of us. For it is through that willingness, that radical nonconformity, that we discover the open-mindedness that is the invitation to truth itself: openness to the Spirit.

I have not told you the whole story about the greater honeyguide, and I must, for like all other honeyguide species, the greater honeyguide is a brood parasite. That means it lays its eggs in the nests of other birds, destroying their eggs in the process, and relies on the host to raise its young. Some forty hole-nesting species have been recorded as its hosts.[28] Shortly after fledging, the young birds find adult honeyguides from whom it is thought they learn the culture of guiding. It is unclear why brood parasites, which include the European cuckoo (whose behavior coined the term *cuckoldry*), have evolved this way of life. The strategy is not without risks, for the future survival of the cuckoo and honeyguide depend on that of their hosts, who may evolve countermeasures. Through a particular, moralizing lens, the behavior of these birds may seem disreputable, but perhaps a different perception emerges when we understand that the dynamics of honeyguide populations are bound up not only with that of their numerous hosts, but with the fruit tree–planting activities of humans (pollinated by bees), trees for which too many nest-hole excavators may become a problem. Whatever the explanation, I suggest that a holistic—a more Gaian—perspective can help. Surely, we do not see as God sees (1 Sam. 16:7). Short and Horne write, "[Nest-parasitism] . . . seems to many to be cruel in the extreme, for every honeyguide is a 'killer,' representing a lost brood of some host. Rather, honeyguides should be respected as highly evolved, efficient brood parasites, and unique among birds in their dependence on beeswax."[29]

Personal Evidence Base

God has always spoken to me through birds. My doctoral research in the 1980s on the fine details of adaptation and the ecomorphology of the bill (beak) of the great tit (*Parus major*)[30] led me to descriptions of the huia (*Heteralocha acutirostris*). The huia, a bird endemic to Aotearoa New Zealand, was remarkable for the difference in form of the male and female's bill. Revered by the Maori, it was driven to extinction by white New Zealander settlers (*pakehas*), and most notably by the ornithologist Walter Buller. Buller was inspired by Darwin to believe that the vulnerability of the endemic birds of New Zealand was symptomatic of their inferiority and that, sad though it was, like Maori culture it was destined to extinction now that a superior culture had arrived.

In January 2019, I gave one of my students a copy of my book *Ethno-ornithology*[31] when he emerged from his doctoral oral exam. I had ordered it gift wrapped from an internet bookshop, and so with all due ceremony in the presence of friends and examiners, I handed it to him. As he opened it, I noticed something peculiar about it. A small block of color plates that should have been invisible in the closed volume and inserted near the center was very visibly inserted in the wrong place. I asked my student if I might quickly inspect the book, as something looked odd. What I found surprised, shocked, amazed, and amused me. In place of four pages of plates and a painting of Maori king Te Aho-o-te-Rangi Wharepu, I found twenty-two pages of Christian icons! Thankfully I hadn't signed the book, so telling him it was faulty and I'd send it back, I later signed a copy for him that I had in the lab.

In trepidation, considering how many copies they might have printed like this, I phoned the publisher. Suitably shocked, they requested pictures of what was and what should have been. I sent them the pictures, and they offered to speak to the printer and call me back in a few days. This they did. The printer had spent two days tracking down what had happened, since clearly these were pictures from another book they had been printing. The comedy of errors that led to this was so convoluted that they didn't want to waste my time with the details, but I should rest assured that this was "the only copy like it." It was unique in the whole world: so, when the publisher apologized and offered to replace it at no charge, I happily declined, pointing out that in fact I was a minister and found this miracle of improbability rather cool!

Later that year, while on a lecture tour in Aotearoa New Zealand, I was visiting the Museum of New Zealand Te Papa Tongarewa with my hosts Reverends Tim and Mel McKenzie. There I saw the painting of King Te Aho-o-te-Rangi Wharepu and told my hosts the story of the icons. Tim later asked if I might talk about it in a service in their church the next day. After the service a local expert on icons asked me if I understood what God was saying to me through this. That God was affirming my work of ethno-ornithology and was in it with me, I had discerned already, but the expert advised me to seek guidance in Oxford about each of the icons. Space does not permit me to expand further on that, but when I returned to Oxford and opened the book to investigate why the icons were at pages 32–33, rather than pages 137–38, I found them placed within my own chapter, indeed within a paragraph describing how neo-Darwinism had sought to distance ornithology from its taxonomic and naturalistic roots!

Upon my return to the United Kingdom, I was sent a gift by my new friends in New Zealand: J. Ruka's wonderful book *Huia Come Home*.[32] The Darwinian assumption about the huia's bill was that the dimorphism evolved to reduce competition between members of the pair. The Maori knew (and revered them for the fact) that huia paired for life and were forever together. They shared in the task of food finding, their differing bills complementing each other as knife is to fork, and they shared the prey they extracted. Rather than Darwin's framework of competition driving evolution, they were the model of devoted mutual dependence.

When we watch a bee pollinating a flower as it searches for nectar, do we see a reciprocal and mutually beneficial interdependency or a cynical manipulation of insect behavior by a plant and a purely self-interested behavior of the bee? As the true purpose of the sexual dimorphism of the huia was obscured through the misdirection of Darwinian assumptions, so the reality of God's creation is obscured by neo-Darwinian cynicism. As I have felt my eyes opened to a truer perception of creation, I have come to regard Christ as my honeyguide.

As I write this, people everywhere are suffering the distress of the COVID-19 pandemic. What have we learned from all this? Many have found comfort in birdsong that they have become aware of for the first time in their lives and in the hope it provides that, despite everything we are suffering, life goes on and God is with us. Many have also turned, perhaps for the first time, to the Bible and found comfort in the knowledge, reflected for example in the book of Lamentations and Psalm 42, that others have suffered and been delivered and in the ministry of Christ and the hope offered by witnesses to the resurrection. But all this reflects a deeper realization of the interconnectedness of all things, that life is the most precious and fragile gift to inanimate matter, that every life hangs by a thread, and that, therefore, all life is sacred and founded not on selfishness but on mutual interdependence, which is truth: the spirit of love and peace.

Chapter 6

An Afrikaner's Faith Pilgrimage

JOHAN ERASMUS

Daring to Ask: Does God Exist?

I GREW UP AS AN Afrikaner in South Africa, which means you play rugby on Saturdays and go to church on Sundays and you are religious about both. If you are an Afrikaner, you are almost by default a Christian,[1] and with the exception of when our national rugby team lost to Japan in the 2015 rugby World Cup, few identify as atheists. The question in that kind of an environment is seldom whether you believe but rather in which church you believe those things.

My family believed those things in a Reformed church in a town about three hours from Johannesburg, and my earliest memories of church were not disbelief but boredom. My main objective on a Sunday (like most of the kids my age) was to not fall asleep and, more importantly, not be caught out in the confusing sitting-and-standing routine of our liturgy.

Things changed dramatically, however, when I was ten years old. My parents were out of town during the school holidays, and one morning my uncle sat me down and told me that my dad had just died of a heart attack on the Zimbabwean border. He was in his early forties. Before that day, when I sat in church I thought about the school cricket or rugby game I played the day before, but after that fateful day, I sat in church (and everywhere else, for that matter) with deep existential questions. All of a sudden, chasing a ball around was not enough to satisfy my ten-year-old self. I had questions about meaning and destiny, and those questions drove me mad.

They also drove my mom mad—primarily because the questions came to me in the early hours of the morning, at which point I would wake her up to discuss them. For some reason my mom was not the best at discussing the existence of God at 2 a.m. Eventually she gave up, and the poor pastor started getting midnight calls from me.

These two had to field questions from all over the place. What about all the other religions? How do we know we are right? How do we know God exists? Why trust the Bible? The list went on. As a good Reformed believer, the pastor assured me that if I was chosen, I had nothing to worry about. That helped for about an hour, after which the terrible thought occurred to me that I might not be chosen! I don't think the technology existed back then, but I am sure that the poor pastor would have blocked our number if he could have. He was a patient man and responded as best he could, but in a culture where these types of questions were taboo, my questions and his answers failed to meet.

Back then (in the late '90s and early 2000s), the Afrikaners believed in three "very real" dangers: the Black danger, the Red danger, and the Roman danger. It does not translate that well into English, but we were terrified of an aggressive Black majority government, the Communists, and the Roman Catholic Church. God help you if you were a Black Catholic with socialist leanings! Any form of apologetics at the time was tailored to these issues, and very little attention was given to the "secular danger" or the "atheist danger."

My search for answers continued throughout my primary school years, and I vividly remember browsing the school library and finding a thin, green book entitled *Does God Exist?* I do not remember the author or the content of that book, but I remember a classmate grabbing the book out of my hands and being utterly disgusted with my reading material. Her words, "How dare you?," were a firm reminder that in this "Christian" Afrikaner culture, you had to take your questions underground—which I did.

Fortunately, I had a very perceptive English teacher in high school who was able to pick up on some of my skepticism in classroom discussions, and instead of outing me to the how-dare-you mob, she gave me a book containing a collection of C. S. Lewis essays. Many skeptics' journeys find an abrupt end in Lewis, but my fourteen-year-old English vocabulary struggled to comprehend most of what he said. I have since become a Lewis addict, but at the time I would have benefited from an Afrikaans translation. Also unfortunately for me, Lewis was Anglican, and Anglicans were basically seen as "Roman Catholics lite" in the Reformed tradition. Hence, an Afrikaans translation was unlikely. The little I could understand was very helpful though, and I remember thinking to myself that if I believed one day, it would probably be because of him.

Imagine my surprise, then, when I was told at a church camp at the end of high school that his Chronicles of Narnia was basically satanic. It turns out, the one guy who was making me hold on to my faith (if only by a thread) was supposedly in cahoots with the devil! An odd strategy by the Prince of Darkness. It seemed unfair to me (and still does, as a matter of fact) that Satan wrote the best books and songs and made the best movies. God was a bit of an underachiever in that category—his songs all sounded the same and his movies were almost unwatchable. (Perhaps one of the strongest arguments against Christianity looks something like this: if God is good, why are Christian movies so bad?)

A Skeptic Among Believers

When it was eventually time to go to university, I hesitantly decided to study theology. I went to what was then called the University of Potchefstroom for Christian Higher Education. You can imagine that a Reformed theology faculty at a university bearing that name is quite serious. And they did not disappoint; in order to be accepted by the school of theology, a student is questioned by a panel of professors. One question stood out: Why do you want to study theology? My answer was, "I want to know if it is true." This, by the way, is the wrong answer. After a minute of awkward silence, one of the professors managed to correct the error and said with authority, "Brother, you don't study theology to gain faith; you have faith and then you study theology."

Everyone in the room agreed that I was in the wrong place. Luckily for me, the humanities department was far less selective. Then again, judging by the small number of fellow classmates, they couldn't really afford to be picky. It was here that I encountered alternative voices to those of Christianity, but ironically they were not the ones that pushed me into skepticism.

I came across a now infamous chap named Kent Hovind, and to my first-year mind, his young-earth creationism was fascinating. At last, here was a Christian who in a simple way answered some of the bigger questions in life. Sadly it turned out his answers were a little too simplistic, and my newly found young-earth-creationist faith was very quickly destroyed in the marketplace of ideas. It was an older friend of mine with a background in the natural sciences who informed me that Hovind's arguments were as opportunistic as his tax returns. Without going into much detail, it is fair to say that if it took God six literal days to create everything, it took less than that to destroy my flimsy faith.

Here is the thing though: I cannot say that I became a hard-core atheist. On the one hand, it was social suicide to confess your skepticism in the wider Afrikaner community back then; on the other hand, I *wasn't* a full-blown atheist. I was something different every day—on Sundays I was mostly a Christian, but on Mondays I became skeptical again. My skepticism was aided by the explosion of atheist literature at the time. I remember reading parts of Christopher Hitchens's *God Is Not Great* in an airport bookshop. A friend of mine in the hostel started reading *Letter to a Christian Nation* by Sam Harris. We weren't American, so technically we were not allowed to read the letter, but South Africa, and especially our little Afrikaner subculture, very much fit Harris's intended audience. These books, coupled with a bit of Dan Brown's *The Da Vinci Code* here and some of Dawkins's *The God Delusion* there, helped articulate my growing skepticism.

I remember trying to discuss some of the atheists' arguments with various Christians I knew, and it was bizarre how the charismatics would reduce the questions to the demonic and how the hard-core Reformed guys stuck to some version of God's sovereignty. Most of the time they were so busy fighting with each other over what to believe that the question of whether it even made sense to believe never emerged.

There was also a part of my skepticism that was not intellectual. For most of my schooling I wanted to believe but found it difficult. It was at university, however, that I realized the benefits of not believing in God. If God was out of the picture, it freed me up to make the most of the sexual freedom that accompanies a campus full of hormonal students. I didn't know the quote at the time, but my heart completely resonated with Aldous Huxley when he said, "I want this world not to have meaning. A meaningless world frees me to pursue my own erotic and political desires."[2] I didn't have any political desires at the time, but like most nineteen-year-old boys, I had a few erotic ones. For many of my friends, it wasn't difficult to hold to some nominal form of Christianity without it impacting their sexual ethics. I found it difficult, and I kid you not, I would recite some of the more convincing arguments against God when there were prospects of acting on these "erotic desires." It was as if there were party buses driving through my mind with the words "There's probably no God. Now stop worrying and enjoy your life" printed on the side of them![3]

Again, at the risk of sensationalizing my testimony, I should clarify that I was no Hugh Hefner. I was raised with the idea that sex belongs in marriage, but as is true for most young people, this idea was often very much at odds with my desires. If the only argument in support of celibacy is found in the Bible, then it is hardly surprising that I would be skeptical of that book. It was as if I wasn't satisfied with the first doctor's diagnosis, and I was looking for a second opinion. At this point, the *problem of evil* and the *hiddenness of God* became very convenient second opinions.

Looking back at all of this and my subsequent reading, I've become convinced that we are not as rational as we claim to be. More often than not, when we want something to be true, we find the relevant arguments to support it. Laurence Peter describes me well: I was looking for God the same way a thief looks for a policeman.[4]

This does not mean that every atheist is actually a sex addict in rational disguise, but it is hopelessly naive to think we are neutral toward truth claims when those claims go against our nature. It is true in many spheres of life. The opulent might like what Jesus has to say about grace, but he has good reason to be uneasy with his teachings on wealth. The angry social justice activist might find Jesus's claims to divinity convincing, but Jesus's command to forgive means he is siding with the oppressor. For both the opulent and the activist there are plenty of reasons to reject Christianity, none of which are rational.

Discovering the New Atheists

Over time, my thin C. S. Lewis book got pushed to the corner, and the latest New Atheist literature started to dominate my small, dorm-room bookshelf. I became more content with God's nonexistence—even though at times it was a terrifying thought. I was annoyed that most of the Christians around me seemed so content in their faith—I wanted them to experience some of my existential angst. Perhaps that is what these New Atheist "street epistemologists" (basically evangelists) feel like—they just want to crack the naivete of happy, uncritical Christians. I might have rattled a few cages of Christians with questions they were not used to, but one winter night it went horribly wrong for me. I was visiting family friends, and the eldest daughter of that family was home from the United States, where she was studying theology. I asked her a little about her studies and whether she knew anything about the likes of Dawkins, Hitchens, and Harris. Those names seldom meant anything to most of the Christians I interacted with, and those brave enough to venture a guess thought they were sports stars. Her answer, however, caught me completely off guard. In a disappointed tone she said, "You seriously need to get yourself some better atheists."

Apparently she had heard of them. She then went on to advise me on those she considered to be "better atheists": "If you are going to be an atheist, at least do it because you were convinced by the likes of Michael Ruse, Thomas Nagel, or Nietzsche, but I am going to be insulted if those guys [Dawkins, Hitchens, and Harris] put the nail in your Christian coffin."

Here was a seminarian advising me that it was okay to use the likes of Harris and Hitchens as a gateway drug but that to stop there would be like being converted through Kent Hovind. It can happen, but have some self-respect—don't give it away that easily.

It was a bizarre encounter. I then pushed her on one or two of the New Atheists' arguments, and instead of dismissing or refuting them, she reformulated their objections to make them stronger. She would have been an amazing atheist had she stopped there, but she seamlessly changed gears and started articulating the ideas of guys named

Thomas Aquinas, Alvin Plantinga, Alister McGrath, and many others. I had never heard their names or ideas, and although most of it went over my head, I hung on her words.

The evening sped by. Seven p.m. became 9 p.m., and at 2 in the morning I still had questions, but at this point my new friend became a lousy apologist, falling asleep halfway through my questions and her answers. The next morning, perhaps somewhat annoyed with my relentless questions, she gave me a CD with lectures by William Lane Craig and others. I went back to my dorm room and immediately started listening. At times I needed the help of a dictionary, but I was glued to it. I remember telling a friend that I'd been looking for something like this all my life. I probably wouldn't have understood much of it earlier, so perhaps the timing was fine. That night with my new friend and the path she set me on turned out to be a fateful one.

It was a path, though, and not a destination. C. S. Lewis talks about taking a bus ride and being a believer by the end of it. I cannot quite identify with that. I had many bus rides—often I came back as a "1" on Dawkins's spectrum of theistic probabilities, other times I scored a "5." It wasn't because I was wrestling with a particular objection or argument; it was just a feeling of doubt or a feeling of belief. I didn't have a single aha moment. It wasn't one particular question that was answered. I never saw a blinding light. I was simply dabbling with Christianity, as Stephen Colbert likes to say. I was reading about it, talking about it, feeling about it. I watched debates and listened to talks, and after a while I sort of calculated that "I believe" more than "I do not believe."

A Manual for Creating Christians

In *A Manual for Creating Atheists*, Peter Boghossian advises atheist "street epistemologists" to identify the most prominent reason the Christian holds to her beliefs and then to problematize that particular issue.[5] I find that a stupid exercise; it's like asking, "What is the main reason you love your wife?" It isn't one reason or five reasons—it is a cumulative case. That question reduces faith to a single little encounter and betrays a complete misunderstanding of what atheists are trying to liberate people from. Instead of "creating atheists," it's just creating a straw man at best and an annoyed, misunderstood Christian at worst.

I would be lying if I told the street epistemologist that I believe because of the cosmological argument; I find it kind of persuasive, but it is hardly the reason. The design argument is sometimes difficult to trust because of the weird culture wars in the United States and my questionable scientific abilities. I really like the moral argument and am not persuaded by secular attempts to justify morality. Then there is N. T. Wright's book on the resurrection, which would cause any true seeker to pause at the very least.[6]

I guess it is all of these and none of them. Part of it was experiencing the Sagrada Familia cathedral in Barcelona. There is something profoundly spiritual about sitting in the not-yet-completed "sermon" of Antoni Gaudi, also affectionately referred to as God's Architect. I recall sitting in it with a friend of mine who is a Christopher Hitchens fanboy. As both of us were marveling at the interior, I couldn't help but lean over to him and say, "Don't you just hate how religion poisons everything?" He smiled and conceded that this might be the one exception.

Then there is the Sistine Chapel, Lord of the Rings, Mumford & Sons, and Bob Dylan. All persuasive theologians—one brushstroke, page, and lyric at a time. Terrence Malick's *A Hidden Life*, one of the most beautiful movies ever made, is a visual homily. All of them make me long for a world outside this one; they whisper in my ear that reality is not as thin as the materialists would have it. "There is something more," they say.

It is also difficult to explain to the street epistemologist the beauty of Scripture. This is something I only discovered later in life, but to see the beauty of a book like Genesis makes me embarrassed of previous simplistic readings. With the help of gifted preachers like Tim Keller and others,[7] I've fallen in love with a book I found very embarrassing before. I am now embarrassed of my embarrassment. There is a coherence and flow in the Bible that cannot be given as a "proof" to the critic. It is something that must be experienced. One must view it from the inside. Once you immerse yourself in the world of Scripture and note the parallelisms, typology, and social commentary, then it becomes hard not to wonder about a divine hand behind the book. Even if I lose my faith tomorrow, I hope I will be sober enough to admit that the Bible is a literary masterpiece. I sometimes yawn when I see the Bill Maher–type of critique against famous Bible stories. Such critics really don't know how to read an ancient text; they may as well critique Shakespeare for not saying anything useful about modern-day plumbing. They don't know it and might not like the comparison, but the New Atheists share striking similarities to many young-earth Christian fundamentalists. Both are super unaware of their Enlightenment lens, and both are not very good at listening.

I therefore would need to show the street epistemologist the world of Scripture. It is not something that will necessarily please the mind of the rationalist, and perhaps it is unfair of me to expect that of him. But if he really wants to rid me of my superstition, then he will have to understand that the Christian faith is not simply a set of propositions; it is a life shaped and lived by Scripture. As Lewis said, "I believe in Christianity as I believe that the Sun has risen, not only because I see it but because by it, I see everything else."[8]

The street epistemologist should also accompany me to a township church. As someone living in Africa, I am confronted with poverty on a daily basis. To see the hope and joy that faith brings to the lives of millions living in the townships is a massive refutation to cynical atheist propaganda. It perhaps shows the imperial arrogance of the New Atheists. It is one thing to argue against the claims of the

Christian faith to try to build a case for atheism based on arguments. But to claim from European and North American ivory towers that Christianity poisons a place like Africa is woefully out of touch with reality. Matthew Parris (himself an atheist) is correct when he says, "In Africa Christianity changes people's hearts. It brings a spiritual transformation. The rebirth is real. The change is good."[9]

Surely part of testing a worldview is looking at its livability. Is it a worldview that provides one with the necessary resources to navigate the complexities of life? Looking at that question through the lens of African complexities, Christianity makes a whole lot more emotional sense than its secular alternatives.

I do not wish to come across as arrogant in my subjective presentation. I have never liked Christian book titles like *I Don't Have Enough Faith to Be an Atheist* or clickbait YouTube videos called "Atheist Owned by Christian" or "John Lennox Destroys Dawkins." To think an eight-minute video clip is going to "destroy" a complex worldview is silly. Christians as a whole, and the apologetics community in particular, will do well to respect the fact that there are brilliant minds, past and present, who ended on the side of atheism. You would be a fool to call a Graham Oppy or a John Gray deluded atheists.

Perhaps the reason I am so annoyed when Christians fall into this polemical vortex is because I know the frustration I feel when atheists make the same move. I guess I can give the New Atheists some slack; they weren't philosophers and perhaps came out of the gates a little too zealous in their rhetoric. However, when I see someone like Peter Boghossian, who *is* a philosopher, argue that faith is a virus,[10] I become less sympathetic. It is breathtakingly ignorant to reduce Christianity and the massive intellectual tradition that accompanies it to a simple virus in need of an Enlightenment vaccine. Thank God for the likes of Tom Holland and James Hannam, who try their best to enlighten those who are still drunk on this Enlightenment myth.

You don't have to be a historian and you don't have to become a Christian, but the most cursory historical glance will reveal that the West remains utterly saturated by Christian assumptions. Our morals and ethics are not universal but are instead the fruits of a very distinctive civilization, whether it be the conviction that church and state should exist as distinct entities or that polygamy is unacceptable. From women's rights to the dignity of the individual and yes, even the darling of the New and the new New Atheists, something like "modern science" are all deeply rooted in a Christian seedbed.[11]

When I think about this historical denial, a movie comes to mind. *The Giver*, starring Jeff Bridges and Meryl Streep, is set in the near future in a seemingly utopian city. Without giving too much away, each citizen is obligated to take a daily sedative that erases their memories. No one, except the Giver, is permitted to remember the colorful but conflictual world that preceded the present "utopia." I can't help but agree with Catholic thinker Robert Barron[12] when he draws a comparison between The Elders of this fictional society and the intellectual gatekeepers of ours. The latter are trying their best to suppress the memory of anything good that might have happened prior to the eighteenth century.

Atheists love to show how unreasonable Christians are by not acknowledging that humans came from monkeys. How ironic then to see the same reluctance among skeptics when it comes to admitting that much of what the New Atheists hold dear today comes from Christianity. It would appear that both the Christian and the skeptic are rather embarrassed of their respective origins.

From New Atheism to New Activism

Try as we might, I don't think traditional apologetics will result in much fruitful engagement with the self-proclaimed Brights, at least not yet. There is a strange phenomenon that has proven to be a far stronger adversary to the New Atheists. It would appear that the New

Left has unceremoniously dethroned the New Atheists. How strange that issues of race, gender, and sexuality have completely hijacked the conversation away from the constant God debates of the early 2000s. The only New Atheist who managed to stay somewhat relevant is Sam Harris, and that is only because he is addressing some of these identity questions. Richard Dawkins has been all but canceled by the social justice activists and is a mere shadow of his former prominent self. It is a surprising twist in this long-standing rivalry between Christian and secular apologists. There was, however, a theologian who predicted all of this in the 1960s: Lesslie Newbigin, a British missiologist who was in India when the Beatles became "more popular than Jesus" by singing of the lonely Father McKenzie who writes sermons no one will ever hear. Later their front man asked millions of adoring fans to imagine a world without God and religion; they didn't need a second invitation.

Reflecting on this rampant secularism, Newbigin predicted that it will simply not hold. He argued that secularism's attempt to attack all sacred orders and live without belief ultimately leads to exhaustion and a lack of meaning that will throw society back to a religious impulse. He sensed that instead of Father McKenzie and Eleanor Rigby, it will be this new secular West who will be "all the lonely people." What will they do with this lonely vacuum created by secularism? According to Newbigin, they will return to the extremes of politics as religion.[13] It is perhaps not exhaustive, but it explains quite a bit of the illiberal politics visible in many parts of the West today.

The journalist Andrew Sullivan says that the need for meaning hasn't gone away, but without Christianity, people look to politics for satisfaction. And these religious impulses, once anchored in and tamed by Christianity, now find expression in various "political cults." Many of these political manifestations of religion are new and crude, as all new cults are. They haven't been experienced and refined and modeled by millennia of practice and thought. They are evolving in real time. And like almost all new cultish impulses, they demand a total and immediate commitment to save the world.[14] It is these meaning-seeking movements that have all but canceled New Atheist epistemology by labeling it white and patriarchal.

I mention this only because I want my imaginary street interlocutor to understand something important. This strange phenomenon of secular fundamentalism might not be the reason why I came to faith, but it is definitely one of the reasons why I am keeping the faith. An honest skeptic must ask himself how we as a global society got to this utterly illiberal point. I think part of an honest reflection would reveal that secular humanism was hopelessly naive when it celebrated humankind as essentially good and argued that human happiness depends only on liberating the self from artificial social constraints. Political scientist Francis Fukuyama (hardly a Christian), in his attempt to make sense of our current cultural moment, is brave enough to venture a guess. He cautiously concedes that maybe the inner self is, as "traditional moralists" believed, the seat of asocial and harmful impulses. Perhaps this is why Nietzsche was concerned about "personal liberation" in a post-Christian morality. The promotion of a naive humanism predicated on a noble savage embodying humanity's innate goodness, free from the corruption of civilization, might lead to a crippling narcissism.[15] In a world where humans are basically all good, it makes sense that people who disagree with me are basically all bad. If I come to my political persuasion because I make my decisions based on love, then I guess people on the other side of the fence make their decisions based on hate. It is within that noise that a "traditional moralist" like Solzhenitsyn tries his best to contribute his two cents of outdated wisdom:

> If only it were all so simple! If only there were evil people somewhere insidiously committing evil deeds, and it were necessary only to separate them from the rest of us and destroy

them. But the line dividing good and evil cuts through the heart of every human being. And who is willing to destroy a piece of his own heart?[16]

Race or Grace?

In my country, South Africa, I am involved in various racial reconciliation initiatives, and from experience I can tell you that if the conversation does not start with some version of what Solzhenitsyn just articulated, it almost always ends in flames.

Critical Theory might have sounded like a good idea to the likes of Foucault and other postmodern thinkers, but it is not bringing white and black South Africans together. As a matter of fact, it is pushing us so far apart that it would have made the apartheid government smile. But when we have these difficult conversations in church, we are reminded of our own selfishness and need for change. We find that we have solidarity in sin. This universality of sin and the primacy of grace have huge consequences when taken into the social arena where humans wage war against each other.[17]

Just notice, for example, how secular attempts to address racial reconciliation differ from Christian ones. John McWhorter talks about three waves of antiracism.[18] The first wave was, according to him, the abolitionist movement, and the second was the civil rights movement. He argues that both these movements had a distinct Christian voice. Frederick Douglass, who can arguably be called the voice of the abolitionist movement in the United States, relied heavily on the prophetic teachings of Jeremiah and Isaiah and the stories of Exodus, Job, Lot's wife, and others, identifying the hypocrisy of a nation calling itself Christian while nakedly oppressing so many of its people.

Likewise, the pinnacle of the civil rights movement was arguably the now-famous "I Have a Dream" speech by Dr. Martin Luther King Jr.—a speech that quotes Bible books such as Amos, Isaiah, Psalms, and Galatians.

McWhorter argues that the latest antiracism wave is different from its forebears in that it is secular. Where the first antiracism movements were driven by an identity politics that appealed to a common humanity, the latest secular wave of antiracism is based on a "common enemy" identity politics. The movements that saw the end of slavery and segregation in the United States and apartheid in South Africa were filled with biblical language. They reminded people that all human beings are created in the image of God. They quoted Paul as saying that there is now no such thing as a Jew or a Greek, a slave or a free man; they are all one in Christ. (Historian Thomas Cahill says that Galatians 3:28 is the first egalitarian statement in literature.[19]) They reminded people how blind nationalism flies in the face of God's redemptive plan, as told in the story of Jonah; that when Jesus tells parables, more often than not the political enemy is the good guy in the story and the so-called good guys end up being the bad guys. Jesus does this to stretch his listeners' moral imagination, and he's still doing just that. Because we are sinners, we know that we gravitate toward selfishness and tribalism. Therefore he reminds us to first take the log out of our own eye. Centuries later, when asked to write an essay on the topic of "What's wrong with the world?," one of his followers says:

> Dear Sir,
> I am.
> Yours, G. K. Chesterton[20]

The Christian knows that before he attempts to change everyone else, he must first change himself. Whatever the problem is, he is part of it—rather, I should say, I am part of it.

In the third wave of antiracism, instead of focusing on a common humanity, there is a focus on a common enemy,[21] an enemy called "whiteness" or "white privilege"—including heteronormativity and patriarchy. People are told that if they are white, male, straight, able-bodied, and so on, they are oppressors, and the opposite of those identities are by default the oppressed. No wonder, then, that the world is as polarized as it is. The Christian will admit that there are many societal problems and that white people have often been a big part of that problem. There are systemic and individual sins, and they must be addressed. Where the Christian approach differs radically from its secular placeholder, though, is that Christians are called to embrace their enemies. We are not called to relentlessly label them. In a world obsessed with terms like *truth* and *justice*, the followers of Jesus will warn that those things do not exist outside the will to embrace your enemy. This is why Paul warns us not to just be interested in the truth but to always speak it in love. If the aim is not to be reconciled to your enemy, then what you call justice will just be a different word for revenge.

This is not necessarily how I came to faith through Dawkins, but it is probably one of the reasons why I will keep my faith through Dawkins. Comparing the secular and biblical ways of addressing racism is enough to drive me to and keep me in the arms of Jesus. I might have jumped the fence because in a qualified sense a combination of the moral, cosmological, and resurrection arguments convinced me. I stay, though, because among many other things, Christianity helps me to navigate the complexities of identity issues in a way that doesn't destroy me or others.

Know Doubt

Having said all of this, I have to admit that I sometimes still doubt. Heck, I am practically an atheist every morning till about 10 a.m., and only after my third cup of coffee do I start regaining my faith. On a serious note, though, I do occasionally (despite my vocation as a pastor) doubt. This may well be a problematic admission in some church circles, but it is true. I often find myself struggling to reconcile the person of Jesus in the New Testament with the violence encountered in the Old Testament. Then there is the problem of evil. When I reflect on some of the pain and suffering in this world, it just seems totally random. Perhaps Tom Cruise's character in the movie *Collateral* was correct when he justified his killing spree by saying, "Millions of galaxies of hundreds of millions of stars, and a speck on one in a blink. That's us, lost in space. The cop, you, me. Who notices?"[22]

It is, at times, hard to imagine that this world was the idea of a loving and omnipotent God who pays attention. Perhaps we are just the product of time plus matter plus chance? There is a scene in the Coen brothers–inspired *Fargo* series where a lady who just lost her husband is washing the dishes, and a friend comes to sympathize. The widow shares the random story of someone she knew who stood in line to get a milkshake and out of nowhere was struck by a softball-sized hailstone that crushed his skull. After a brief silence, the friend asks, "What flavor?" "Strawberry, I think," the widow replies.[23] This arbitrary dialogue just hangs in the air, but the message is clear. Her husband's death and the death she recounts are as random as the milkshake flavor the unfortunate chap was to enjoy before his life was snuffed out.

I also have my "strawberry moments," but it really does help to think through the implications of that idea. It might be cute to reflect on nihilism in a French street café while sipping your expensive wine, but in the real world the implications are staggering. If it is true that this world is but a slow-sinking ship and one day there will be nobody left to remember it, then it is hard to think that our behavior matters very much on this side of the water. Five minutes before the *Titanic* sank below the water's surface, it wouldn't have mattered much if people ran around hugging each other or mugging each other. It all ends the same, irrespective of whether you lived your life as a mugger or a hugger.

It is also, perhaps, no coincidence that Europe has fewer believers than Africa. Africans have fewer street cafés and other comforts to occupy the mind. How interesting to see after the Christchurch earthquake in New Zealand that the city itself became more religious compared with the rest of the country.[24]

Here is the thing. If God is mainly interested in our holiness and character, then the research suggests that suffering cultivates this more than not suffering. I wonder whether the Canadian worship singer, now famous apostate, Jon Steingard would have kept his faith had he been a South African worship singer. You don't often read headlines that read "Somalian Pastor Now Atheist After Reflecting on the Problem of Evil in His Underground Church." I don't want to trivialize North American and European suffering, but there is such a thing as "imagined suffering."[25] This is where you experience the pain of others more intensely than they do.

I once had an imagined sufferer in my church; he was voicing the problem of evil, and because I knew he had read all there is to read about the topic, I simply asked him what he was doing about it. I suggested to him that if the suffering of the poor is causing him this deep angst, then perhaps we should stop talking *about* them and start talking *to* them. He agreed and accompanied me to Tembisa, a township halfway between Pretoria and Johannesburg. We visited friends and basically just spent the day there. Before the day was done, it became evident that the man's doubt was residential: in other words, the doubt stayed home in his cozy, middle-class suburb and didn't accompany him to the township. It would appear that doubt is very middle class and a tad snobbish—it avoids poverty.

I cannot single out this friend of mine because I occasionally experience the same doubt when I suffer from imagined suffering. This is why I try to be intentional about placing myself in poverty-stricken environments. It is good for me and bad for my doubt. When I look at people's circumstances from a distance, I do not see any rhyme or reason in them; but I can assure you those on the inside do not have a meaning problem. Although their lives are hard, they also make sense. There was a famous guy who once said, "Blessed are the poor in spirit." I'm beginning to think he had a point.

Let me try and bring my ramblings to a conclusion. My faith plays a big role in my life. I get it wrong most of the time, but its footprints are everywhere in the books I read, movies I enjoy, and conversations I have. With the benefit of hindsight, I am not sure that I would have gotten on this path had it not been for the New Atheists' popularity. I say this not to mock or ridicule their efforts, but they became prominent at a time when I started becoming more and more apathetic to questions of faith. They ensured that in many circles questions of God and meaning were discussed—even as far away as the bottom part of Africa. Their questions contributed to my discovering the rich Christian intellectual tradition.

At one stage, many Christians considered the New Atheism as the biggest threat to the church. They were wrong. Atheism is not the problem; apathy is. For quite a few, atheism is just the beginning of the journey.

Chapter 7

Coming to Faith via
The God Delusion

NICK BERRYMAN

BECOMING A CHRISTIAN WAS NOT something I expected, wanted, or even thought was possible. It was a complete surprise. This really was a major U-turn in my life; it surprised all of my friends, my family, and myself. For a significant part of my life, I had dismissed religion as incompatible with an intellectual mind. For me, science and religion were in opposition, and I had chosen the side of science. My life as an atheist made sense, and I was happy with it. My story is of rational thinking leading to a surprising conclusion, and I am grateful for the opportunity to tell this account.

For the first thirty years of my life, I gave very little thought to faith and religion. In our family, churchgoing was largely reserved for christenings, weddings, and funerals. The exception to that was that my parents sent me to Sunday school when I was very young. Around the age of five or six, I started objecting and was no longer required to attend. My family was close-knit; my parents remained married until the death of my father. My father was a bricklayer, and

I have fond childhood memories of assisting on weekend jobs, in only the way a child can!

I was fortunate to have a decent mind and did well academically. I progressed through school, college, and university more easily than most of the people around me. I have a technical, analytical mind, and it was mathematics and the sciences that I had an aptitude for. I am also quite practical, and it was engineering, in the form of electronics, that I chose to study at university. When I graduated, university course leaders encouraged me to stay in academia. However, my graduation coincided with a boom time in the high-tech sector, and I chose to enter industry.

The story of my twenties was one of graduation, gaining employment, and enjoying life. Professionally I was doing well, and I became a chartered engineer pretty much as young as it is possible to do so. I was happy in my personal life too. I got married at twenty-six and very much enjoyed socializing with friends.

A Turning Point

Life was progressing nicely, and then the wheels came off. I found myself separated and divorced by thirty, a truly traumatic life event. The divorce left me broken, adrift, and with strong feelings of failure. At that time, I had my first invitation to a church, by a kind Christian neighbor. I could not comprehend how that might help my situation; I was polite but refused without serious consideration. With the help of a few very good friends, I started to rebuild my life and form new social circles.

During my twenties I had become an atheist. Why? Where had the atheism come from? Not from childhood. Not from my scientific and engineering studies. No, it came from one book I read as a young adult. I was sometimes required to travel for work and was often on my own for a week or longer. Long flights and hotel stays gave me good opportunities to read. On one of those trips, I picked up *The*

God Delusion from the bestseller rack in Heathrow. At that time I was not particularly aware of the author, Richard Dawkins, but the title intrigued me.

The book was easy to read and seemed to explain big questions of the world in a convincing way. It put into words what I had subconsciously already accepted—there is no god. I viewed religion as a crutch for the weak or a means of keeping parents happy. My view was that a keen scientific mind had no business even discussing religion.

I was not as antireligious as Dawkins or particularly zealous for atheism. I thought Dawkins went too far in condemning all religion as evil. I was definitely an atheist though. Dawkins thoroughly convinced me that "there almost certainly is no God."[1]

Some of the more compelling aspects of Dawkins's case included a criticism of a "God of the gaps."[2] "God of the gaps" invokes God as an explanation of something science does not have an answer for. It is true that religion has sought to do this with "we don't know, so God must have done it" answers. The problem with this is that as science advances, those gaps get smaller. I resonated with this; I did not require God to explain things—science did that for me.

I also chimed with Dawkins's answer to the "who made everything?" question. Religion explains the existence of everything with God. Dawkins claims that does not explain anything, as "God" still requires an explanation, that invoking God is only one step further back in a regression of causes.[3]

Dawkins also underlines some significant moral failings of religious leaders and church organizations. In themselves, these did not make intellectual reasons to discard religion, but they did make me less inclined to associate with any religious organization.

An Investigative Journey

The year 2009 was significant for me. My father was diagnosed with lung cancer, a battle he lost several months later. For some reason I also decided to move. For several years after the divorce, I had remained in the house my wife and I had shared. There was clearly a bit of closure going on, as one chapter of my life was ending.

As the eldest child, a son, I felt a sense of leadership growing within me. I wanted to be a support for my mother and sister. Grief is a funny thing; it affects people differently and sometimes in strange ways. I certainly had times of crying and mourning about losing my father, who had been my childhood hero. I grieved not just at his passing but also in the months before. Those months in 2009 also built a strength in me.

Moving to a new house was a new start. I had wanted it to mean new friendships, which is what transpired. Shortly after moving, I went to a house party in the new neighborhood. At the party, I talked with a friend of a friend. This new friend worked as a missionary and asked me what I thought about Jesus. This was new territory, but my mind rallied, and I started repeating some of Dawkins's arguments. I enjoyed our conversation, but I did end the evening feeling that I had not done myself, or Dawkins, justice. As I walked home afterward, I resolved to reread *The God Delusion*.

The loss of my father is part of my story, and for some it will weaken my conversion story because it offers a reason why I would need a crutch. I may well have taken that view of myself as an outsider. Several of my friends did come to that conclusion or the one that my conversion was an emotional reaction to grief. I am comfortable with their opinions. A profession of faith is difficult to explain to an atheist—it does not make sense. And thus, if there is a readily available reason, it is likely to be pressed into service. But the investigation that I would embark on was an intellectual one. There was no emotional comfort. I missed my father then, and I still do. My profession is engineering; I often refer to myself as a problem solver—I am well accustomed to being analytical with evidence. What I did then, and what I ask my readers to do now, is to look at the details and follow the evidence.

That chance encounter at a house party became the trigger for an investigative journey. This new friend, clearly an evangelist for the Christian faith, gave me a couple of books to read. The first was *Mere Christianity* by C. S. Lewis. I was eager to read it and wasted no time, partly because I arrogantly thought I would find holes in it. I did not. In fact, I realized that the Christian story was more coherent than I had been led to believe. This was the first thing I changed my mind about. Agree with him or not, C. S. Lewis was a first-rate mind. He had an excellent ability to think and communicate logically. He was no fool.

Reading *Mere Christianity* gave me a hunger to find out more. It had not changed my mind; I was still an atheist. But I could no longer with integrity dismiss Christianity as a fairy tale or myth. The book took me to a place where I recognized that there are legitimate questions to be asked of the Christian faith. I considered whether those questions should extend to other religions. However, I had started questioning Christianity, and that seemed enough to consider for now. I resolved to come to my own considered position and not to adopt Dawkins's or anybody else's.

I read many more books that often had a science and religion theme. I also watched a debate between Richard Dawkins and John Lennox, the latter a professor of mathematics and Christian apologist. I was especially interested in how Dawkins would respond to challenges by Christian academics. I strongly believe that you need to hear both sides of any debate. When I have not done that and have made an ill-informed decision, I have suffered the cost. The cost is often in wasted time of having to do a more thorough job the second time around.

This is what I had not done with my initial reading of *The God*

Delusion. I had not thought critically about the claims made; I had accepted them. My reading of that book had been both the start and the end of a very brief investigation. I had not asked, "What would the opposition say?" I wish I had.

For the first time in my life, I was hearing a persuasive argument for the Christian faith. I was considering the merit of those arguments and the rebuttals to many of Dawkins's claims. I realized that the issues at stake were worthy of further thought.

I started to see warning signs in *The God Delusion.* One in particular grew in my mind: Why did Dawkins ruthlessly ridicule anyone who professes a faith? There is a constant pattern of ridicule in *The God Delusion,* both from his own pen and others he quotes. Dawkins is clearly passionate, and that in itself does not make him wrong. None of us completely disentangles our passions and our intellect. But scientific inquiry is based on calm, logical, analytical interpretation of the evidence. Preconceptions, biases, and emotions are best left at the door. Dawkins seemed to bring a lot of emotion to the discussion, which became a growing red flag for me.

I looked into more of Dawkins's writing, specifically *The Selfish Gene.* That book is a masterpiece. By use of illustration and the author's expertise, it makes complex science accessible. That said, there is one exception, an anomaly. Sprinkled throughout the book are a few attacks on Christianity. He negatively compares the early copying of the Gospel manuscripts with the reliability of RNA/DNA reproduction. This stood out to me. It seemed a very odd illustration. The historicity of the New Testament manuscripts is far superior to any other ancient text, and by quite some distance.

Why would Dawkins use reproduction of the Gospels as an example of bad-quality copying? The body of manuscript evidence does show some copying errors. It also shows the subsequent correction of many errors in other manuscripts. It also contains very early manuscripts, evidence from before some of those errors occurred.

To include human copying of manuscripts is reasonable. To then use copying of the Gospels is a very poor choice. Why use it?

The Selfish Gene did, however, enlighten my thinking about genetics. Furthermore, it made me want to understand even more and read further. I genuinely believe that Richard Dawkins is a gifted teacher of science. He does what many good teachers do. He illuminates his subject in a winsome manner. He not only educates the readers but leaves them hungry for more learning. *The Selfish Gene* is a brilliant example of that.

But when it comes to *The God Delusion*, there are many examples of Dawkins using ridicule. Dawkins dedicates his book to Douglas Adams (1952–2001), author of *The Hitchhiker's Guide to the Galaxy*, and his quote from Adams right at the front sets the tone: "Isn't it enough to see that a garden is beautiful without having to believe that there are fairies at the bottom of it too?"[4] The underlying narrative is that religion should be discarded without too much consideration. It is of the same substance as myth and fairy tale: nonsense.

I do understand the ease by which an atheist can revert to ridicule. I have been there and remember well that even the notion of "god" can seem ridiculous. But ridicule is never helpful to learning. Many of us learned at primary school not to ask any question that may result in us looking foolish. The fear of unwanted attention prevents curious questions. The best teachers are the ones who communicate a belief that no question is too silly.

Dawkins himself criticizes a previous culture that ridiculed atheists for their nonbelief. He also criticizes religion for not encouraging people to question or think. Yet, by his own use of ridicule, he is surely guilty of the same crime. The continued use of ridicule actually weakened Dawkins's case for me. I concluded that Dawkins was allowing passion and emotion into his thinking.

There is another way that Dawkins discourages further investigation: the notion that the burden of proof lies with a believer to show that a god does exist. Burden of proof is a necessary legal concept, an important one; it provides a safe default answer. However, the concept is not helpful to science or general investigation. Burden of proof is rarely associated with scientific inquiry. Scientific advancement has come about by a spirit of wonder and of questioning. It was certainly more of an innate curiosity that was now driving my investigation. I felt that an atheist claiming there was no burden of proof on him flew in the face of any sense of thirst for knowledge. So in a strange way, Dawkins's words to discourage further study on the topic of God only served to encourage me.

A Questioning of *The God Delusion*

I decided to study *The God Delusion* many years after my first reading. There were many arguments I now saw in a completely different light. The first of Dawkins's arguments that I came to disagree with was "the Ultimate 747." The basic question Dawkins raises is, Who designed the designer? This is his response to theists who posit God as the ultimate cause of everything.[5] It sounds like a reasonable response. The key for me to unlocking this is in the nature of the cause: that is, is it within time or eternal?

Scientists understand that you cannot talk of infinity as simply the next step of time. It is legitimate and sensible to question the cause of something that came into being. It is not sensible to question the cause of something that has always existed.

The creation of the universe is a good example. Scientists have long debated whether it came into being or has always existed. If it has always existed, it is not sensible to ask what or who caused it, as there was never a time when it did not exist. Current scientific thinking, that is, the Big Bang theory, suggests that it did have a beginning. As such, it is eminently sensible to ask what, or who, caused it. Christianity claims that an eternal God created the universe.

It does not make sense to ask what caused God, as God is eternal.

This is the same logic that would apply to an eternal universe. This is not simply one step backward as Dawkins suggests. This might seem convenient in the eyes of an atheist. But Christianity has always claimed that God is eternal. There are many biblical references, even in the Old Testament. One such example is from Psalm 90:2, "Before the mountains were brought forth, or ever you had formed the earth and the world, from everlasting to everlasting you are God."

"Who designed the designer?" turns out to be a nonsensible question applied to an eternal designer. I concluded that postulating God as one step further back in a regression was incorrect.

The next area where I found Dawkins's reasoning falling short was morality. Dawkins recognizes that humanity is capable of amazing acts of kindness to others. This kindness also extends to strangers and even to animals.

Dawkins acknowledges that a simple survival-of-the-fittest explanation is not sufficient to explain morality. He posits four mechanisms to explain the evolution of morality, listing genetic kinship as the first.[6] This explains kindness to those who share our genes, kindness to our relations. The second method is reciprocation and explains kindness to strangers. Even a small probability of "payback" is the motivation. The third is an extension of the second. It states that gaining a reputation for being kind can be advantageous for survival. The fourth postulated method is advertisement. Demonstrating we have the resources to be generous is actually self-publicity. All four methods are ultimately self-serving.

I do not disagree that these mechanisms occur. If I am honest, I am sure I could find examples in my own life. However, the nagging question as I reread this was: Is it a *sufficient* explanation? I did not think it was. The common factor in the four mechanisms is economics. The basic premise is people will do something that costs them providing there is the potential for gain. The cost can be hard to define: time spent, loss of earnings, risk to health. The gain can be equally hard to define but must have a benefit for genetic propagation.

The deeper question on morality, though, is who defines what is right and wrong. There is a much stronger case for God here than I ever realized. The Christian answer is that God who is outside of time and space is the creator and the rule-giver. If that is true, then morality is absolute, and what is right and wrong is true for all people, in all places, at all times.

For the atheistic answer, without a global rule maker there are not too many options left. One option is a consensus-based approach on what is right and wrong. Another option is an evolution of rules that serve humanity best.

The problem with the consensus approach is twofold. First, what happens if the consensus changes its mind? It is possible to change laws, but is it really possible to redefine morality itself? The second is this: most advances in human rights laws have actually come from a campaigning minority. Women's rights activists from a century ago, pro-life campaigners, champions of racial equality—they all base their arguments on an absolute moral truth, such as the equal value of all human life.

The problem with an explanation of morality that evolves for the good of humanity is as follows. The set of rules or laws that evolves is not what is right and wrong but what is helpful. This is not morality. Absolute morality cannot come from evolution. It can only come from an external lawmaker or judge.

The third area where I came to disagree with Dawkins was over digital information in nature. I owe a debt of gratitude to Richard Dawkins for the understanding of genetics that I have. As already mentioned, I found *The Selfish Gene* incredibly helpful. Digital information piqued my interest. A lot of what I do in engineering involves transmission and reception of digital information. All the building blocks of life contain vast swaths of digital information. RNA and

DNA both contain incredible amounts of coded, or digital, information. "A set of instructions" is such a good analogy for DNA that it is perhaps more accurate to say it is a definition. Even the simplest life-forms contain a quantity of coded information that is hard to comprehend. This information tells the living structure how to build a copy of itself.

At the heart of the matter is the question of the source of that information.

The Christian explanation is that an intelligent designer is the ultimate source. This is not a "God of the gaps" argument. Coded information when found is always regarded as evidence of an intelligent source. This is true when archaeologists discover ancient symbols. It would be true if scientists discovered a coded message from outer space.

Dawkins admits that chance alone could not explain this digital information. The age of the universe does not give enough time for that process to be random. Dawkins uses the idea of "climbing Mount Improbable." He proposes an alternative to one step of astronomically high improbability. Mount Improbable can be climbed by taking many small steps along a rising path. Each individual step is of much lower improbability.[7] The analogy resonates easily. Most of us can walk up a mountain path over the course of a day but cannot scale a near vertical face.

John Lennox, in his book *God's Undertaker*, helped me see the flaw in Dawkins's reasoning. The analogy frequently used is that of randomly selecting letters, often pictured as monkeys hitting keys on a typewriter. Ending up with a work of Shakespeare by randomly hitting keys is very unlikely, to say the least.[8] It is analogous to climbing Mount Improbable on the vertical face. Dawkins breaks the problem up into small chunks. A monkey may well get the first letter correct— analogous to a small step up the slope of Mount Improbable. This is where the theory fails though. Dawkins attempts to then "lock" the correct letter in. Having gotten the first letter correct, the monkey can move on to having a go at the next. But this is not a valid step without invoking intelligence. To "lock in" the first letter, it must be declared "correct," and that can only happen by comparing it to the "right answer." Having the "right answer" is to have added the intelligence Dawkins is seeking to deny. Without "locking in" that first step, the second random step is just as likely to take you back down the mountain as it is up.

It was becoming obvious that my thinking was significantly diverging from Dawkins's. My assumption that rational thinking was not compatible with religion was being challenged, and I am grateful to those Christian academic authors who helped illuminate my thinking and who appeared to display the greater rationality.

Weighing Up Christianity

However, disagreeing with an atheist does not make one a Christian; it does not even make one a nonatheist. So what next?

I decided to investigate Christianity for myself. I googled churches close by and visited one. It was advertising an Alpha course, which is a course for people who want to find out more about Christianity. I enrolled. It met for ten weeks after work on Wednesday evenings. I did not have high expectations. I arrogantly assumed I would be more educated than others there. But I was surprised at how much I enjoyed it. It was illuminating; I learned a lot. I learned about the authenticity and reliability of the New Testament documents. At the beginning I did not ask many questions, assuming they would be unanswerable. Other guests asked questions of the Christian faith, many I had not considered. The answers given by the leaders were not only credible but often convincing. As the course went on, I engaged at a deeper level myself. I also continued reading books and online material. These were largely from Christian authors addressing issues of science. But there was still much I held true that seemed incompatible with God.

During this time, an atheist friend asked me a challenging question: Why was I only investigating Christianity and not other religions? He used the analogy of shopping, saying that if I was shopping for a religion, I should at least shop around and choose the best one. It seemed like a fair challenge. If I was going to open my mind to possibilities that previously seemed far-fetched, where should I stop?

My research into other religions was not completely absent, but it was to a much lesser degree than I was investigating Christianity. Was that because the country of my birth has a strong heritage of Christendom? Was it because I had happened to meet a Christian evangelist who asked some questions? Would things be different if I lived in a country dominated by Islam? I did grapple with these questions, but for me, shopping was not analogous to my investigation. I was searching for truth, knowledge, and understanding. I thought of my investigation more as applying the scientific method. It is good science to replace a theory with a new one when the latter has greater explanatory power. This holds true even if there are other theories you have not yet investigated.

A tipping of the scales was happening. Dawkins's atheism was losing explanatory power; the Christian faith was gaining it. As the scales tipped, I chose to abandon my atheism and accept the teachings of Christ as true. Whatever terminology makes sense to you: I became a Christian. I submitted my life to Christ. I was born again. I became a man of faith.

I now understood that word, *faith*, in a different way. It would previously have made me roll my eyes in disdain. But faith did not mean the blind faith that Richard Dawkins pours scorn on. This new faith did not require normally rational people to ignore the evidence; I still have no time for that faith.

The faith that I now had had been born out of my rational questioning of Christianity. The evidence for me pointed toward Christianity rather than away from it. I did not have an inherited faith that

I was trying to reconcile with science, logic, and reason. It was my questioning of science, logic, and reason that had been the largest part of my conversion.

Faith is, of course, more than evidence and reason. I started to test some of the biblical claims around prayer. I made some decisions based on what the Bible says. God showed himself to me in amazing ways during the early months of praying. To say even a short prayer was a very alien thing to do in the beginning. The very first prayer I said was to ask God for help in a situation that was outside of my influence. Within a week that situation changed significantly for the better. A few weeks later another situation occurred, and I prayed again. Again circumstances changed for the better. I was effectively asking God if he was there and got an answer that demanded acknowledgment.

Faith is more than evidence and reason, but it is not less. My faith was born out of an academic exercise, and it has grown to embrace things that I cannot fully explain. My faith still has space for rigorous intellectual challenge. I always welcome a good, spirited debate! That same faith also has space for a spiritual dimension, a trust in and love of a God who rescued me. I have now been studying the Bible for over a decade. The things I accepted lightly at first I now have a deeper understanding of.

I have found the Bible to be more coherent than I had ever imagined. The Bible is a collection of books authored by different people at different times. And yet it has threads woven through that are hard to explain without a single inspiration. I have found the Bible to be beautifully curated. Some of the passages have a richly architected structure. I have found the Bible to be more relevant than I had ever thought. It describes a humanity that can be simultaneously good and broken. Humanity demonstrates traits of kindness, creativity, generosity, and love. And yet that humanity is flawed—it also demonstrates selfishness, greed, envy, a dangerous disregard for our environment. Self-centeredness is proven true time and time again. These are timeless truths, evidenced by what we see around and within ourselves.

The Bible teaches that putting your faith in Jesus is the start of a new life. In those who follow Jesus, God grows the fruit of the Spirit: love, joy, peace, patience, kindness, goodness, faithfulness, gentleness, and self-control. This has been my experience, that in each of these ways I have changed for the better since I became a Christian. Please do not misread me. I am not claiming to be a better person than any of my atheist friends. I am claiming to be a better person than I, myself, used to be. All because God is working in me to transform my desires to be more godly, more like Jesus.

After declaring my faith in Jesus, I got baptized. I have experienced a fuller life—not always a happier life, but a fuller life. As Jesus said, "I have come that they may have life, and have it to the full" (John 10:10 NIV).

The God Delusion still has a place on my bookshelf. I am sure Dawkins would dislike the fact, but it had a role to play in my becoming a Christian. I have recently read it again, and something new struck me. It was what was absent rather than what was written.

For a book that refutes the veracity of the Christian religion, it hardly mentions Jesus. This now seems odd to me, given he is the person on whom the faith is centered. The title and many of the claims are about faith and God generically, but there is also much focused on Christianity specifically. Dawkins attributes the central doctrine of atonement to the apostle Paul. Perhaps he finds Paul easier to dismiss. What Dawkins does say about Jesus is actually complimentary: "The Sermon on the Mount is way ahead of its time" is Dawkins's nod that the teachings of Jesus are full of wisdom and goodness.[9] That said, Dawkins subtly questions the very existence of Jesus: "Jesus, if he existed . . ." is dropped in, without any support.[10] It is almost universally accepted by historians that Jesus the Nazarene existed. There are historical sources from non-Christians.

Those writings even report of Jesus that people said he did miracles and, furthermore, that his followers claimed he rose from the dead. To glibly question the existence of Jesus is to depart from the bulk of academic research on the question.

During the Alpha course I took part in, I concluded what many have before me—that the Christian faith stands or falls on whether the resurrection actually happened. *The God Delusion* is an interesting book. It discusses the probability of the existence of God. It underlines moral failings of many churches, vicars, and priests over the ages. It hypothesizes why people create religions. What it does not do is confront the central pillar of the Christian faith, which any serious attempt to dismantle that faith must do to be successful.

The truth of the Christian faith does not depend upon the moral goodness of its followers. I can see why those failings make it less attractive, but they do not make the historical claims false. If it can be shown that Jesus is wrong, a liar, or evil, then that undermines the claims of Christianity. More importantly, if it can be shown that Jesus did not rise from the dead, then Christianity is shown to be false.

We can postulate all we like about how probable or improbable things are. Many events in history have come as a surprise and were improbable before they occurred. Assessing the probability of an event as low does not mean it did not happen. Dawkins fails to make the transition from thought experiments on probability to history. He concludes that some historical claims are false solely because they are improbable. That transition must involve making judgments on the veracity of historical claims. The relevant tools come from historians, such as textual criticism experts. There are compelling reasons to trust that the New Testament documents are authentic. That the names of people and places are genuine. That the authors knew the culture, the geography, and the history of the region. That the earliest manuscripts date from only decades after the death of Jesus.

These aspects, and others, are hallmarks of authenticity. The New Testament scores high in these tests for authenticity.

Even Richard Dawkins has very little negative to say about Jesus. Jesus made some very bold claims about who he was, or is. In my view they are worthy of consideration. My final words to anybody reading this are from a quote in *The God Delusion*. Dawkins offers a "new" list of Ten Commandments, one of which is, "Form independent opinions on the basis of your own reason and experience; do not allow yourself to be led blindly by others."[11] I could not agree more.

Chapter 8

The God Delusion and Probability

LOUISE MABILLE

IN THE FOURTH GRADE, I attended a barbecue. As is customary on such summer occasions, there was ice cream, swimming, and music. It was during a break in the music when I—finding myself between childhood and the beginning of young adulthood—decided to ask (addressing both groups) what it means to say that "God is dead." I was not a popular child.

However, I had always been an inquisitive one. Growing up during South Africa's period of transition from apartheid to democracy and within a thoroughly secular family, I had a comparatively easy time of it. Being part of a truly significant stage in my country's political history saved me from the coming-of-age clichés that seem to initiate the careers of quite a few antireligious fanatics. Add to that the information explosion of the new millennium and my encounter with Francis Fukuyama's thesis (drawing on Hegel) that "history" had come to an end, and I thought that all the great questions had been settled. The West had settled into a kind of comfortable disbelief. Religious belief was for the slightly backward, and atheism was embraced by the bright and inquisitive. Then came *The God Delusion.*

By the time *The God Delusion* was published, I was already lecturing in philosophy and therefore literate in the fundamental principles behind logical arguments. I had also been steeped for a significant time in the thoughts of Friedrich Nietzsche. Given the level of attention *The God Delusion* had received, I expected sparkling new arguments, a commitment to free thought, and above all, a commitment to science and logical thought. However, I came to see that *The God Delusion* is not only a shallow attack on a grand old tradition but also badly constructed and ultimately an expression of what Nietzsche called *ressentiment*—resentment—a feeling exhibited by those who find themselves outside of traditional power structures. There will be those who say that the New Atheists are far from excluded outsiders: they are highly respected academics and bestselling authors. In the parlance that became popular in the decade after they were the most controversial figures on the bestseller lists, they are very *privileged* indeed. But resentment is present everywhere, even among the most immediately privileged. In the case of the New Atheists, there should be no hesitation in pointing it out.

What bothered me most about *The God Delusion*, and what contributed most to my eventual turn to Christianity, was that it made enormous claims upon which it then failed to deliver. I have always been a rational person. Arguments are like relationships to me: they have to work. For a significant time, I was truly convinced that atheism had "won," that the future belonged solely to the scientifically minded and to no one else. For me personally, this meant I needed to read widely and make sure that I understood the foundations of the field that was to be the arbiter of human values. However, this meant that the public defenders of science themselves had to measure up to the standards they claimed to defend.

What is more, *The God Delusion* was delivered in such a condescending and negative tone that one is forced to reconsider the validity of all this rage: it just could not form a whole, coherent worldview. I am by nature a very inquisitive person, and contrary to Dawkins's assertion that believers do not submit their worldviews to critical analysis, I think most of us do. It certainly means Dawkins's own thoughts should also be carefully scrutinized. While I work in the humanities, I have an avid interest in the natural sciences—the other source of getting to know God—and I believe when one places *The God Delusion* in relation to the other sciences, its arguments go nowhere. If anything, they point right back at God. However, this will mean some serious engagement with other fields of science, such as probability theory. Kindly bear with me—it will be rewarding, I promise!

The Central Claim of *The God Delusion*

The God Delusion had its origins in the attempt to deal once and for all with what Dawkins sees as the ultimate unscientific attempt to answer the question as to why things are the way they are—namely, that some Creator, or some Divine Intellect, has designed the universe and everything in it. Nature provides the one point of agreement between the radical evolutionists (who believe that evolution explains everything) and those who believe that the universe is designed: nature is very complex. Even those who stand aloof to the entire debate would concur upon this point. Yet our relationship with our incredibly complex world is in itself at least equally complex: we are prepared to acknowledge the complexity of the unknown, the sublime, the exceptional, and sometimes the just plain immense, yet often overlook the wondrous complexity of living beings right in front of us. Walt Whitman famously said that a leaf of grass is no less than the journeywork of the stars.[1] And the human being reading this statement is more complex still. It is very hard to believe that all of this, including us, could simply have fallen together by chance— taking the word in its broader metaphysical sense—over time, let alone continue so successfully. Some Mind had to be involved.

Fred Hoyle also thought so. In a now-famous radio lecture, the astrophysicist argues that the improbability of life occurring sponta- neously compels us to accept the notion of life being designed by an intelligent being, God, as opposed to adopting the seemingly random occurrence of natural selection. Hoyle's argument basically states that the probability of life occurring through pure chance alone is no greater than a hurricane sweeping through a scrap yard and as- sembling a Boeing 747. The original passage, first published in 1982, reads, "A junkyard contains all the bits and pieces of a Boeing-747, dismembered and in disarray. A whirlwind happens to blow through the yard. What is the chance that after its passage a fully assembled 747, ready to fly, will be found standing there?"[2]

This famous statement is probably one of the most controversial in the history of the so-called Darwin wars. It is also one of the most misunderstood. Biological complexity has never been one of those quiet Sartrean questions on which philosophy undergrads could test their skills over a few glasses of wine. For biologists it is *the* question, and both those who believe that the universe is designed and the Dawkinites seem to agree that (1) as a complex phenomenon, life is statistically highly improbable, and (2) as improbable as it is, chance (in its metaphysical sense) is not a satisfactory explanation as to how the wondrous complexity of life on Planet Earth came about. Fred Hoyle was so confident of this that he felt convinced that the level of complexity present in nature suggests a force over and above random processes. The suggestion of a guiding hand left Hoyle, an atheist up until that point, badly shaken and convinced that there must be some guiding intelligence behind the properties of matter (as it also did in my case). When reflecting on the precise conditions that render possible the synthesis of carbon in the heat of the stars (nucleosynthesis), Hoyle writes:

> Would you not say to yourself, "Some super-calculating intellect must have designed the properties of the carbon atom, otherwise the chance of my finding such an atom through the blind forces of nature would be utterly minuscule." A common sense interpretation of the facts suggests that a superintellect has monkeyed with physics, as well as with chemistry and biology, and that there are no blind forces worth speaking about in nature. The numbers one calculates from the facts seem to me so overwhelming as to put this conclusion almost beyond question.[3]

For Dawkins, the notion that mere random activity might lie at the root of biological complexity is as unacceptable as it was for Hoyle. Something as complex as the human being did not just fall together on a fine sunny day in March. One of Dawkins's aims in writing his book *The Blind Watchmaker*, as he states in the preface, is "to destroy this eagerly believed myth that Darwinism is a theory of 'chance.'"[4] However, with his consciousness thoroughly raised by Charles Darwin, the idea that God intentionally created humankind is equally unacceptable. For as statistically improbable as organized complexity is, a designer would have to be at least as complex—and experience tells us so far that designers are always more complex than that which they have designed. As Dawkins famously opines, "However statistically improbable the entity you seek to explain by invoking a designer, the designer himself has got to be at least as improbable."[5] At a workshop held for journalists in Cambridge, Dawkins repeated his challenge, this time on a cosmological scale: a God capable of creating the universe would have to be so complex as to be statistically improbable.[6]

At first, this appears to make perfect sense. Even the laws of probability appear to support this. One of the most basic laws of probability, succinctly stated by Leonard Mlodinow in *The Drunkard's Walk*, reads: "The probability that two events will both occur can never be greater than the probability that each will occur individually."[7] In the language of probability theory, joint probability is never more likely than classical probability. The chances of a simple thing forming on its own are greater than a complex thing because a complex phenomenon would require the coming about of more than one event. A single cell is more likely to form than an antelope jumping into existence. If the antelope's coming about is an unlikely event, it implies that anything that might have been responsible for the antelope, such as a divine Creator, is even more unlikely than the ex nihilo appearance of the antelope itself.

Daniel Dennett has called this argument "irrebuttable," and Dawkins himself considers it to be "unanswerable."[8] However, this is anything but the case. What Dawkins appears to be saying is that the cause of an improbable event must be improbable itself, or that the algorithm responsible for complexity must be responsible itself. If winning the New York lottery is highly improbable, then the random activity that is responsible for the winning result must also be improbable. In short, if the odds of winning the New York lottery were 18,009,460 to 1, for example, then the likelihood of randomness being involved in the coming about of the result must also be at least 18,009,460 to 1. But if this is the case, then why is there any need to overcome the problem of randomness? The chances of the existence of the phenomenon of randomness are then virtually zero!

Dawkins or his disciples are bound to respond that this is a category mistake and that random activity does not "cause" the lottery in the same way that natural selection brings about complex biological diversity. If the disciple in question had taken in the first chapter of *The Blind Watchmaker*, it should be clear that I, just like Dawkins, engage in *hierarchical reductionism*.[9] Reductionism in this context, of course, has nothing to do with that infamous phantom that trendy theorists in the human sciences see everywhere when they are unable to offer a proper refutation of an argument they do not like. Such a reductionist would blithely ignore important facts in favor of trying to "explain complicated things *directly* in terms of the *smallest* parts, even, in some extreme versions of the myth, as the *sum* of the parts!"[10] This form of reductionism can rightly be denounced as crude thinking. The hierarchical reductionist, on the other hand, attempts to explain something complex on a particular level in terms of the next, more essential level of complexity until the explanatory possibilities of that level is exhausted. Obeying Occam's razor, he continues down the line until he finds the simplest explanation possible. Naturally, it goes without saying that the kinds of explanations that are suitable at high levels in the hierarchy are quite different from the kinds of explanations that are suitable at lower levels. It depends on the context, of course: "This was the point of explaining cars in terms of carburettors rather than quarks."[11] However, when one makes ultimate, fundamental claims about the nature of reality, one has to go all the way down. After all, "reductionism, in this sense, is just another name for an honest desire to understand how things work."[12] What makes our attempt so significant is that we are prepared to go down the organizational hierarchy to a point where explanations in concrete terms no longer work, where the obvious and tangible become abstract and counter-instinctual.

What makes the lottery, or gambling in general, possible is not the balls, cards, roulette table, or lotto machine. If this were true, one could simply throw all the balls one can find on a heap and sell tickets. But we all know that a heap of balls does not make a lottery. So what does? Certainly not the quasi-celebrity presenters. It is, among others, the *movement* of the balls and one's inability to predict the outcome that make it a lottery: in other words, random activity. Randomness is a lack of order, purpose, cause, or predictability. A random process is a repeating process with outcomes that follow no describable deterministic pattern. But what is the relationship between an abstract principle like randomness and the *concreteness* of the balls and gambling paraphernalia? This brings us to the ultimate *aporia* or double bind: any attempt at a final explanation of reality in materialist terms is at once doomed to fail, because it would simply throw up more material entities requiring explanation or, alternatively, would be bound to be encapsulated by abstractions like randomness and symmetry. Dawkins's problem is that he takes the first principles of his own field, biology, to be the first principles of science *as such*. This is one of our main objections: Dawkins has misunderstood the first principles of his own subject. Most of the contradictions and double binds that we encountered can be traced to a failure to acknowledge the fact that biology is *not* a fundamental science and can*not*—by definition—give us first principles.

It is precisely because randomness, for example, is such a basic feature of earthly existence that no nonrandom process such as natural selection—defined by Dawkins in the *Microsoft Encarta* encyclopedia as "non-random survival of randomly varying hereditary units, resulting in the evolution and maintenance of adaptive improvements"[13]—can ever truly serve as a foundation for the scientific edifice, let alone as a source for the meaning of our existence. Contrary to Dawkins's claims, natural selection does not overcome the problem of the statistical improbability of the occurrence of life. In fact, it does not even touch upon it. It still means that natural selection is a valid theory and that Charles Darwin was a remarkable scientist whose enormous contribution should be celebrated by contemporary science, but it is not fair to expect that his work should hold the answer to *everything*.

The Law of Large Numbers

It is no use appealing to the law of large numbers either. It is the kind of thing you appeal to when you are unsure of the success of your more particular arguments. Dawkins appears to use it as the final nail in the coffin of religious belief, blithely stating that "if the odds of life originating spontaneously on a planet were a billion to one against, nevertheless that stupefying improbable event will still happen on a billion planets."[14]

However, like his other attempts at probability theory, this also fails abysmally. Again, Dawkins appears to use it as an absolute law when, just like the other instances of probability theory, it only makes sense when used in a demarcated sample space. A. J. Ayer reminds us that "the upshot of this law, which is mathematically demonstrable, is that in the case of any sufficiently large sample which is drawn from a larger population, there is a high probability that the ratio in which a given character is distributed in the sample approximately matches the distribution in the parent population; as the size of the sample increases, this probability approaches unity."[15] All that the law of large numbers really means is that the more studies you conduct, the more you will find certain trends pitching up. What those trends may be are, of course, determined by the nature of the subject under discussion. In the context of trying to account for the origins of life, the law of large numbers means virtually nothing. It is only a statistical aid, not a "get out of jail free" card. This is how the science of probability theory works.

It is clear that once more, the Dawkinites need to be reminded that there is nothing necessary about the coming about of life. If the wind continues to blow over the sand surfaces of an infinite number of planets for an infinite number of years, it still does not entail that life will spring from such action. And if we are to take Dawkins at his word and apply the law of large numbers to the universe in general, we may just as well say that not only will life pitch up sooner or later but so will the Flying Spaghetti Monster, Batman, E.T., and Darth Vader. If the law of large numbers as Dawkins understands it is consistently applied, it means in effect that sooner or later, given the infinity of time and space, *everything* will turn up. This implies that, sooner or later, a redeemer will be born from a virgin. Who says you need Stephen Jay Gould's non-overlapping magisteria to reconcile science and religion? Apparently, according to the law of large numbers, anything is quite literally possible.

The Category Mistake

The question that now suggests itself is, How does the Ultimate Boeing 747 argument yield such absurdities? The reason for this is the category mistake. The category mistake was identified by the British intellectual Gilbert Ryle during the mid-twentieth century in his book *The Concept of Mind*. This mistake occurs when two different categorical terms are treated as if they are categorically equivalent. Ryle uses the following example: "She came home in a flood of tears and a sedan-chair."[16] The reader would have noticed that this statement sounds very strange, and for good reason. The category "to be in a flood of tears" is not the same as the category "to be in a sedan chair." This difference is also found in phrases like "the tide is rising" and "hopes are rising." Another example of a category mistake is when one puts forth the argument that one cannot blame soldiers for the wars they fight any more than you can blame firemen for the fires they fight. Obviously "fighting" in the sense of fighting fires and engaging in combat is not the same thing.

Dawkins commits the category mistake by treating probability as a property of complexity. Probability refers to the degree of likelihood that a particular event will occur. However, probability is not a property in the same sense that mass, color, or even complexity are properties. Biological events may be extremely rare, and it may not be inevitable that they will occur on a planet or in a universe, but when you describe the cause of an entity in terms of probability in the way Dawkins does, you treat probability as if it is a property. It becomes a "property" of complexity. You are stating that probability is a property that is inherited alongside complexity and that complexity and improbability are inherited from that cause. In effect, you are stating that the reason biological organisms are complex is because they inherited the property of complexity from their designer, and because improbability goes alongside complexity, improbability is also inherited from the designer. However, the problem is that if probability is treated as a property that is inherited from a cause, then that cause must be improbable as well. In short, committing the category mistake of treating probability either as a property, which is inherent in an entity, or as an occurrence that has an improbable cause removes any possible cause for that effect.

The Ultimate Boeing 747 gambit raises yet another interesting question: Why is the question of the occurrence of life couched in terms of probability theory at all? After all, in its stronger version, the anthropic principle states that if the right factors did not combine in the right way, we would not be here asking the question about the origins of either life or the universe. It is rather like asking, "Why do I always find roads where I am driving?" It makes no sense to speak of the probability of something that *has* already happened. In such a case, one would be quibbling over the probability of an event that has already been accorded the status of 1. Strangest of all for a biologist is to treat life purely in hypothetical terms, when, in fact, as the anthropic principle reminds us, the fact that we as living beings are here talking about the likelihood of life's occurrence renders the question meaningless. The strong version of the anthropic principle, with a healthy idealistic vibe, refers to the parameters of physics and reads as follows: "The Universe (and hence the fundamental parameters on which it depends) must be such as to admit the creation of observers within it at some stage."[17] In the Australian physicist

Brandon Carter's Cartesian terms, *cogito ergo mundus talis est* ("I think, therefore the world is such [as it is]").[18] This is a very significant statement since, from a logical point of view, it demonstrates that Dawkins is trying to saw sawdust: the fact that we as observers and representatives of life are here to ask the question about the origin of life renders the question about the improbability of life occurring superfluous.

In fact, the very reason for the biologist's existence—both for his physical existence as well as the existence of his profession—is derived from an event that *has definitely happened at some stage in the past*, rendering the vocabulary of probability irrelevant. There is a very interesting literary parallel here known as the grandfather paradox, named after the famous scenario where a man travels back in time, kills his own grandfather before his parents are conceived, and thereby cancels out his own existence.

Once again we find ourselves upon the Greek road to nowhere, the aporia. The anthropic argument states that there must be living beings with a fairly sophisticated form of consciousness in order to ask the question of the origins of life. In other words, there has to be life and a form of consciousness at a distance from the origins of life, since the question of the origin of life can be asked only when there is an observer of life available to ask that question. Even if the actual probability of a universe that supports intelligent life is very low, the conditional probability of supporting intelligent life, given our existence in it, is 1. Even if there could be other universes, less "fine-tuned" and so devoid of life, there would be no one there to observe them.

This brings us to yet another instance of the category mistake. Dawkins appears to regard the questions of the probability of complexity and that of the occurrence of life as identical. But demonstrating that natural selection renders complex phenomena more likely by breaking one big case of improbability into several small simple instances of the (more) probable does not mean that the question of the origin of life is solved. Natural selection, whether in its classic Darwinian variant or couched in the hip vocabulary of *The Selfish Gene*, is not a theory of abiogenesis but a theory about life's history. It does not solve the improbability question at all. It is like the medical examiner who arrives at a crime scene: it gives us a great many details about the history of events, but only after the action has already occurred.

Dawkins's question can be rephrased in proper Darwinian terms. Natural selection tells us a lot about what happened within the primordial soup can, but it tells us nothing about the probability or improbability of there being a primordial soup can in the first place. What are the odds for and against the soup, that is, for the complex falling together of the physical elements? What are the odds for and against the coming together in this particular way? Do we have this information? It looks as if we are right back in Hoyle territory. And to be painfully existentialist again, what are the odds for and against a single element, such as hydrogen, coming about? Whether you climb Mount Improbable or not, you are still stuck with pretty much the same problem.

Not only has Dawkins done away with both the possibility of human creation and the treasured notion of natural selection, he has almost pulled off the impressive metaphysical feat of doing away with the notion of cause altogether. Not only are complex phenomena like the Venus flower basket statistically improbable, but practically *everything* is. What is the probability of a stone, for example? What are the factors for and against the coming about of a stone? Or sand? Is sand statistically probable or not? What about matter as a whole? This is known in the much-despised regions of continental philosophy as the "why is there something rather than nothing?" question. If you really think about it, just about everything has the odds stacked against its existence. The anthropic principle is not just about humans and life; it is about the world itself. Hopefully you have not grown too attached to the easy answers science purports to give, for every answer encloses a further mystery within it. I believe the mystery can only ultimately be solved by turning to the original mystery writer.

Chapter 9

My Egyptian Journey to Faith

RAFIK SAMUEL

I GREW UP IN ALEXANDRIA, Egypt, and currently live in Cairo, where I studied philosophy and political science at the American University of Cairo and now work in government at the Ministry of International Cooperation. I have found my deepest hope in life in the person and in the life of Jesus Christ, and my passion is to become shaped more according to his image.

In this chapter, I want to present three main sections. The first is a brief narration of how, as a teenager, I became in awe of the New Atheists and completely lost my faith for about two years. The second is how through apologetics and following Christian philosophers, and through avidly following the New Atheists, I gradually came to the impression that the latter were more charisma than substance. And parallel to that impression was a realization that there were plenty of Christian minds that were nothing less than genius. This allowed me to accept that I could reembrace my faith while still seeking to be a rational and clear-minded person. Finally, the third section is about how it was an encounter with the person of Jesus, and not the arguments, that ultimately changed my life, brought me to reconciliation with God, and helped me regain my faith.

Becoming in Awe of the New Atheists and Losing My Faith

I am the son of a professional psychiatrist and a Christian preacher, and my childhood was a unique mix of both Christian life and an openness to science, critical thinking, and explorative deep questions. My dad is a well-known figure in the Christian Arab evangelical world, and throughout my childhood he was a role model to me and still is today. I grew up in a home where I always felt encouraged to think critically and where my rather large number of daily questions were embraced. Up until the age of thirteen, I was comfortable identifying as a Christian. This was true until one night during the summer of 2012. I was off from school, which allowed me to stay up late, and I had a habit of searching for interesting YouTube videos, sometimes into the early hours of the morning. On that particular night, I stumbled upon a video of famous atheist and political talk show host, Bill Maher, who in turn introduced me to videos of Richard Dawkins, Christopher Hitchens, Sam Harris, and Daniel Dennett—the so-called Four Horsemen of New Atheism. I started watching some of their interviews, talks, and debates. And as they poured out their attacks on God and the Christian faith, I suddenly started wondering, Why am I Christian? In that moment it felt like I did not have quick, clear, and convincing responses to any of the arguments the New Atheists were making. In fact, I started to like them. Their charisma and influence, especially that of Christopher Hitchens, quickly impressed me and convinced me that rationality was on the side of atheism.

That night I decided to no longer identify as a Christian and felt a sense of relief. It was as if a weight had been lifted off my shoulders. I had a feeling that trying to remain close to God was a burden. Not only did religion trigger too many questions and doubts that made me intellectually uncomfortable holding on to faith, but the spiritual life of trying to stay close to God was also emotionally uncomfortable. Rarely did I ever feel a desire or have an interest to pray or read Scripture. And more importantly, I was never really touched by the message of the gospel. As a thirteen-year-old boy, I did not really feel like I was a sinner, as I was not sure what exactly I had done wrong in life. The Christian message seemed tailored to those who identified as sinners. If you are not a guilty sinner, then the whole story about grace becomes irrelevant to you. And that was very much how I felt about Christianity, so much so that I vividly recall going up to my dad and telling him, "Dad, you all like this so much because you are sinners. I am not a sinner, and so this is not for me." Needless to say, I was an insufferable teenager.

I was not merely a pain to my family; I was also one to my church. I decided to continue attending youth group. In fact, I decided that I would not be a quiet atheist teenager but that I had to spread my atheism. At that point the Four Horsemen of New Atheism were very much my heroes. I remember having their picture as the wallpaper on my desktop-computer background. Much like my newfound heroes, I had to have a group of atheist buddies who were also concerned with spreading the message of atheism and challenging the precepts of religion. I thus began a rigorous process of recruitment. I approached three of my closest friends, explaining to them why I had lost my faith and why it was crucial for them to follow my example. Unprepared for my onslaught of attacks on Christianity, two of them made the decision to convert to atheism. I was deeply proud of myself. Together we regularly attended our church's youth group with the sole goal of challenging every invited speaker and working to challenge the faith of all our fellow youth group participants. I constantly raised my hand during these youth group meetings and made sure to rigorously ask questions that made everyone uncomfortable: What is the evidence for God's existence? How would a good God allow so much pain and suffering? How can you trust Scripture and also claim to respect science? I asked questions like these and many more.

My obnoxious atheistic inquiries at church reached a point where things got somewhat embarrassing for my family. In the summer of 2013, my youth group's leaders, in part influenced by my turn against religion, decided to organize an apologetics camp to address the kinds of questions I was asking. Sessions were on topics such as evolution, God's existence, and the reliability of Scripture. My two atheist friends and I were, of course, enthusiastic campers. I wanted this camp to be an opportunity to show my entire youth group that the questions I had were valid and that the case for Christianity was weak. The first session was on evolution. I remember thinking that the speaker was unprepared. I had a list of questions and objections that I loudly voiced. The speaker had a difficult time responding to my questions, and I recall sensing that people in the room were convinced that I had the much stronger case. I went back to my room feeling victorious. But as I changed my clothes to get ready for sports night, my phone rang. It was my father. In a somewhat firm tone, he explained that the youth leaders had called him and complained about my behavior. He asked me to keep my questions for when I got back home and to give space to the speakers to present their case. I thought my leaders were cowardly and so unable to refute my objections that they had to complain to my parents to have them silence me.

In retrospect, I realize I was being selfish. I cannot begin to imagine the difficult position I put my father in. A renowned Christian speaker and apologist was getting complaints about his atheist son spreading atheism in his own church. But at the time I was completely unempathetic toward the awkward position I created for him. Looking back, I have a deep sense of gratitude toward both my parents. Despite the embarrassment that I must have caused my father especially, he not only continuously showed me kindness and patience but also encouraged me to think, and he respected that I was going through my own journey and pursuit of truth. His love and kindness to me helped me go from a position where I was self-righteous and arrogant in my questioning of faith to being more in awe of a life lived with God than of the life and message of the New Atheists.

My excitement for my newfound atheism was short lived. I quickly started to struggle with a deep sense of emptiness; I was a cause of pain to both my family and my church. And I was gradually growing aware of my own pride and sin. I was not concerned with the needs of those who were around me; I was not interested in serving them as much as I was interested in flexing my intellectual muscles and showcasing my knowledge of arguments about God. And throughout my journey, I must stress that experiencing the love of people like my parents helped me gradually change my set of values and what I ultimately admired in life. It is for this reason that I think that being Christlike must always be understood as the strongest apologetic.

Disillusionment with the New Atheists and Reconciliation Between Reason and Faith

One of the key moments that pushed me to reexamine my impression that rationality was on the side of the New Atheists was when I watched Christopher Hitchens debate William Lane Craig. I would take very careful notes during these types of debates and then review my notes to decide on a debate winner. But this debate was so clearly won by Craig that I was almost embarrassed to say I was on Hitchens's side. I was bewildered by my admiration for Hitchens. I was not aware, until that point, that what I really liked about him had more to do with his wit, and probably his deep voice along with the famous British accent, than it had to do with the substance of what he had to say. William Lane Craig was in a sense the opposite. Much like a college professor, he presented his case in a clear-cut series of valid arguments (his famous "five arguments for God's existence" introduction), explained simply and in a persuasive manner that, unlike Hitchens, was based more on substance than on his delivery. The two main arguments that specifically caught my attention were the cosmological argument and the argument from the existence of objective moral values. In the following, I will explain my disappointment with the way Hitchens straw-manned those two arguments and responded in a manner that seemed to evade the key premises.

Craig presented the classical Kalam cosmological argument, which rests on the premises that "whatever begins to exist has a cause" and that "the universe began to exist." Like Dawkins,[1] Hitchens responded to the argument with the traditional "who designed the designer?" comeback. Hitchens's exact words were:

> Who designed the designer? Don't you run the risk with the presumption of a god and a designer and an originator of asking, "Well, where does that come from, where does that come from?" and locking yourself into an infinite regress?[2]

This response, however, misses the key point, which is that the argument specifically stresses that "whatever begins to exist has a cause" in its very first premise. Notice that God does not fall under the category of "things that have begun to exist." Hence, the question of what caused God is in fact illogical. God is, by definition, an uncaused causer, and thus to ask what caused the uncaused is clearly contradictory. If the argument had a premise which said that "everything has a cause," then Hitchens's response would be valid: God must have a cause, since the divine falls under the broad category of "everything." However, since the argument is making the qualification that *whatever begins to exist* has a cause, Hitchens's response gave the impression that he was not carefully assessing each premise of the argument. In contrast, Craig presented philosophical and scientific reasons to think that the universe began to exist, which makes it perfectly legitimate to inquire about what caused the universe. In this case, it seemed clear to me that Craig was a philosopher who understood how to make valid and sound arguments, where the conclusion followed from the premises and the premises were well supported by facts, whereas Hitchens was misreading the argument and thus offering a fallacious response.

Craig also presented the argument from the existence of objective moral values. In this case there were also two clear premises: "if God does not exist, objective moral values do not exist" and "objective moral values do exist." The conclusion is that thus God does exist. Hitchens's rebuttal was the classic challenge that he often likes to put forward and that he always insists no religious thinker is ever able to overcome:

> There are two questions that I've asked in public and I'll try them again because I try them on every audience. They're very simple ones: First, you have to name for me an ethical action or an ethical statement or moral action or moral statement made or undertaken by a believer that I couldn't undertake or say, I couldn't state or do. I haven't yet had an example pointed out of that to me. In other words, that a person of faith would have an advantage by being able to call upon divine sanction. Whereas if I ask you to think of a wicked act undertaken by someone in the name of God or because of their faith or a wicked statement made, you wouldn't have that much difficulty, I think, in coming up with an example right away. The genital mutilation community, for example, is almost exclusively religious; the suicide bombing community is almost exclusively religious; there are injunctions for genocide in the Old Testament; there are injunctions, warrants for slavery and racism in the Old

Testament too. There's simply no way of deriving morality and ethics from the supernatural.[3]

Hitchens's challenge, by pointing out that atheists are well capable of performing moral acts just like theists and that theists perform certain evils that atheists would not, simply says that religious people are not ethically superior to atheists. Hence, he claims, "There's simply no way of deriving morality and ethics from the supernatural." Notice again how Hitchens makes a mistake similar to the one he makes regarding the cosmological argument. Just as the prior argument did not have a premise that said "everything has a cause," this argument does not have a premise that says "belief in God entails an ethically superior life." Instead, the argument is simply stating that for morality to be objective, a transcendent point of reference such as God is necessary—otherwise, morality is subjective. Again, it feels as if Hitchens has misread the argument and instead of carefully assessing and refuting the premises, is simply throwing rhetorical jabs that would irritate a believer.

Throughout the debate, I genuinely struggled. I could not deny the clear reality that the man I considered my intellectual hero was presenting the much weaker case. I was frustrated. The problem was not that he gave weak responses but rather that he did not engage the arguments. He gave responses that failed to even address the premises. For brief moments, I tried to convince myself that Hitchens was somehow making a solid case, but as I reviewed my notes, it became very clear to me that I really liked Craig's arguments. I was not fascinated by his voice nor his rhetoric, but I knew that his arguments were valid and worthy of reflection. And I suddenly became aware that in this case it was not reason that was on the side of atheism; it was rhetoric. Reason, at least in this context, was rather very much on the side of Christianity.

It was not this one debate that caused me to become disillusioned with the New Atheists and to work to reconcile reason with faith. This was just a turning point. It is not within the scope of this chapter to fully explain how I studied the arguments for Christianity and how I concluded that the Christian case is more justifiable than its atheist counterpart. Having said that, this chapter is a testimony to my journey to faith. And in this journey, there was a gradual realization that, to put it simply, there were plenty of highly intelligent scientists and philosophers who embraced their faith and who had good reasons to accept it. William Lane Craig was one good example. But there were many more. I spent time looking into Gary Habermas's and Michael Licona's minimal-facts approach to defending the resurrection of Jesus.[4] I could not deny that Christ's resurrection was an interesting explanation for historically verifiable facts that were otherwise difficult to explain. On the other hand, I was frustrated when, for example, Dawkins repeatedly insisted on not debating with Craig, with the justification that Craig was not a worthy opponent. I could see that there was arrogance—and in some cases, anger—on one side, while there were sound, calm arguments on the other.

About a year and a half into my atheist season in life, I reached a point where I realized that it was rationally warranted to accept that there were good arguments for God's existence and good reasons to think that Christ's resurrection was a powerful explanation for the historical facts. Based on these two matters alone, I could at least theoretically become a Christian. However, I was still not ready to do so. I worried that there might be good responses to the arguments for God's existence and for Christ's resurrection that I was simply unaware of. Moreover, I was uncomfortable committing myself to a position of faith. Despite becoming disillusioned with the New Atheists, I still felt more inclined to be agnostic about the claims of religion and to spend my life exploring the different sides of the debate. I acknowledged that many of my criticisms of religion had been addressed, but to make a personal commitment to Christ felt like a complex decision that required something beyond studying apologetics. How do I commit my life to someone I do not really know?

No matter how convincing the Christian case seemed to be, God's hiddenness was still my fundamental stumbling block. Becoming a Christian was not an intellectual decision; I needed to develop a sense of love and intimacy toward Jesus, to submit to him as my Lord and Savior. In the final section, I will explain how I not only came to see Christianity as rationally warranted but also encountered Christ and fell in love with him.

Encountering Christ and Regaining My Faith

Alongside my struggle with arguments for and against Christianity was a constant longing to encounter God. I wanted to see him, to feel him, to touch him, and to hear him. My atheism began as an exciting adventure, but eventually it turned into a scary state of confusion. I wanted to know the truth. I was uncomfortable with my own cynicism and arrogance, and I was weary of not knowing whether a God existed out there who could love and save me. During this tough time, it angered and even hurt me when my parents asked me to approach and talk to God—as if it were some easy and simple task, and almost as if we had a guest that I was being unkind to or ignoring and that they were asking me to befriend. I would sarcastically ask, "Oh, do you want me to talk to God? That sounds great! Please share a phone number or an email, and I promise to contact him right away." I was not only trying to be sarcastic; I wanted to express that I was being asked to do something that I just had no clue how to do. I was being asked to befriend a person in a way that is unlike any friendship that I had ever experienced. I was being asked to think stuff, assume God heard it, and then, like some detective, look for clues that might reveal God's answers. That just seemed ridiculous. There was no way to be sure God was listening to me when I spoke to him. And, assuming he listened, there was no way to be sure of what his answers were—if there were any answers to begin with. This was not an easy task, if not totally impossible. It felt reasonable to just disregard God altogether. What is the point of enduring the daunting task of speaking to the invisible, inaudible, and untouchable?

It seemed to me that I did not need God. In fact, God represented a burden to me. Seeing, however, that some of the people closest to me, those whom I loved and trusted the most, found so much pleasure and intimacy with God was almost heartbreaking. I could not accuse them of lying to me—I was sure they were genuine in their faith. It was either that the people I loved the most were delusional or that the God they experienced did not care about me. He was a wonderful friend to them and an invisible thing to me. Thinking about the latter would push me to hate the very idea of God, if not God himself.

In 2014, I started listening to several sermons about the person of Jesus. I also began to read the Gospels with fresh eyes. I yearned to meet God. I meditated on Jesus in the Gospels so deeply that it felt like I was trying to pull him out of the pages of the Bible and talk to him myself. In the summer of that year, I was at a camp where my father was preaching. His sermons were about the life of Jesus, and it began to dawn on me that I was not just someone who thought it was rationally warranted to be a Christian—I also really liked Jesus.

During that camp something happened that helped change my attitude toward God. One morning, I went to my father's room to say hi. I walked in and found him sitting at a desk, preparing his notes for the morning sermon. He was slightly distressed and explained to me that his brand-new laptop had suddenly shut down and would simply not turn back on. I felt bad for Dad, and I did everything to fix it, but to no avail—the laptop just would not turn on. This was very inconvenient, as he had a full PowerPoint presentation prepared, along with sermon notes he had written, on this device. I apologized that I could not help and left his room. As I walked out, I sarcastically thought, "Poor Dad, he is trying his best to serve God, but God won't even fix his laptop."

Later that morning, Dad preached—without the laptop—and the message was powerful and touched me deeply. Afterward, I went again to his room. As we chatted about the sermon, he explained to me that he thought God intentionally turned off the laptop because he wanted Dad to give a different message than the one he had prepared earlier. I suddenly saw a fun challenge. I said, "Dad, if God turned off the laptop so that you would preach a different message, then the laptop should work fine now. Since the purpose was for you to change course in the sermon, then the purpose is now achieved, and the laptop should work." Dad nodded. I suggested that I should try to turn on the laptop. To my bewilderment, the laptop powered up at my first touch of the power button. Dad smiled. I could not believe my eyes.

This may seem like a trivial story. But for me, it answered a deep longing to see and feel the divine working near me. The message I sensed God conveying to me was, "I want you to know who I am; I am in control, and I am ready to intervene to see that you discover the truth and encounter me." As the camp continued, I kept meditating on the person of Christ. Jesus was almost everything I wanted God to be. He loved and defended people like me, broken and sinful people. I was unfulfilled and disgusted with my own moral reprehension, pride, and cynicism. I needed hope. And Jesus represented that hope. He represented grace, and that was everything I needed. I could relate to a prodigal son, a tax collector, and a prostitute. These were the people I belonged to, and he loved them. That meant only one thing to me: Jesus could love me!

I repeatedly stress that the best way to describe my experience at that time is to say I fell in love with Jesus. The reason I do so is because I have come to think that God is more interested in people getting to know and love him than in people just "believing" in him.

Of course, in order to love God, you must believe in him. But my point here is that God was very capable of convincing me of his existence right away on that night in the summer of 2012 when I first started having doubts. In fact, God is capable of demolishing atheism altogether with powerful signs of his existence. He could just write in the skies that he exists or have it inscribed on the cells of our bodies. However, I think God was more interested in leading me on a journey where I ultimately pursued him and thus encountered the person of Christ. I think that is the fundamental way in which we ought to think about the problem of God's hiddenness. He may be hidden, but he guides those who are searching for him and leads them toward a relationship with him. To put it simply: God is more interested in having a relationship with us than he is in proving his existence.

A month after this camp, I was with my family on vacation in Miami, Florida. On the final day of our trip, Dad woke me up early in the morning and gently asked if I would like to go for a quick swim. I jumped out of bed as if I had been waiting for him. While we were in the water, he asked me a pointed question: What more do you need to accept Christ as your Lord and Savior? My mind immediately flashed back to that night in the summer of 2012 when I started to watch the New Atheists. On that night, I could not answer the question, Why am I Christian? But now, on this morning, I could not answer the opposite question, Why am I *not* a Christian? I had accepted that it was rationally justifiable to accept the fundamental claims of Christianity. I had discovered my own sinful nature and my need for a Savior. And I had found the person of Christ to be worthy of praise and awe. In that moment I told Dad that I was ready to accept Christ as my Savior. We prayed together in the water, and I came out knowing something fundamental had just changed about my life. My prayers were no longer random requests to an invisible person, asking him to reveal himself. Instead, they were specific requests to Jesus. I wanted to be his follower. I fell in love with him, and I wanted him to love me, to be sovereign over my life. I began asking for that, and I began to notice him guiding my life and deepening my affection for him.

I then studied philosophy and political science with the goal of finding out how Christ could be an answer to society's most pressing questions. Currently, in my work in the office of Egypt's Minister of International Cooperation, I aspire to show that in government—despite how a myriad of difficult questions can be raised, how confusion can be widespread, and how darkness can run deep—the grace and love of the person of Jesus Christ can be the ultimate rest from all the pains of life. In the past eight years that I have had with God, I can attest that his acts of providence continue to overwhelm me. I still struggle with his hiddenness, but his interventions in my life are undeniable. He has guided me in my education and is orchestrating my career. I still find talking to him sometimes exhausting and strange. I think Christians should better learn to express this difficulty. However, Christ is my ultimate hope, the thing that is most worth holding on to. I recognize his fingerprints more and more in my life. And he keeps reminding me of his amazing, loving grace. I love him because he loves me!

Chapter 10

From Lukewarm Theism to Committed Faith

JUDITH R. BABARSKY

WHEN ASKED TO CONTRIBUTE A chapter for this book, I never imagined how challenging it would be to give a complete account of my conversion. Where to begin? At each point in reflecting upon my story, I realized I needed to take a step back. I could begin with the moment I picked up Richard Dawkins's book *The God Delusion*, but I believe that leaves out a big piece of the picture. We all come to a book with various preconceived notions, a certain mindset, and expectations. Preparing to write about my conversion to Roman Catholicism, I returned to a rereading of *The God Delusion*,[1] as well as Joseph Ratzinger's *Jesus of Nazareth*.[2] It was the former that led me to the latter, but the story begins long before those events.

A Lukewarm Theist

It is only fair that I provide a bit of my background. A comment to a previous blog piece I wrote noted that I was never truly an atheist, so Dawkins, in all fairness and contrary to what I claimed in my post, did not "convert" me to theism. It is certain, however, that he did not convince me of any truth in atheism. In any case, I approached my reading of *The God Delusion* with an open and inquiring mind. If Dawkins could make a solid case for the nonexistence of God, I was prepared to accept that.

While I never self-identified as an atheist, I was, for a good part of my life, a lukewarm theist at best. Dawkins speaks of these theists in his book. They are those who embrace the familiar stories of the Bible with a childlike nostalgia and identify as "religious" for mostly social reasons. I'm sure there are many of these people in our churches today, and Dawkins delights in noting as well that such people as Michelangelo and Raphael and many others from centuries ago likely had no choice in the matter since social custom demanded religious piety or at least public practice—not to mention that the artists needed to win commissions to practice their art. Seriously, though, how could Dawkins know the mind of Michelangelo? I found such presumptions throughout Dawkins's book, and they did little to make his case for atheism, absent as they were of any semblance of objectivity or scientific rigor.

Baptized in April 1964 at the age of nine (along with my father and brother) in Old First Presbyterian Church on Long Island, New York, I remember very few instances of church attendance throughout my childhood. Certainly, there were the Easter Sundays when I excitedly donned a new Easter dress and hat (hats were "in" back then), and I looked forward to the visit of the Easter Bunny. The fact that Christ rose from the dead was not a significant event in my lexicon of meanings attached to the day. My parents certainly never inculcated in me an appreciation for the religious significance of Easter. As Protestants, there was no mention of Lent, nor of any spiritual preparation in advance of the celebration of Easter Sunday.

My family was never particularly invested in any specific denomination, although we did seem to favor the Presbyterian church. My mother had grown up in the Episcopal church. My paternal grandmother, for all my recollection, always identified as a Christian Scientist and was a proud member of the First Church of Christ, Scientist, in Boston, Massachusetts. Many Christian Scientist beliefs seeped into my childhood, notably an avoidance of doctors except in cases of extreme need and a healthy skepticism of medications as opposed to simple, healthy living. This avoidance, however, was never tied to any religious belief, as is found in more dogmatic adherents to Christian Scientism. Throughout high school and college, I was, on and off, drawn to various systems of religious belief (Christian Scientism and various Eastern religions in high school and Judaism in college), as well as to various schools of philosophy, predominantly phenomenology and existentialism.

My parents divorced following my graduation from high school; a year later my mother married a lifelong Lutheran, and my father married a Thai Buddhist (who, I learned years later, had a mixed-belief system; she professed Christianity while at the same time offering oblation to Buddha). Drawn into the Lutheran church for social reasons (my parents' network of friends and the wonderful choir parties), I married a lapsed Catholic in a Lutheran marriage ceremony. All three of our children were baptized in the Lutheran church; I was more the driving force behind any religious practice in our family, although we did not attend services regularly nor did we practice religious customs in our home. I divorced, taught Sunday school at our Lutheran church for a brief period, and had a crisis of faith, during which I embraced Judaism. I could wrap my head around a Supreme Being but not around the God-man, Jesus Christ. I questioned the virgin birth and the resurrection. During this time, I met my second husband (another lapsed Catholic—was God leading me somewhere?), and although I never converted and only twice attended synagogue services, I spearheaded the practice of various Jewish rituals in our home (Shabbat, Passover, Hanukkah); my husband graciously acquiesced. His first marriage had been in the Catholic

Church to a nonbeliever; he had never baptized his daughters and never practiced his faith.

Discovering Dawkins

In the meantime, family friends (our boys played baseball together) were slowly sowing seeds with their quiet witness. Never loud in the proclamation of their faith, nonetheless they never hid the fact that they attended Mass on a regular basis and would often tweak their arrival times for our postgame BBQs to attend Saturday vigil church services. We would part ways for the summer and reconnect once baseball began again, sharing our summer doings. Our friends spoke of "work camp" and how enriching their experiences had been—there was very little "religious" about their stories; mostly they talked about the people they met and helped and the communities they visited. Eventually, after three or four years, I asked, "What's work camp?" Something their church did every summer with a group of teenagers, kind of like a Christian Habitat for Humanity. "Do I have to be a member of your church to go?" "No." "Do I have to be Catholic?" "No." Okay, great, this was sounding better and better. Our friends forwarded me a link with information about the following summer's destination, a First Nation on Walpole Island, Canada.

So off I went, never expecting that the work-camp experience would be the catalyst for my ultimate conversion and reception into full communion with the Catholic Church. At camp I oversaw five teenagers in completing our assigned project of building a handicapped ramp. It was hot; it was exhausting. And it was transformative. I returned home determined to learn more about Catholicism. Although I made every attempt to temper my enthusiasm, it was self-evident and provoked my stepdaughter to recommend Dawkins's book to me. At the time she was a college student; her boyfriend (raised Catholic and educated in Catholic schools but no longer practicing) had brought the book to her attention.

In fairness to Dawkins, I suppose I was, at least to a certain degree, indoctrinated into my beliefs. But, honestly, who isn't? Certainly the atheist child is indoctrinated into his or her beliefs. It would be naive to think that any child could be raised in a vacuum of parental beliefs. A completely objective environment is an impossibility; the very fact of what is or is not a focus of attention is a result of subjective choice. As for me, without any catechetical education, without any significant lived faith in my childhood home, nevertheless there was a tacit understanding that we were "Christian," and being Christian, we were Protestant. Beyond that, I could not have articulated any understanding of what I believed beyond the (primary-school edition) Easter and Christmas stories, in addition to the stories of creation, Noah, and Moses. But these stories simply formed part of my cultural upbringing with little impact on how I lived my life or how I thought about who I was. There was never an expectation on the part of my parents that I profess any specific religious beliefs.

Unconvinced by *The God Delusion*

From the outset, perhaps the biggest problem I had with *The God Delusion* is its decidedly unacademic presentation of the—largely antiquated—arguments for atheism and against theism. Dawkins lays his foundation for atheism by discrediting belief in God through identifying multiple individual cases, as in the form "so and so believes this, and this is how they are wrong, stupid, imbecilic, and the like," or the reverse form, "such and such very smart, educated, intelligent scientist/politician" is an atheist. He does this over and over again. The further I read, the less impressed I was, due to his lack of any reasoning process at all. Rather, he delights in quoting others (often well-known people, scientists, politicians, etc.) regarding their lack of faith and repeating their denigrating comments about various religious practices, faith, and belief.

Ultimately I found these arguments unconvincing. First, I wasn't looking for a compendium of individuals and their beliefs regarding religious belief. Second, I didn't see what these individual beliefs had to do with Dawkins's argument that belief in a supernatural being was delusional. It was a tautological argument: if you believed in a supernatural God, you were delusional; if you didn't, then you weren't. It proved nothing. I was reminded of Socrates's discourse with Euthyphro wherein the attempt is made to define "piety." Euthyphro, much like Dawkins in both method and arrogance, resorts to a series of characterizations of piety. To each, Socrates posits an alternative viewpoint, always searching for a universal "form" by which one will always properly identify piety. "Bear in mind then that I did not bid you tell me one or two of the many pious actions but that form itself that makes all pious actions pious."[3] Dawkins fails to identify the form by which religious belief would be discredited, relying instead on anecdotal stories.

Dawkins easily dismisses anything he deems unworthy of contemplation (read "religious" or "faith-based" here), commenting, "Here is the message that an imaginary 'intelligent design theorist' might broadcast to scientists: 'If you don't understand how something works, never mind: just give up and say God did it. You don't know how the nerve impulse works? Good! You don't understand how memories are laid down in the brain? Excellent! Is photosynthesis a bafflingly complex process? Wonderful! Please don't go to work on the problem, just give up, and appeal to God. Dear scientist, don't *work* on your mysteries.'"[4] It was these nonarguments that left me with no deeper understanding of why atheism was a better choice over belief in a supernatural being. And in any event, such God-of-the-gaps type of arguments are generally dismissed by Christians as being of little value in understanding what we mean by God as creator.

Dawkins claims to be a scientist, and as such he discounts anything not capable of being proven by the scientific method. He absolutely fails to approach the subject of religious belief, the historicity of the

Christian story, and the occurrence of miracles with any degree of open-mindedness that might allow for honest scientific inquiry—or even reasoned thought. He simply dismisses them out of hand as not even worthy of inquiry, the nonsense of silly, uneducated individuals. Dawkins's science is perhaps more rightly "scientism," in its adherence to the belief that only scientific knowledge is authentic knowledge—and authentic knowledge is only that which can be affirmed by the scientific method. Dawkins's scientism seems to embrace a dogma that would equate science with reason itself.

Undoubtedly there are fundamentalist thinkers on both sides of the aisle—religious and nonreligious. But for anyone who has delved at all into Catholic thought through the ages, it is clear that the Catholic Church is not antiscience. As early as the eleventh century, Saint Anselm of Canterbury, whose motto was "faith seeking understanding," spoke of the alliance between faith and reason; they are not in opposition but work together in a grand choreography. Pope John Paul II devoted an entire encyclical to elucidating how faith and reason not only are not mutually exclusive (as Dawkins would have his reader believe) but are mutually dependent upon each other. In the same manner that I discount those fundamentalist religious thinkers who are antiscience, I discount fundamentalist atheists (and I count Dawkins among these) who are dogmatically anti-God. G. K. Chesterton speaks to this very phenomenon: "It puzzled me very much, even at that early stage, to imagine why people bringing controversial charges against a powerful and prominent institution should thus neglect to test their own case and should draw in this random way on their own imagination. It did not make me any more inclined to be a Catholic; in those days the very idea of such a thing would have seemed crazy. . . . I never dreamed that the Roman religion was true; but I knew that its accusers, for some reason or other, were curiously inaccurate."[5] Dawkins's inaccuracies range from facile descriptions of Scripture (Paul of Tarsus as the founder of Christianity, God as the

Old Testament's "psychotic delinquent") to the lumping together of all three Abrahamic religions (Judaism, Christianity, Islam) as being able to be treated as "indistinguishable."[6]

Dawkins's arguments based on Scripture are similarly uncompelling. Writing about, seemingly, biblical fundamentalists, he claims that Scripture is "persuasive to people not used to asking questions like: 'Who wrote it, and when?' 'How did they know what to write?' 'Did they, in their time, really mean what we, in our time, understand them to be saying?'"[7] Such comments ignore the vast amount of rigorous biblical scholarship being carried out in universities around the world, not least in Dawkins's own University of Oxford. Further, that the Gospels "were written long after the death of Jesus"[8] is misleading, as dating places them within fifty to sixty-five years of the death of Jesus, based on the fact that they were written by the apostles or those close to the apostles and cited by various other contemporaries whose writings we have. It is these and similar convenient insertions in the book that left me unconvinced of any objectivity on the part of Dawkins to fairly examine the evidence for or against faith. Certainly, if Dawkins expected to mount a credible attack on religious, specifically Christian, belief, it would not be unreasonable to expect that he would have studied his opponent extensively enough to present the arguments fairly and objectively. The fact that he clearly failed to do so left me with the firm conviction that his was not a credible witness and certainly not scientific.

Finally, in chapter 4, after three chapters of invective against religious belief, Dawkins lays out his main argument. He summarizes this argument in six points:

1. One of the greatest challenges to the human intellect, over the centuries, has been to explain how the complex, improbable appearance of design in the universe arises.

2. The natural temptation is to attribute the appearance of design

to actual design itself. In the case of a man-made artifact such as a watch, the designer really was an intelligent engineer. It is tempting to apply the same logic to an eye or a wing, a spider or a person.

3. The temptation is a false one, because the designer hypothesis immediately raises the larger problem of who designed the designer. The whole problem we started out with was the problem of explaining statistical improbability. It is obviously no solution to postulate something even more improbable. We need a "crane," not a "skyhook," for only a crane can do the business of working up gradually and plausibly from simplicity to otherwise improbable complexity.

4. The most ingenious and powerful crane so far discovered is Darwinian evolution by natural selection. Darwin and his successors have shown how living creatures, with their spectacular statistical improbability and appearance of design, have evolved by slow, gradual degrees from simple beginnings. We can now safely say that the illusion of design in living creatures is just that—an illusion.

5. We don't yet have an equivalent crane for physics. Some kind of multiverse theory could in principle do for physics the same explanatory work as Darwinism does for biology. This kind of explanation is superficially less satisfying than the biological version of Darwinism, because it makes heavier demands on luck. But the anthropic principle entitles us to postulate far more luck than our limited human intuition is comfortable with.

6. We should not give up hope of a better crane arising in physics, something as powerful as Darwinism is for biology. But even in the absence of a strongly satisfying crane to match the biological one, the relatively weak cranes we have at present are, when abetted by the anthropic principle, self-evidently better

than the self-defeating skyhook hypothesis of an intelligent designer.[9]

Here at last Dawkins lays out his thinking. But he commits the same errors he accuses the theists of. He cannot imagine who might have designed the designer (God); yet in the same way he omits any explanation of how evolution initially got underway. Where did the initial "slime" that evolved, ultimately, into human life come from? He hopes for an explanation from physics and chemistry and even says, "I shall not be surprised if, within the next few years, chemists report that they have successfully midwifed a new origin of life in the laboratory. Nevertheless, it hasn't happened yet, and it is still possible to maintain that the probability of its happening is, and always was, exceedingly low—although it did happen once!"[10] Furthermore, he tells us that it is "utterly illogical to demand complete documentation of every step of any narrative, whether in evolution or any other science."[11] Yet isn't this the very demand he makes of theists—complete documentation? Of miracles? Or of anything else that Dawkins claims is "delusional"?

Even as a well-established theory, evolution still begs the question as to how it all got started in the first place. How come we exist in a universe that is so anthropically fruitful that our own existence becomes possible? Dawkins, an evolutionary biologist, places great hope in evolutionary physicists—although they are no closer than the biologists to a credible theory of how the universe and life itself began. Multiverse theories are just that—theories—and in large part they fail the test of Occam's razor, which states that the simplest explanation is usually the correct explanation. The theory of the Big Bang, a more parsimonious explanation for the advent of the universe, is not incompatible with the spontaneous creation that is depicted in the book of Genesis.

COMING TO FAITH THROUGH DAWKINS

The Case for Belief

With a sigh of relief, I turned to Joseph Ratzinger's (Pope Benedict XVI) *Jesus of Nazareth*. In the foreword, he writes, "Unless there had been something extraordinary in what happened, unless the person and the words of Jesus radically surpassed the hopes and expectations of the time, there is no way to explain why he was crucified or why he made such an impact."[12] Ratzinger identifies the "great question that will be with us throughout this entire book: What did Jesus actually bring, if not world peace, universal prosperity, and a better world? What has he brought?" And he answers the question by noting, "The answer is very simple: God. He has brought God."[13]

Ultimately, I found in *Jesus of Nazareth* a clear answer to the question, Who is Jesus? It was an answer that was logical and made sense to me. For starters, Ratzinger clearly outlines his methodology in approaching his subject (something Dawkins does not do)—utilizing the historical-critical method (placing Scripture in the context of history, authorship, etc.) and bolstering it with canonical exegesis (reading the individual biblical texts in the context of the whole). Viewing Scripture through this lens, it becomes apparent that the Old and New Testaments proclaim a unified message—Jesus Christ is the key to understanding both. Proceeding directly from Scripture and the Gospels, Ratzinger places Jesus in the context of his times, without "modernizing" him and therein destroying the figure of Jesus. To avoid this error, we must not discount the ability of God to act in history—if we do that, we relegate everything to do with God to a subjective understanding where "*we* alone speak and decide what God can do and what we will and should do"[14] (italics mine). If we discount miracles and anything we cannot verify with our own eyes, then "we have developed a concept of reality that excludes reality's translucence to God. The only thing that counts as real is what can be experimentally proven."[15] There is a humility in Ratzinger's book that is lacking in Dawkins. Granted, Ratzinger did not set out to write a polemic against atheism, as Dawkins set out to write against theism. Nonetheless, the Cardinal makes a strong and logical case for the reasonableness of belief in Jesus as the Son of God.

At this point, I found myself in a surprising place—a place I never imagined I would be. I began to believe in the Christian message. And further, I began to draw near to the Catholic Church. Chesterton speaks of the three stages through which most converts pass: (1) detachment/indifference ("I had no more idea of becoming a Catholic than of becoming a cannibal"); (2) awareness of far more truth than falsehood in the Catholic message; and (3) in being "fair" to the church, one is drawn to it.[16] Previous to reading Dawkins and Ratzinger, I had dismissed the Catholic Church as bigoted at worst, anachronous at best—something that no one who could think for themselves would ever embrace except as a social/familial custom. As Bishop Fulton Sheen once said, "There are not one hundred people in the United States who hate the Catholic Church, but there are millions who hate what they wrongly perceive the Catholic Church to be."[17]

As I moved between Chesterton's second and third stages, I found that the Christian message as proclaimed by the Catholic Church was a consistent and unified message. As the prophet Jeremiah says, "Your words were found, and I ate them, and your words became to me a joy and the delight of my heart" (Jer. 15:16). I felt my mind broadening and expanding. Particularly in our modern world, where so much passes for "real" because it feels good in the moment, I found myself drawn to a way of thinking that was logical. Again, Chesterton, in his unique way, sheds light on this issue: "As the world goes, especially at present, it is the other people, the heathen and the heretics, who seem to have every virtue except the power of connected thought. . . . What is now called free thought is valued, not because it is free thought, but because it is freedom from thought; because it is free thoughtlessness."[18] Many, including Dawkins, deride religion as irrational, something needed to quell fears of death, a belief system for those who don't think for themselves. But I found the opposite to be true; rather than ceasing to think being the result of my conversion, I came to understand the truth in Chesterton's words: "To become a Catholic is not to leave off thinking, but to learn how to think."[19] Rather than my education ceasing upon my conversion, I found my mind broadened with a desire to learn more about all that I didn't know—particularly history, philosophy, and, yes, science.

Chesterton writes of the speculation of others as to when the convert will give up any newfound convictions and give up the embrace of the church. This was certainly true in my case, as a number of friends and acquaintances (having known me in my Catholic-denying days and my previous endless search and embrace of myriad belief systems on my spiritual journey) figured it was simply a matter of time before I'd give up on Catholicism. Chesterton makes the beautiful analogy:

> The outsiders, stand by and see, or think they see, the convert entering with bowed head a sort of small temple which they are convinced is fitted up inside like a prison, if not a torture-chamber. But all they really know about it is that he has passed through a door. They do not know that he has not gone into the inner darkness, but out into the broad daylight. It is he who is, in the beautiful and beatific sense of the word, an outsider. He does not want to go into a larger room, because he does not know of any larger room to go into. He knows of a large number of much smaller rooms, each of which is labeled as being very large; but he is quite sure he would be cramped in any of them.[20]

When Dawkins writes of the God *delusion*, he is referring specifically to a belief in a supernatural being, a creative intelligence, that operates behind the observable universe. An atheist, on the other

hand, believes there is nothing beyond the observable, natural, physical world—it is a belief system rooted in empiricism and positivist
philosophies. Ultimately, considering the choice between a world
where only the natural exists and a world with two orders—the supernatural and the natural—the convert, living in that larger world,
has no desire to retreat to a smaller world circumscribed by what can
be proved through experimental science.

For me, the church is a timeless institution. What other worldwide
institution is as old or older than the church? And when one considers that the church is the continuation/culmination of a process
begun in antiquity many thousands of years ago—in truth the story
goes all the way back to the beginning, to creation—with what can
we possibly compare that? When we root ourselves as individuals in
this timeline of history—rather than think of ourselves as children
only of our own age—we gain a perspective that benefits from the
wisdom of the ages. This is a wisdom that is eternal, not ephemeral
and based on emotional responses to concerns specific to our moment in time. By adhering to an eternal wisdom, we are better able to
navigate the trials that cross our paths during the short time we are
here on earth: "The years of our life are threescore and ten, or even
by reason of strength fourscore; yet their span is but toil and trouble;
they are soon gone, and we fly away" (Ps. 90:10 RSV).

If people approach faith in a supernatural being, God, with skepticism, it is certain that they will find many ways to feed that skepticism, particularly given the proclivities of our modern culture. This
is the scientism as evidenced in Dawkins—and scientism is little different than fundamentalism. I choose to embrace belief in both the
natural and the supernatural, with the certitude that one day both
will be understood to be not only reasonable but compatible beliefs.
Faith is a supernatural gift, whereas reason is a natural gift—both
are gifts from God, and as such, it would be unreasonable to expect
that they would be in conflict. To have one gift without the other

disallows a reasonable approach to life—one becomes either a religious fanatic (denying reason) or a materialist (denying the reality of anything that cannot be empirically studied).

More than anything, my conversion was a result of learning to think in a different way over a period of several years. Mine was more of an intellectual conversion than anything else, and I've often said that I read my way into the faith. It was provoked by a process of reasoning—it most certainly was not an emotional conversion (although I would have welcomed that). While I say it was an intellectual conversion, I do not want to discount the spiritual impact the process had on me. I remember feeling as if my brain had short-circuited when I grasped the implications of believing in the Jesus that Ratzinger presented in his book.

Lest one think an "intellectual" conversion is simply changing the way one thinks about any particular subject—in this case Jesus Christ and the Catholic Church—it is important to note that such an intellectual conversion comes with a price. The price is that if one accepts the Christian faith as the one, true faith, there is a moral and ethical component. Of necessity, it demands changes in how one goes about living one's life as well as how one views oneself. It comes down to adherence concerning where we place our allegiance. As Jesus tells the Pharisees in answer to their question about the greatest commandment in the Jewish law, "You shall love the Lord your God with all your heart and with all your soul and with all your mind. This is the great and first commandment. And a second is like it: You shall love your neighbor as yourself. On these two commandments depend all the Law and the Prophets" (Matt. 22:37–40).

Dawkins's arguments, I suspect, appeal to those who are drawn to catchy quotes that seek to discredit any arguments for the existence of God. *The God Delusion* is one of those books that preaches to the choir with little of intellectual value. I have found this to be true also of some books written by Catholic apologists, although, generally, books on Catholic apologetics are professionally written with strong arguments made for the reasonableness of religious/Christian/Catholic belief. But there is little reasoned argumentation in *The God Delusion*, and this is what ultimately led me to find little of value in the book. *Jesus of Nazareth*, on the other hand, didn't have a bone to pick.

Ratzinger doesn't demand that one has to have faith to read his book; he only says that if one allows oneself to approach the book with an openness to the idea of faith, the figure of Jesus will be seen to be worthy of belief. It is presented in a much more neutral sense, allowing and inviting the reader to form his or her own opinion. Dawkins never allows for this—he discredits theist belief from the start.

Ultimately, I embraced all of Catholicism. Not because I must, based on some outside authority, but because the teachings make sense; they are logical and reasonable, even if difficult. In our modern, increasingly secular world, the practice of religion is often simply a performance, an adherence to a set of rules—such seems to be the religion in Dawkins's mind. The religion of the early Christians was vastly different—it was a lived faith, a transformative faith. And it was often a faith that one practiced at great risk. Here in the United States, where I live, any current religious "persecution" is in the form of the ongoing political battles between liberals and conservatives as they argue over what constitutes separation of church and state and whose rights will prevail. It is easy to forget that there are many places in the world today where Christians practice their religion under threat of death. In fact, it is estimated that more than three hundred million Christians live in areas with high levels of persecution. Throughout Chesterton's writings, and especially in *The Catholic Church and Conversion*, he intimates that the measure of truth in Christianity is the fact that people are still converting to the faith, two thousand years after Christ.

My journey did not end with my conversion to the Catholic faith.

Realizing that I needed to be part of a Christian community beyond my parish in order to inform and strengthen my faith, I discerned a vocation as a lay (or Third Order) Dominican, making full profession in 2020. Drawn to the Dominicans because of their emphasis on study—as well as prayer, community, and an apostolate—I find the order to be a good place for me to grow in holiness.

In the years since my conversion, I have become increasingly convicted of the truth of the gospel message: the truth of Christ. Do not think, however, that it is always an easy conviction. Faith, at least for me, is not and has not always been straightforward. I admit that I stray at times—not so much from belief as from commitment to practice. I rarely (only because I am reluctant to use the word "never") question the value of the Christian life rooted in love, but I do, at times, balk in the face of miracles, in the folly of the cross, in the secret and hidden wisdom of God (see 1 Cor. 1). Yet, time and time again, I return to the words of Simon Peter, "Lord, to whom shall we go? You have the words of eternal life, and we have believed, and have come to know, that you are the Holy One of God" (John 6:68–69). Inevitably, I find that there is no greater truth than the Word of God, culminating in the incarnation of our Lord and Savior.

Chapter 11

From Religion to Agnosticism to Faith in Christ via Dawkins

WALDO SWART

I GREW UP IN SOUTH Africa in a loving, typical Afrikaans Christian home. For Afrikaners, being Protestant is part of our cultural identity, and it is uncommon to meet an Afrikaans family who is not at least nominally Christian. If you live in an Afrikaans community and go to an Afrikaans school, you cannot escape Christianity. Like most Afrikaans children, I was raised to believe in "the Big Man in the sky." I cannot remember a time when we did not have Bible study and prayer as a family. As a young child, even though I was probably too young to really grasp any of it, I thoroughly enjoyed the epic and heroic stories from the Bible. Despite my limited understanding of all it entailed, I gave my heart to Jesus when I was five years old. I was told during a Bible session at kindergarten that Jesus is the Son of God and that he died for my sins. The teacher told me that if I love Jesus, I should invite him into my life. I can still remember repeating the prayer after her.

I was brought up in an Apostolic Faith Mission (AFM) congregation, South Africa's largest Pentecostal church. Every Sunday we went to church as a family. People raising their hands and speaking in tongues during worship services was nothing strange. There was also the occasional sharing of wisdom from the members of the church, if they felt called by God to do so. Emphasis was placed on experiencing God through the Holy Spirit during worship and prayer. After the worship session, the children went to Sunday school while the main church service continued.

I don't remember much about Sunday school classes, but I do remember that I was quite frightened when I heard about the devil and hell—the eternal fiery place for people who did not accept Jesus as their personal Lord and Savior. I was also told that people from other religions were "lost" and misled by the devil and his demons. For the most part, however, the Sunday school teachers focused on discussions about having Jesus in your life. The church's social activities, such as camping, were a lot of fun for me and my friends. So much fun that by the end of primary school, I received a certificate for faithful Sunday school attendance.

Beginning to Question

I was raised in an affectionate home by doting and warmhearted parents. As my family was very religious, I was given my first Bible for my seventh birthday. At home, the majority of books and music were by Christian authors and artists. My parents rarely questioned the teachings of the church or the religious authors that they looked up to. Christianity was a way of life for them, confirmed by their personal experiences. There was no need for them to question their faith.

Supernatural-themed media was considered evil in our household, a serious complication for a young boy who loved superheroes and fantasy films. My parents forbade my brothers and me from playing with Pokémon cards, reading the Harry Potter series, or doing anything that Christian friends or Christian magazines told them were evil influences on children. I believe that this was from an inherent propensity to protect us. I thought that my friends' parents were so cool because my friends were allowed to watch the Harry Potter films. I remember watching the first Harry Potter movie with my friend at his house. He didn't want me to miss out. Spoiler alert: I didn't dabble in witchcraft after seeing it.

When I began to develop my own taste for music, outside the gospel genre, my father and older brother regularly warned me of all the evil in the hard rock and metal music that I loved listening to. In fact, my parents had a booklet, titled *Maak Skoon Jou Huis*[1] (literally translated as "Clean Your Home"), which contained a list of "evil" musicians. This later became a collection of my favorite bands. I regularly turned to this trusty little booklet when I wanted to discover new metal music to listen to. Again, there was no discussion on whether the views in this booklet were correct or even debatable.

My grandmother told me time after time about the rapture and end times—and that current world events meant that Jesus would be returning soon, prophecies about which she had absolute conviction. She saw political events and technological progress as clear signs of the end times.

It was rather strange to me that no one in my family questioned these ideas, but I tended to go along with it. My faith was a very "personal" thing for me, and I didn't feel the need to argue any points where I differed from my family. Though I often quietly disagreed with my family's views, I still believed in God and Jesus.

I began to deal more seriously with this religion of mine in high school. During a youth service altar call, I, like many other teens, gave my heart to the Lord—for real this time. And I was crying. A lot. For me, it was time to get serious. To symbolize my new commitment to Jesus, I decided to be baptized at the age of sixteen. I started attending youth cell groups and church services every week. Most of the informal talks and discussions centered around how to practice

Christianity in our daily lives and live out the fruit of the Spirit. We occasionally watched Christian sermons and films. Theology and doctrine were never discussed in depth, but questions were welcomed, within reason. I'm not exactly sure why, but it was just assumed that everyone had the right views about God and Jesus. Although it was rarely discussed openly, I am convinced that many of the teenagers in the youth group believed that we were living in the end times and that much of the secular media was evil. And obviously, this included the belief that the theory of evolution was a hoax, made up by god-less men who wanted to lead people astray. I was exposed to a lot of young-earth creationism media during this time. Despite all of this, I really enjoyed socializing with my Christian friends and even visited the youth groups of my school friends' churches. Many of my best friends I met during church-related events.

A Loss of Faith

Later that same year, a man broke into my grandparents' home and attacked them. They both ended up in comas and died shortly after. It was the first time I doubted God's goodness. My grandparents were the most devout Christians I knew, so I didn't understand how a loving God could just stand by and allow this to happen. The pain and suffering in the world began to bother me. I was bitter toward God for many years, but somehow I still trusted that he had a plan for everything.

Make no mistake, I was still very involved in the church, despite my bitterness. I helped out where I could and assisted with preparations for youth services at the church. I even participated in church plays—a very challenging task for an introvert like myself. I wanted to learn more about God and be closer to him, so I spent more time in prayer. I also started to read the Old Testament. But this had an opposite effect than intended.

What I read in the Bible didn't align with how I personally experienced God. I was taught to believe that the Bible is the Word of God. I was told that it is infallible—trustworthy and reliable—and inerrant, free from any contradictions. Yet, the more I read the Bible, the less things made sense. I realized that this was a very, very strange book—that the world of the Bible was not the world I lived in.

The conflicts between what I read in the Bible and what I knew about science became much more apparent. The order of the creation days in Genesis was wrong; it didn't fit with what we now know about the world, what I learned from science books and documentaries.

I came across many passages that I never realized were in the Bible, ones that we were certainly not taught in Sunday school classes. I had so many questions. Why would God drown the whole world, children included, except for a few people (Gen. 7:23–24)? Why did God harden Pharaoh's heart (Exod. 9:12)? Why did God order a whole people group killed, including babies and camels (1 Sam. 15:3)? I mean, what horribly immoral thing did the babies and camels do? God seemed a bit psychotic.

Even in the New Testament, I found passages that bothered me. Why did Jesus curse a fig tree (Matt. 21:18–22)? Why did Jesus have to die? Why eternal torment (Rev. 14:11)? Why would God write such a confusing book? Overall, the Bible seemed quite primitive and brutal.

I took my troubles with the Bible to God in prayer, eagerly expecting a clear explanation (preferably an audible one). But prayer felt like I was talking to myself, with no answers and not even a feeling of inner peace.

I was confused. Christianity had given me so much joy in the past, but now it just didn't make sense to me. I began to question the Bible's content but soon realized that I was apparently the only one among my Christian friends who was struggling with this. I discussed my objections with some of the youth leaders from my church but only got cheap answers: Have faith like a child. God is testing you. It's the devil who is making you doubt your faith. Just believe.

One youth pastor did lend me a few books, but all the books assumed Christianity and the Bible to be true. They were not satisfactory at all.

I started keeping my questions about Christianity to myself. I only discussed them with my girlfriend and best friend on occasion. Why was I the only one thinking that these things in the Bible were mad? I felt crazy and very alone. I couldn't discuss my questions about Christianity with my parents; I didn't want to disappoint them.

In my last year of high school, I walked out of the church building during a youth worship service, crying. My girlfriend followed me and asked what was wrong. In tears, I told her I no longer believed these things. At that moment I realized that I wasn't a Christian anymore. That was the last time I attended the AFM church faithfully.

Exploring Other Faiths

After that night, I went on a spiritual journey—a very academic one. I was convinced that there had to be a god, but I wasn't sure if the traditional Christian view of God was the right one. I clearly remember browsing through all the different "-isms" on Wikipedia, searching for the one worldview that resonated with me. I briefly dabbled in Unitarianism, the belief that God is one entity instead of a Trinity (as taught by mainstream Christianity). But the worldview that best described my beliefs at that time was deism: belief in God based on reason and nature, not revelation. Deists believe that the universe was created by God but reject claims that he intervened with the world via supernatural means. Deists do not make specific claims about the nature of God; they also reject any revealed claims from holy books. It was a relief to discover a name for what I believed, or at least didn't believe. Thomas Paine's *Age of Reason*[2] became my new Bible. My fear of eternal damnation faded away as well.

During my last year of high school and first year of university, my deistic beliefs were fairly constant. I wanted to learn more about God and his creation and, as a result, read many popular science books. I also bought a remastered DVD collection of Carl Sagan's *Cosmos* and watched many nature and space documentaries on the National Geographic channel. They blew my mind.

During this time, I came across apologetics, arguments defending Christianity, by watching YouTube videos that came up in the recommended videos lists. This was probably because I watched many videos on science and theology. I found it rather amusing at the time that theologians thought there was evidence for their belief in God. I usually agreed with the classical arguments for the existence of a god, but the arguments regarding the historicity of the Gospels didn't convince me. At this stage, I was quite certain that Jesus, like many other gods, was just another myth.[3]

I became slightly more outspoken about my deistic beliefs in religious discussions and, as a result, caused tension in my relationships. In fact, my girlfriend broke up with me by saying, "I love you, but I love Jesus more."

Embracing Atheism

I began a more in-depth study on cosmology and evolution. Being told from a young age that evolution was one big hoax, I finally decided to investigate what the big "evolution versus creation" fuss was about. Doing some self-study, I realized that all the reasons I still believed in a creator god sounded less and less convincing. Evolution by natural selection explained the diversity of life quite elegantly. I watched *The Blind Watchmaker* documentary by Richard Dawkins, as well as his series on Charles Darwin.[4] Shortly after this, I watched all his other documentaries and any talks and interviews I could find. I found his arguments very powerful and convincing. He was also very pleasant to listen to. He did not seem as bitter and angry as many of my Christian friends thought he was. I, unfortunately, did not read *The God Delusion* at this stage because I wasn't sure how I would be able to sneak it into my parents' house. Instead, I watched his documentary[5] on the subject, and it was enough to sway me in a different direction.

I don't remember there being an exact moment when I eventually decided that God, whether a theistic or deistic god, did not exist. During my second year of studies, I made peace with the fact that I was an atheist. My long-held deistic views were a stepping stone to complete unbelief. Although I lost my belief in God, I still found the world quite beautiful. It was a great privilege to be alive, to experience this short existence on this speck of dust in our vast universe.

I argued away faith quite easily: life is scary and death is scary, which is why people made up gods throughout the centuries to help them cope with life. I was confident that everyone would be an atheist if they really reflected deeply on the world around them. I was certain that I knew too much to consider a Christian worldview again. Christianity was just wishful thinking.

Of course, I didn't share my unbelief with most of my friends and family. I had committed social suicide too many times in the past just by questioning my faith and sharing my doubts. Fortunately, I made some new, similarly nonbelieving friends. It was such a relief to be able to have open discussions without any pretensions. These friends, like me, thought that faith was irrational and unintellectual. They were also very friendly people. They didn't seem to be angry at the world, contrary to what I'd been taught about godless people. They were just unconvinced.

During my years at university, I became increasingly militant about my atheistic views. I read books and watched many debates and talks from well-known atheists and skeptics besides Richard Dawkins, such as Sam Harris, Christopher Hitchens, Michael Shermer, Dan Barker, and Richard Carrier. But I was quite stubborn, to be honest. I often fast-forwarded the debates just to hear the atheists' arguments. Being already convinced that Christianity was false, I wasn't interested in apologetics and hearing the arguments for Christian theism. I just wanted to get ammunition so that I would never be caught off guard when a believer confronted me. However, one of my friends who studied theology challenged my views, and we had regular lively discussions. I did not understand the terminology he used, though, so I rolled up my sleeves and started studying basic theology in my spare time to better defend my views.

Ayn Rand's *Atlas Shrugged* triggered my interest in philosophy. I didn't agree with all her views, but her writing made me think. I decided to read more books on basic philosophy. While studying within the humanities, I was exposed to other worldviews in more detail. One worldview I could immediately identify with during one class was nihilism: the view that man and life have no ultimate meaning and purpose. I struggled to see how life could have objective meaning in a naturalistic worldview. If I wanted to be consistent with my views, I had to accept that life is absurd. I was convinced that God does not exist; I just had to accept it as a fact.

What Was Missing?

Despite this stark belief that the universe was indifferent, I longed for something more. To keep my sanity during this time, I deliberately occupied myself with studies and social activities, just to avoid thinking too much about the deeper questions of existence. I went out a lot more in the evenings, and I lived more hedonistically. Although I had a healthy social life and great years at university, deep down I felt empty.

In 2012, my final year at university, I had a theory class where we discussed ethics. After that class, I started reading about morality and other issues again. In the process, I stumbled upon apologetics again and watched a few lectures and debates around the subject. Things were different this time, probably because I had more knowledge of science, theology, and philosophy. I listened to a lot of debates and talks from William Lane Craig, John Lennox, Peter Kreeft, Alister McGrath, J. P. Moreland, and Frank Turek, often the same debates that I had fast-forwarded through previously.[6] I also read some of their books. Their reasons for faith were now quite compelling, and while two years earlier I had thought that the atheists destroyed the theists' arguments, I found my thinking regarding these debates flipped.

These Christians were actually rational—this wasn't the Christianity I knew from my childhood. My former atheist heroes' arguments seemed poor compared with the coherency of Christian theism. I didn't think the two sides were always arguing about the same type of God. I also picked up on logical fallacies in the debates, something I hadn't noticed before. I noticed some common trends and claims made by atheists that I had found compelling a few years before but now started to question in light of the apologists' arguments. Here are a few of them[7] (these are my own words; theologians and philosophers would be able to answer these objections in a much more insightful and sophisticated way):

- *People tend to believe in the religion of their parents or culture.* Although I was raised to believe in a Christian God, this does not undermine its validity. You can say the same thing regarding any worldview, even an atheistic one. How you come to believe something has no bearing on whether that belief is true or not.
- *Science explains the world better than religion.* This is a bit of a broad, sweeping statement, so I wasn't always exactly sure what atheists were referring to when making this claim. Sure, science explains an aspect of reality and our experience of it, but science doesn't answer my existential questions satisfactorily. Literature, art, music, beauty, values, morality—how do I make sense of these aspects of life from a completely naturalistic worldview?

- *The universe came from nothing.* Reflecting on the universe's origin now, it makes sense to me to believe that something spaceless, timeless, and nonphysical brought the universe into existence 13.8 billion years ago (sounds a lot like the classical idea of God).

- *Who created God?* This question came up frequently. It sounded quite compelling at first, but the more I thought about it, the more it did not make sense. God is not one of many beings in the world. It makes sense to think that something necessary and not dependent on anything must exist.

- *Faith is blind belief without evidence. Christians are intellectually lazy.* The apologists that I came across gave good reasons when defending their worldview and explaining why they trusted Christianity to be true. They didn't seem anti-intellectual at all.

- *Religion is dangerous and the cause of wars.* It can be dangerous, but it doesn't have to be. People throughout the ages have always abused ideas to support their own agendas.

- *We can be good without God.* Given a naturalistic, evolutionary worldview, how can I say that there are objective standards of right and wrong? If there are no objective moral standards, how can I condemn the harassment of minorities, for example? How can I think raising a child in a particular faith is morally wrong? Also, on what grounds can I condemn the Christian God's actions in the Old Testament?

- *The Bible is primitive.* I realized that I grew up with a very literal reading of the Bible. I'd read it in a very simplistic way, ignoring the genre and cultural context of specific books. I had many assumptions about what the Bible should be and placed impossible standards upon it.

- *Jesus didn't exist.* Many scholars, even non-Christians, believe at least that Jesus was a real person. The point of contention is

usually the resurrection. The resurrection has a lot of explanatory power compared with other theories regarding the empty
tomb.[8]

Thinking more critically about the claims above, I was completely
rattled. Considering all the arguments, God's existence seemed very
probable. It upset me that a theistic worldview made so much sense,
because it meant that I was wrong this whole time. I could not, however, bring myself to believe in God again. But at least such a belief
didn't seem that irrational anymore.

I sat on my bed one night, very emotional, and accepted that there
might be a god because the cosmological and moral arguments for
a god's existence were sound. The conclusions of the arguments just
made sense to me. Feeling confused and a bit lost, I sought a more
spiritual path, but not through the Christianity that I grew up with.
This was when I came across a spiritual community for free thinkers—a church that accepted various spiritual truths but did not as-
cribe to one particular "way." I started visiting this church regularly.

A few months later, through a lecturer, I also discovered an
apologetics-focused church and felt very at home there, as I met
other people who also struggled with faith. This was a different kind
of church. I had never heard Afrikaans people speak so articulately
about their faith. Asking questions during a church service? Wow.
This was quite novel. I was intrigued.

I did not feel crazy anymore. I appreciated that this group of people was not afraid to ask difficult questions about God, Jesus, and
the Bible. My new girlfriend and I became regular visitors. I got my
spiritual fix at the spiritual community and my intellectual fix at the
apologetics church. At this stage, I was nowhere near Christianity
spiritually. Still, it seemed to me that there could at least be a rational
basis for faith in the Christian God.

In my new relationship, I grew spiritually along with my girlfriend. She exposed me to the emotional side of faith, and I exposed her to the intellectual side. We watched various talks and debates and balanced them out with Rob Bell's NOOMA series when we wanted to take a break. I wasn't always open in my relationship about my ever-present struggles with faith. I pretended to have more faith than I did. I didn't want to have that kind of conflict in a relationship again. The relationship eventually ended. However, I will always be very grateful that this woman allowed me to explore my faith freely.

I became more involved at the apologetics church. By now I had become good friends with many of the members there. I got involved with the men's cell group. I even presented a few talks, even though I didn't really believe in Christianity. Although I knew all the arguments, I couldn't quite buy the Jesus story. Salvation by grace seemed too good to be true. I read about liberal theology and Gnostic Christianity, seeking a new understanding of the Gospels. I became very comfortable with the idea of a mythological and symbolic resurrection.

From Eastern Spirituality to Christianity

I was agnostic at this stage of my life, in 2014. Christianity did not bring me any emotional peace, and it was still quite strange to me that it made intellectual sense. For no specific reason that I can recall, I began to read about Eastern religions, specifically Taoism and Buddhism. I think I started exploring these religions purely out of curiosity, since I wasn't exposed to them when I was young. I guess I wanted to explore all my options before committing, given that I had come to believe that agnosticism was unsustainable and confusing.

I started to read the *Tao Te Ching.* I read the Dhammapada shortly after. These books were so simple and wise. They did not contain strange, violent stories or difficult verses that needed explanations. Eastern religions also seemed far more tolerant to me.

I started meditating daily, trying different techniques. I listened to Alan Watts's lectures on a daily basis. Although I had a sense of calm, I realized that Eastern ideas were not always intellectually sophisticated or satisfactory. The more I studied these ideas, the more I realized that many aspects, such as reincarnation and karma, should just be accepted.

Throughout my Eastern journey, I still visited my new church. I experienced an information overload and no longer knew what to believe. I came up with various ideas from different faiths and belief systems and basically created "Waldo-ism."

Some days I felt spiritually enlightened, and other days I felt like I was making things up as I went along. At the end of 2014, I was not in a good place spiritually. I experienced anxiety that reminded me of my nihilistic days during university.

In early 2015, I decided to stop attending my church. It felt like a waste of time. Just as I was about to leave the church, I heard they had arranged for Ellis Potter, a former Buddhist monk from America, to present a series of talks. Of course, I was very interested. *Why would a Buddhist become a Christian?* I was invited to a retreat where he was the speaker.

I found the sessions at the retreat very meaningful. It was especially interesting to hear how Potter approached Christianity from an Eastern perspective. I had deep conversations with other people, and I could freely share my ever-present objections with them. I also had an engaging conversation with Ellis Potter. He pushed me to identify the questions behind my questions.

I especially enjoyed talking with one of my agnostic roommates who was very articulate and skeptical. We got along right away, since we felt similarly about life and religion. But there was one thing that was striking to me in our conversations. Like me, he had read up on different religions and was aware of the main arguments for and against the existence of God. However, it soon became clear that for all his knowledge, he was unwilling to let any convincing argument sway him. Instead, whenever he conceded a point, he directly moved on to the next objection. I realized that what he wanted was not answers to his questions but an ongoing argument that would never lead to a conviction on anything. During one of our conversations, I vividly remember that this felt like looking in a mirror. I had been so happy to cherry-pick my -isms and to hold up my well-versed objections one after the other, rather than allowing a positive answer to sway me in a particular direction. It struck me how frustrating it must have been for my Christian friends to argue any point with me, exactly because it would never stay at that one point. I, like this roommate of mine, was constantly moving the goalposts.

I felt empty after the retreat. I realized how erratic my mixed worldview really was. I was actually being very stubborn and silly. It was so unnecessary because I knew that there were good enough reasons for me to accept Christianity. Ironically, it was not a Christian's belief that convinced me in the end but rather an agnostic's unrelenting unbelief.

On a Saturday night, February 21, 2015, I decided to give up, surrender myself to the Lord, so to speak, and take that step into faith. I didn't hear a voice, see a white light, or even get a fuzzy feeling. I just experienced an aha moment where everything fell into place. I was, however, overwhelmed with peace. There was a reality in my life that was not there before. It felt like I finally knew God.

The Impact

After making my decision, I started to "get" things that hadn't made sense before. Christian doctrines like the Trinity and the atonement started to make a bit more sense. What was particularly striking to me was my eagerness to pray and read the Bible.

These days, I read the Bible more critically. Though it is rarely easy reading, I consider the cultural context of the passage, the audience for whom it was written, and the reason why it was written. Keeping this in mind, I find it easier to deal with difficult passages.

To me, Christianity makes God approachable, more than just some indifferent force. I think I finally understand what it means to have a relationship with God.

I see a more complete picture of God and reality when I incorporate science, theology, and philosophy into my worldview. I aim to have a more holistic and integrated view of the world.

Since becoming a Christian, my life has become a bit more complicated. Christianity has changed my view on family and relationships. It has also changed how I think about my career and how I spend my money. I'm less self-centered. I think I'm more patient as well. Christian Waldo doesn't seem to be so angry anymore. Faith hasn't made me a saint, and I don't always do what I think God expects of me, but my life seems a lot clearer since I started believing in God.

I have come to realize that life is, or will be, difficult for everyone. Everyone will suffer in one way or another. But for me, Christianity means that there is hope in this suffering.

I now challenge myself to follow my grandmother's advice: "Pray and read your Bible every day, and go to church every week." I've even visited my old AFM church again, assisting with an apologetics series for their youth service.

When I look back on all the -isms and worldviews that I traveled through, Christianity is the one that gives me the most intellectual and emotional peace. I think there are three main reasons why I believe in God and adhere to Christianity. First, to me Christianity best describes reality and the human condition. I admit that many aspects of Christianity are difficult to make sense of. It is comforting to know that I'm in good company with many respected theologians and philosophers—I'm not the only one struggling to make sense of certain aspects of the faith. Second, Christianity works practically, when its teachings are actually followed. And third, personally, it gives meaning to my life. Atheists might say that I am deluding my-self. But since there are good reasons to believe that Christianity is true, believing adds meaning to my life in an otherwise absurd, nat-uralistic world.

I still have many questions, and there are still things I wonder about. I have again struggled with my faith since becoming a Chris-tian in 2015. Issues and difficulties that I thought I had sorted out for myself still trouble me from time to time. I sometimes wonder why I bother with faith at all. But when I consider the alternatives, Christi-anity seems more probable to me. I can't seem to escape the idea that Jesus is a reality in my life. Despite all the ups and downs and lapsing once or twice in unbelief, I haven't regretted my decision to follow Jesus. So far, it has been quite a wild ride.

Chapter 12

Seeking the Truth via New Atheism and Psychedelic Drugs

ASHLEY LANDE

I WAS TEN YEARS OLD when I first met a real, live atheist. Sort of, anyway—I heard one on the radio. I was riding in my brother's car down the Pacific Coast Highway in California, just a quarter mile or so away from the ocean, which asserted itself in a faint crashing and blustering and salting of the air. A curious song came on, at first quiet out of the speakers and then building to a roar. Before long, my entire world was uncomfortably rocked.

The song began innocuously enough: a morose acoustic guitar, a child's dulcet voice. But as I listened, I quickly realized the words were no sweet innocent hymn; they were a scandalous screed against God himself. The folksy thrums gave way to a jangling, cascading melody, and an angry snare kept time while a man, with a tenor smooth enough to rival the child's voice, lamented the gross dereliction of God and howled accusatory questions at him. A growl skulked low and menacing behind the purity of the tenor tone, sometimes erupting into a raw animalistic bawl.

My eyes widened as Mr. Andy Partridge of the band XTC savagely

222

indicted the Almighty, and I hazarded what I hoped was a nonchalant glance at my brother. He was an affable agnostic, fifteen years my senior and unassailably cool because, well, he was a surfer and older than me. A day or two earlier my sister and I had giggled hysterically after we goaded him into saying, in his best SoCal surfer accent, "I'm a Gen X slaaaacker," a phrase we no doubt cribbed from MTV. He was always unruffled, easygoing.

And now he was undisturbed by the radical act of rebellion broadcasting over his car radio. He even idly tapped the steering wheel to the beat as he drove. I was scandalized, not only by his indifference but also by the reality that the ground had not cracked and yawned open to swallow us in our complicit heresy. The ocean continued to churn and foam in its indomitable vastness to our left; the world had not ended. Yet my malleable little mind was blown because here was someone committing nearly gleeful blasphemy. They *didn't believe in God*. And they were saying so, out loud, in song, on the radio!

It's not that my family was particularly religious. Sure, we went to church periodically, and I'd attended Sunday school and vacation Bible school when I was younger. I was a compliant child, and that meant I sang along contentedly with songs such as "Jesus Loves Me" as a teacher led us with the comedic exuberance reserved for young children. It seemed to me she laid it on a little thick, her eyes wide and her arms flapping in exaggerated pantomime—wrapping around her shoulders for "Jesus loves me" and dramatically opening a book for "the Bible tells me so." But I gladly sang for the promise of snow cones and jaunts around the Big Wheel tricycle track outside.

You *had* to believe in God . . . right? It was compulsory, an unspoken rule; you might dissolve into nothingness if you didn't. Just as I couldn't fathom the idea of breaking a rule at school (the very thought of it made my face flush with shame), I couldn't fathom *not* believing in God, though I hadn't the slightest idea what it all meant. I remember discussing the concept of infinity before bed some nights with my father, and I had some idea that it was tangentially related to God, but God felt equally remote and incomprehensible.

The Allure of Atheism

I was fifteen when I decided that I, too, was an atheist, and in stereotypical teenage fashion I was compelled to declare so to my parents precisely because I knew it would outrage them. I ambushed them in our family room where they were enjoying a nightly broadcast of *The McLaughlin Group* on PBS. "I have something to say," I announced, standing at the top of the stairs with self-important bluster. "I am . . . an *atheist*." The very word felt dangerous tripping off the end of my tongue, the handful of syllables forbidden, ugly, and thrilling. My dad sighed heavily and told me I didn't know what I was talking about, which further entrenched my resolve. My mother closed her eyes in exasperation and brought her hand to her forehead. While a debate over NAFTA droned on in the background, my dad and I argued bitterly over my declaration before I retreated to my room to cry and renew my commitment to godlessness.

Hearing "Dear God" for the first time on that breezy coastal highway didn't make me an atheist. But maybe it chinked the beginning of a fissure in my world and electrified me with a frisson of possibility: I didn't *have* to believe this stuff, which never made sense to me anyway—something about sacrifice and sin and atonement, a muddle of mystery that I didn't get and didn't care to probe. As I grew older, Jesus seemed about as thrilling and edgy to me as the ladies' monthly bell choir performance; but raging diatribes such as "Dear God" had passion and bite.

It was perhaps seven or eight years after hearing Andy Partridge upbraid God that I encountered another great British provocateur: Christopher Hitchens. In what seemed a strange paradox to me, my father liked Hitchens—for Hitchens's peripherally conservative political views and for what seemed to me his strangely inconsistent and emotionally motivated stance against abortion. I'd long since adopted left-wing dogma on abortion, much to the dismay of my father.

Hitchens excited me. He was whip-smart, smarmy, cocksure, full of rhetorical bluster, and able to conjure up stultifying retorts on the spot. He eviscerated his opponents with ease and smirking impunity. So what if he was a little brutal sometimes? You had to be when dealing with these backward, religious rubes. Truth be told, I delighted in his brutality. He seemed to spare no one with spiritual delusions of any kind, and rightfully so, I believed.

I was twenty-three when *God Is Not Great: How Religion Poisons Everything* was published. It would be the last Hitchens book I ever read. I'd graduated from college a year earlier and begun working as a reporter at a local newspaper. My commitment to atheism had only intensified with time and experience—I'd spent most of my college years partying, and although hedonism nearly destroyed me, with all the arrogant vigor of youth I was determined never to take refuge in what I'd long ago decided was a lie. I needed to codify my atheism, I believed. I began poring over the work of Richard Dawkins and Sam Harris and found much of the former's scientific explanations impenetrable (I had barely passed high school chemistry and cruised through biology doing the bare minimum with a very kind and lenient teacher), and the latter's ponderousness was simply irritating.

But Hitch—Hitch was the one. Glorious in his polemical savagery, winsome in his trenchant *bons mots*. His forthcoming book became a kind of idol to me; I didn't recognize the idolatry was in concert with the increasing desperation I refused to acknowledge. Hitchens would make me *sure*. Hitchens had the answers, the hard and definitive certainty I craved and needed. It never occurred to me that perhaps I should investigate the "other side" out of intellectual fairness; I needed only to bolster my prejudice and arm myself with greater ammunition to demolish the absurd pretenses of religion. After all, atheism was a foregone conclusion for any erudite person, wasn't it? And my greatest aspiration was to be considered a smart person.

I was so breathlessly eager for the publication of *God Is Not Great* that I preordered a copy on Amazon, and then when I realized that it would not arrive the day of publication, I went to a bookstore after work to buy a second copy. I didn't yet see that my willingness to dump money on two copies of a hardcover book was born out of my intensifying need to prove God didn't exist.

The words shouted shamelessly from the bright yellow cover: *God Is Not Great*. I seized a copy and carried it to the checkout, where the young woman behind the counter handled it like it was a hot coal. Her eyes went wide, and she scrutinized me for a brief moment before taking my money; she handed me the receipt and faintly murmured, "Thank you." Her reaction bolstered my arrogance; I pulled my shoulders back, lifted my chin, and marched out of the store into the shopping mall colonnade. I clutched the volume of contraband tightly, cover facing outward—past the candy shop, past the Gap, past Claire's Boutique. What a rebel.

I was practically salivating to read the thing by the time I got home. And so I did, sixty or so pages of it, my heart slowly sinking to my gut as I realized that Hitchens's style seemed nastier than I remembered. He called C. S. Lewis "pathetic."[1] I had no allegiance to Lewis, having never read his work, despite the gentle prompting of a counselor at church camp. I'd been dragged to camp with my best friend in the eighth grade, and I declared to a circle of shocked teenagers around the campfire that I was not a believer. Years later, I was taken aback when informed that *The Chronicles of Narnia* cartoon I'd watched as a child was some sort of Christian allegory and Aslan the lion was supposed to be a Christ figure. Even so, *pathetic* seemed an awfully strong and, well, *mean* word. Hitchens said religious people belonged to "the infancy of our species." He called *The Passion of the Christ* "homoerotic,"[2] which I felt was strong as well (as much as I loathed Mel Gibson and in fact had marched out of a college class when I thought I was about to be subjected to a scene from *The Passion*).

Hitchens concludes the opening chapter, with the tongue-in-cheek title of "Putting It Mildly," thus: "As I write these words, and as you read them, people of faith are in their different ways planning your and my destruction, and the destruction of all the hard-won human attainments that I have touched upon. Religion poisons everything."[3] As much as I might have concurred with the ideas that religion was silly, infantile, and wont to attract those of weak intellect, I couldn't quite concur with his abject certainty that religion was the root of all evil. Indeed, I was particularly struck by his ironic contempt for "certainty" when he himself put forth an intractable air of surety.

But more than any of these minor qualms, I was uneasy about what he proffered as hard truth. On paper, as the expression goes, I agreed with many of his ideas. But on paper, in the book I held in my hands, his "truth" rang hollow and dissonant, a thing devoid of beauty, devoid of tenderness, devoid of life itself. Here was truth at long last, codified, attractively packaged, delivered with decisive authority and consummate rhetorical flair. But still, Hitchens's truth clattered like words into a vacuum, a void. Shouldn't the truth be . . . beautiful? Poignantly resonant? Was it possible that capital-T Truth itself was as ugly as all this?

It had never occurred to me to long for the coincidence of beauty and truth. Truth was its own thing, existing whether you liked it or not, and my definition of beauty was woefully anemic; I don't know that I'd ever appreciated the beauty of something in itself without lusting after what it could offer me. I certainly thought myself physically beautiful and zeroed in on men I found attractive while I envied women I feared were prettier. My prodigious self-absorption eclipsed my ability to behold true beauty elsewhere. The human gambit was nothing but a contest with constantly shifting criteria, a cutthroat rat race to win a contest that can never be won because death always looms on the horizon. I'd inadvertently embraced a shallow grab bag of social Darwinism, nihilism, and thanatotic hedonism. Underlying it all was a ravening fear that I tamped down with booze and hatred.

It was almost as though my own jadedness—or, at least, my concerted rejection of transcendence, except in the false and fleeting fugue of drunkenness—had carried me here nearly against my will. Nearly.

I clapped the book shut. I sighed and slid it just underneath my bed, where, eventually forgotten, it would recede into the obscurity of dust bunnies and dog hair. When my Amazon package with the second copy arrived a week later, I traded it in at a used bookstore. My discontent with hardline atheism had begun, and newly untethered, I languished in a hinterland between rejecting both atheism and God for several months. Then everything changed, including my faith in my ability to apprehend truth at all.

Looking for the Magic in Mushrooms

I'd eaten psilocybin mushrooms a few times, first in college and then on a couple occasions with friends, and I'd had fun. Great fun—a glittering visual cavalcade of pinball-machine kineticism, where all surfaces whirred and spun and melted, a swirling, swooping mash-up of cut-and-paste auditory distortions, plenty of hallucinatory time travel, and oddball hilarity arising from the simplest objects or situations. I loved the experience, and once I tasted it, I craved it. But mushrooms were only around when they were around, with availability whispered at parties or, if you were lucky, reported in code in a solicitous phone call from an acquaintance.

It was fun, yes, but that was all it was for me. The experiences didn't have a spiritual or transcendent dimension; they were just a good time, a party, a very welcome exceptional treat to the tired old bacchanal offered by drink. So when an acquaintance offered me

LSD on the condition that I take it with him, I readily accepted. I had just lost my job as a desk drone at a company that sold office furniture. They'd been glad to fire me, and I was glad to have been fired—there were only so many exotic descriptors I could attribute to office furniture, which was my primary task—*sleekly ergonomic, dreamily luxurious but eminently practical, old world charm meets modern sensibility*—and I was feeling like playing fast and loose with my brain, with my reality, with my very life.

Still, despite my recklessness, I was confident in my ability to navigate the waters into which I was about to dive headlong. My acquaintance came to my apartment with a comical armory of hippie accoutrements: a singing bowl that issued ghostly tones when its rim was ringed by a wooden pestle, a set of bongos, *The Tibetan Book of the Dead*, and a mysterious, square, purple book with brown butcher-paper pages entitled *Be Here Now*.

I was still an atheist, and Christopher Hitchens was still under my bed, somewhere. My quest for Truth had led nowhere, and now my thirst for certainty had given way to a libertine apathy. Perhaps it was a bad idea to take a powerful mind-altering drug with someone I'd just met, but I put the acid-saturated Smartie on my tongue anyway. The tang piqued my jaw as the chalky candy dissolved in my mouth. The drug's chemicals were tasteless as they made their way into my bloodstream.

We waited. Well, I waited. He chanted, insisting that taking LSD was a ceremonial rite. His magisterial air annoyed me, and I laid back and stared at the ceiling where a trapezoid of late-afternoon light bent and stretched at the seam of the wall. After a time, a prismatic waterfall began to stream down the wall, ever increasing in intensity and color. A sense of prevailing calm came over me, a sense that seemed absolutely impenetrable, and so I turned to my friend where he sat on the couch next to me and breathed incredulously, "How does anyone ever even have a bad trip?!"

He turned toward me, and his eyes widened in horror. "Well, don't *think* about it!" he exclaimed, as if the mere thought would send me spiraling into oblivion.

It turned out he was right. Psychedelics make one intensely vulnerable to suggestion, and so I went and thought about it, a lot. I thought about it as I traipsed to the kitchen to get myself another ice cube—it was high summer, and the ancient humming air conditioning unit in my window provided only moderate relief. Suddenly the skittering of my little terrier behind me took on a sinister tone. Resentful of the patchouli-and-marijuana-scented stranger who had invaded his space, my dog followed vigilantly on my heels whenever I moved. The checkered linoleum of my kitchen floor listed and swayed beneath his little paws, and he barked at me. He never barked at me. He regularly staccato-barked for the squirrels that scaled the trees outside and for humans with the gall to appear within sight of his perch at the front windows, but never for *me*. Something was wrong, drastically wrong. It was as though a deep, doom-laden note had sounded from the heart of the universe—if the universe indeed even had a heart and not merely a void at its center, which seemed far more likely—and that note reverberated throughout all this hollow, meaningless form.

I scurried to the bathroom to hide, to find some refuge from the unbearably high-pitched terror that sounded everywhere, even though I feared—no, I knew—that there was none. No escape. No way out. I was in hell, and I would be here forever and ever and ever.

I looked in the mirror, not my first mistake of the evening but perhaps one of my gravest. I beheld a face neither human nor corpse but caught up in an interminable, cyclical death-groove somewhere between. Livid gobs of flesh fell off my face, and my skull throbbed. The pieces of flesh reconstituted themselves only to decay and fall again, and again, and again. I was dying. I was dead. I was dying. I was dead. There was no life, only a relentless circuit of decomposition that never truly ended and never truly began.

I staggered back to where the stranger I'd invited into my apartment and now into my moment of greatest crisis, my death itself, was seated in the same place on my couch. "We need to call an ambulance," I howled. "I'm dying, I'm losing my mind, I'm . . . I don't know."

His eyes grew wider, making even greater black discs of his blown-out pupils. "No, no, no, we don't need to call an ambulance," he said, likely just as fearful of getting arrested as he was of mediating my full-blown freak-out. "Look at me," he demanded. I reluctantly turned toward him, trembling, wanting to look anywhere but into the eyes of another human at the peak of my eternal torment. "You. Are. On. A. Drug," he said, slowly and emphatically, leaving a pregnant pause between each word as though he were talking to a child or a foreigner. And he was: I'd been reduced to a helpless, fear-riddled child and an alien lost in a hostile land.

My eyes rolled like those of a cornered animal; I hyperventilated; my mind froze in thrall of this nameless, everlasting despair. There was no peace anywhere. No comfort. No soul-slaking draught of living water to quench this terrible thirst. I threw back my head and wished for death. And then the sky split open with an awful flash of light. The world ended, and I died.

An Awakening

"Wow, I mean, wow," he was saying, an awed chuckle in his voice. "Do you even know all the stuff you were saying to me? Like, you were telling me about your childhood, and how you cried every day in the first grade, all this crazy stuff!"

I sat in a heap where I'd slid off the couch onto the hardwood floor, shell-shocked from whatever smiting had just befallen me. I remembered the flash of light, then I remembered weeping. "I—yeah. I remember, I guess," I mumbled.

"Wow," he said, shaking his head at me with a mix of incredulity and mystification. "Just WOW."

I spent much of the rest of the night trying to withdraw from conversation, embarrassed by the cataract of vulnerable memories I'd apparently unloaded on him but also eager to retreat and try to process what had just happened to me. Was it good? Was it bad? I didn't know. I no longer knew which way was up, what was real, who I was. I finally retired to my bedroom. The branches on the trees outside my windows vibrated menacingly, and even the light that shined under the door—from where the stranger in my apartment did whatever he was doing in the living room while getting catatonically high—felt like a profound intrusion.

God Is Not Great still lay beneath my bed, fraternizing with terrier hair, while I lay above, my mind grasping for thought but finding only empty space. Atheism was no longer a viable option, I knew. But what was? What was anything? The most vacuous-sounding, stoner-caliber questions seemed astonishing relevant now: What was time? What was reality? What was life, what was death?

I finally fell into a blackout kind of sleep. But my desire for answers to those questions, and my incipient conviction that LSD held the answers, would lead to a years-long love affair with psychedelic drugs. I was terrified, but I was also hooked. And the barbs would nearly destroy me before I finally found the truth I'd been seeking in the very last place I thought to look.

Resisting Church

It was nearly six years later when I walked into the one place I'd sworn I'd never go again, the one place I was certain contained no answers: a church. Hugely pregnant with my husband's and my second child, a daughter, I held a protective hand over my swollen belly as I shuffled into a pew and sat on the red velvety cushion.

My husband and I had met, fittingly, at our acid dealer's house five years earlier. We'd gotten married after a couple of months and took acid three times over the course of our four-day honeymoon. Our yoga teacher married us in a rose garden, our pupils magnified from the heady draught of love's initial high and, of course, the LSD we'd taken the previous night. Acid was our sacrament, but it was also our recreational activity, and as long as we were riding the intoxicating wave of infatuation, all was well. Or so we thought. But waves inevitably crash, and soon we were shocked to find ourselves with the same problems as everyone else—conflict, distance, the necessity of negotiating the mundanity of life. Furthermore, we were mired in a spiritual darkness that shocked both of us.

I began having panic attacks in my yoga classes, an ominous sense of fear and dread overtaking me as I sat in lotus position, each foot nestled into its opposing hip. The oceanic drone of rounded "oms" throughout the classroom, which was supposed to transport me into ego-obliterating bliss, sounded shallow against the onslaught of evil I felt emanating from every corner, every crevice of the cosmos.

I was helpless, and in my worldview there was no one to help—no conquering power beyond the amorphous, impersonal prana, the universal life force that was ultimately neither good nor bad but coolly amoral and beyond duality. In my early days of psychedelic wonder, I'd viewed this distinction as sophisticated and evolved, but now it seemed terrifyingly deficient and even evil. As much as I strained to move "beyond duality" myself, the reality of evil persistently reasserted itself, and with no personal deity, I had no recourse.

I tried kundalini yoga. I visualized the serpent coiling up my spine as I sucked in sharp, hyperventilatory breath, contracting my ab muscles, working my inhales and exhales into such a frantic rhythm that I nearly fainted—a state that was supposed to approximate ecstasy. But nothing helped, nothing worked. There was no peace anywhere, even in the places I'd previously found it (or thought I had).

Even in my desperation, I resisted going to church and resisted hard, but my husband's therapist had challenged him to quit smoking weed every day and try Christianity, and though hesitant, he was determined to try "this whole Jesus thing" where nothing else had sufficed.

One night we reached a breaking point: "I don't know if any of this is true, but I feel compelled to pursue it," he said.

"Don't leave me behind," I begged, through tears.

"Then come with me!" he exclaimed, frustration in his voice.

I whimpered and hedged and finally spoke the truth, my voice cracking: "I don't know how." And I didn't—didn't know how to surrender to something I'd been rebelling against and avoiding for more than a decade, something I'd convinced myself was infantile and facile and silly.

But here we were, finally, together, in a *church* of all places. I was hostile, to say the least. I barely veiled my contempt as we walked in, returning a tight, closed-lip smile in response to every greeting we received. I insisted that we sit at the very back of the sanctuary. But as the worship music cued up and the morning light shown through the stained glass, projecting mosaic pools onto the pews in front of me, something cracked in me. I was startled to feel some long-tamped-down emotion erupting. Nearly before I knew what was happening, tears were streaming down my cheeks. It was humiliating in the worst way. All my yoga, all my meditation, all my assailing of my brain with chemicals, all my posturing, all my parroting of New Age platitudes and Sanskrit chants—*love and light, there's no such thing as a bad trip, om mani padme hum*, on and on and on and on, all the insane circuitous religious babble that never took me anywhere but left me pacing like a rat on a track. All of it had left me here, crawling toward the cross, protesting and begging for some other way, some other rescue from the hell of my own creation than "this Jesus person."

The sermon on Galatians confounded me. We are not under law? We live by the Spirit, by grace? What does that even mean? I'd lived by rules for so long—"Do not handle, Do not taste, Do not touch," as Paul quotes in Colossians 2:21—that I could see no other way to salvation, even though my quest for as much through rules had miserably failed. I was a vegetarian, then I was a vegan, then I was a raw vegan. I obsessed over what I put in and on my body and my son's body. I attended yoga religiously, three times a week, shunning any commitment that might infringe on these sessions. I still took acid when I could, when our son was with grandparents. Some dark force compelled me onward, even though I knew with increasing dread that it was all for nothing: *go farther, do better, be perfect.* The promise of freedom and peace receded ever farther into the distance the harder I ran, and despair settled in like a still, black cloud.

But part of me balked in offense at this message too. What do you mean, "the only thing that counts is faith expressing itself through love" (Gal. 5:6 NIV)? I had embraced Ram Dass's maxim that the best thing you can do for other people is work on yourself. I'd worked and worked and worked, and now here some Christian was trying to tell me it didn't matter, that the only righteousness I could ever have was accomplished for me by an itinerant Jewish preacher who'd lived two thousand years ago. It was absurd. But as I crossed my arms in indignation, I didn't know that my last bastion of righteousness, the performance on which I'd made my last paltry gamble of worthiness, was about to crumble.

A few weeks later, my icon of the Hindu goddess Kali leered from her perch as I screamed and heaved our daughter out of my body into a birthing pool in our living room. Kali's tongue protruded lasciviously from her fanged, blood-flecked mouth, and she grasped the thatch of hair atop the severed head of her enemy in one of her manifold fists, her blue arms fanning out in victory. A necklace of severed heads ringed her neck, a gruesome lei. Her name translates as "she who is death."

I thought of her as a female warrior, an icon of what women are capable of as I again entered the gauntlet of childbirth. But part of my New Age dogma was that childbirth was a positively transformative passage, a battle that would leave me feeling as triumphant and victorious, as powerful as Kali reveling in her carnage. I also viewed it as a measure of my worth as a woman and as a human being. I idolized a midwife who proselytized it as such, and I was crushed when, during a retreat hosted by her in my second trimester, a bizarre birth-reenactment hazing ritual had left me a sobbing heap on the ground and she'd turned away in disgust, refusing to speak to me the rest of the weekend. It solidified my resolve: my worth was wrapped up in natural childbirth. I had to prove myself.

But when my daughter finally came, first a sanguine little face, then an arm, then her sweet little body, I was shell-shocked, trembling in the wake of shattering pain. I thought my daughter's home-birth would be a blissful experience, an ecstatic counterpoint to the traumatic delivery I experienced in the hospital with my first child, my son. Childbirth in any context was not, as I had brainwashed myself to believe, a blissful, transcendent, psychedelic experience; it was a fiery, staggeringly painful, bloody, messy, humiliating trial, albeit with a wonderful prize at the end. It was a broken process in a deeply broken world, awaiting the fullness of its redemption like everything else in this roiling crucible of a life. And I didn't feel victorious—I felt deeply humbled. I knew I hadn't survived the ordeal by my own power, and it was certainly nothing to brag about.

From Hollowness to Wholeness

We returned to church, again and again. We both tried to find ways around surrendering to the whole truth of the gospel: my husband called himself a "non-Trinitarian Christian" for a time, and I strove to hang on to the last shreds of my own righteousness, galled at the idea of accepting that I was a sinner, as bereft of goodness in my flesh as anyone else who hadn't spent countless hours illuminating their chakras or chanting mantras into empty space, offerings to gods who were not there.

But finally I wept with relief at reading Paul's words in 1 Timothy 1:15: "Here is a trustworthy saying that deserves full acceptance: Christ Jesus came into the world to save sinners—of whom I am the worst" (NIV). Several months after a childhood friend's toddler died of leukemia—a childhood friend whom I'd seen periodically over the years and who rebuked my New Age prattling with Scripture so gently that I'd never even seen any of it as a rebuke—she recommended that I listen to the hymn "It Is Well with My Soul." It had served both her and her husband deeply in the aftermath of their daughter's death.

I put it on a playlist and forgot about it, but one mild spring day several months after my daughter was born, I was sitting on our front porch, and the song came wafting through the window. Suddenly the words pulsed like glowing embers in my heart and gut:

My sin, oh the bliss, of this glorious thought!
My sin not in part but the whole,
Is nailed to the cross and I bear it no more
Praise the Lord, praise the Lord, O my soul![4]

I wept, sobs wracking my whole body. Oh blessed relief, oh the precious priceless treasure that is Jesus, the only hope we could ever have in this fevered, monstrous, beautiful wreck of a world, in our own wretched, stony hearts. I didn't care anymore about enlightenment, about chakras, about triweekly yoga and raw food and Vipassana meditation. I chucked them aside like the filthy rags they were. I only wanted Jesus. I needed Jesus. In a lightning-rod revelation that was pure grace, I finally saw the truth; nothing and no one else would ever do.

That evening when my husband came home from work, I gathered all our physical idols: the bronze Ganesh statue, the Kali icon, and the little Buddha figurine, whose contented smirk now appeared as a mask of cold indifference rather than a mien of placidity. What contrast to Christ on the cross, his face contorted with suffering—with mine, with yours, with the suffering and sin of the whole wide world for which he died and that through only him could be redeemed. I knew the gospel was the only story big enough to account for all of it, both my own sin that threatened to eat me alive and the sin of the human race.

"We need to get rid of these," I told my husband, hefting the little statues in my hand. Yes, yes, we do, he said. We filled a trash bag with books and idols, relics of the old creation that we were glad to leave behind. We had decided to follow Jesus, as the old hymn says—no turning back. And somehow it felt more wild and daring and dangerous than any leap I'd taken before, including into the blind oblivion of drugs. But I trusted Jesus, in a way I had never trusted acid or yoga or meditation, because he was a person, and furthermore a person who had died for me, a person for whom and through whom and in whom everything was created.

The claims he made were so bold, almost impossible, and even as he offered me everything, he demanded my whole self—nothing more than this one wretched heart. He would accept nothing less. I remember vividly the night I realized that Christianity makes a claim on the whole of reality, that the Bible says Jesus Christ himself is the ground of it, and that this is not merely another belief system I was adding to my grab bag of cosmologies. This was one to which *I* was subject. I felt something of the fear of the Lord, and trembled. But I could finally sing it with earnestness, holding nothing back: *even so, it is well with my soul.*

A New Way of Viewing Hitchens

Now that I revisit Hitchens, his ideas don't seem nearly as dangerous as they once did, his invective not nearly as cutting, and his insightfulness not nearly as, well, insightful. But two separate passages toward the end of the book struck me—one a quote from Gotthold Lessing that Hitchens chose to include, another an incident at a speaking event he recounts in the afterword.

The Lessing quote asserts, "The true value of a man is not determined by his possession, supposed or real, of the Truth, but rather by his sincere exertion to get to the Truth. . . . If God were to hold all Truth concealed in his right hand, and in his left only the steady and diligent drive for Truth, albeit with the proviso that I would always and forever err in the process, and to offer me the choice, I would with all humility take the left hand."[5]

Hitchens argues, of course, that absolute truth is not available to be apprehended, but he nonetheless appreciates the Lessing quote because, as he says, even though the choice is something of an illusion, "it is better and healthier for the mind to 'choose' the path of skepticism and inquiry in any case, because only by continual exercise of these faculties can we hope to achieve anything."[6]

Really? I ask. Are we humans doomed to perpetually strive toward truth without any hope of ever obtaining it, or even being able to make the most tenuous claims as to its dimensions? And how did Hitchens justify even this striving when ultimately, in his view, it is completely futile?

I am reminded of the character in C. S. Lewis's *The Great Divorce* who, when confronted with the reality of heaven, persists in hemming and hawing about its merely figurative nature and pleading his case with pseudo-humility that we, in the cause of so-called intellectual honesty, can never really "know" anything at all. When told he can finally see the face of God at last, he says, "Ah, but we must all interpret those beautiful words in our own way! For me there is no such thing as a final answer. The free wind of inquiry must always continue to blow through the mind, must it not? 'Prove all things'. . . to travel hopefully is better than to arrive." When the "ghost" speaking to him—a friend he knew during his university days who now resides in heaven—reminds him, "Once you knew what inquiry was for. . . . Thirst was made for water; inquiry for truth," the man brushes it off. In the end, he chooses to return to hell, where he says he'll be presenting a paper at their "little Theological Society down there," rather than travel farther into the mountains with his friend and behold the face of God.[7]

I hear eerie echoes of Hitchens's voice in the character. To choose faith over doubt, Hitchens argues, continuing to elaborate on the Lessing quote, is akin to choosing Kool-Aid over a finely aging wine. But I had found that the wine of inquiry, though swoon inducing at first draught, turned rancid the more I glugged. It became boring, hollow, repetitive, a single dimension in fading black and white.

The truth held in the mystery of the gospel, however, is like a gem that offers flashes of light and glades of shadow at every turn. The mystery deepens rather than runs out; it becomes not more complicated but more complex—deeper, richer, truer, as more and more threads run to it and from it, as it reveals itself in greater and more prismatically varied details of our lives, as we grow in understanding that Jesus cannot be grasped intellectually but must be held, prized, and worshipped as an invaluable treasure.

In the afterword, Hitchens recounts a brief but curious anecdote from a book tour engagement in Little Rock, Arkansas, shortly before the publication of *God Is Not Great*. "On the road from the Little Rock airport is an enormous black-and-yellow billboard bearing the single word jesus. . . . I start [the speaking engagement] by mentioning the sign. I know the name, I say, and I have used the expression. But on its own the word 'Jesus' seems to say both too much and (somehow) too little. This gets more of a laugh than I might have predicted."[8]

I can almost hear that laughter: chattering, light, adoring of this atheist hero. But I also imagine in it a nervous edge, perhaps even a tinge of hesitation. Because while some of us laugh off God, we cannot laugh off Jesus. Some of us can pshaw at the parting of the Red Sea, picturing Charlton Heston as Moses holding out his arms as the waters gather into foaming towers (special effects that now appear woefully low-tech). We modern people can laugh at Noah, at a deranged religious lunatic building an ark, or at the story of Adam and Eve, a pair punished severely by a fascist overlord for mere intellectual curiosity, Hitchens might say.

But even the most cynical among us can't fully laugh at Jesus, the rogue Jewish preacher condemned to death by torture, the fully human man with the spit of contempt mingling with sweat on his destroyed brow as he gasps and strains, the cost of each meager breath a blackout fugue of agony as he pushes up on his impaled feet. No, most of us, even the unbelievers, can't laugh.

Hitchens is right: the name, on its own, says both too much and too little. Too much, because in two syllables it arrests us, it crushes us, it strikes into the deepest parts of us, to our fears and anxieties, perhaps to the child in us who remembers believing simply and purely. It cuts through our vulnerable flesh that still clings to its belief in its own worthiness, its own righteousness, its own middling conviction that we are basically good people who would never be complicit in the death of the Truth himself.

It's embarrassing, this naked word, Jesus, which we imagine freighted with accusation while simultaneously resonant with truth we may not want. "We wince," Frederick Buechner writes, in a sermon based around the phrase "Jesus Saves" scrawled on a cliff in the Hollywood Hills (and given decades before Hitchens's incident in Little Rock), "because there is something in the name 'Jesus' itself that embarrasses us when it stands naked and alone like that, just *Jesus* with no title to soften the blow. . . . 'Jesus Saves' seems cringingly, painfully personal—somebody named Jesus, of all names, saving somebody named whatever your name happens to be. It is something very personal written up in a place that is very public, like the names of lovers carved into the back of a park bench or on an outhouse wall."[9]

It also says (somehow) too little because we can, by sheer force of will, block it out, speed past the billboard to our many engagements and appointments. We can ignore it and go on pursuing whatever we think might give us peace, whatever we think might confer some degree of intellectual gratification at the end of the day and quiet the insomniac buzz of anxiety we feel when we awaken in the middle of the night. We can, like one of the commoners of Jesus's day, shrug at just another crucifixion, a display that should horrify us but to which we've gradually become inured. But we can't quite bring ourselves to laugh at him, even if we think of him as a deluded rebel who became entangled with the Roman Empire and met an unfortunate, grisly end. And for all his harsh insults, all his biting criticism, his abject hatred of religion and its adherents, I'm not sure Hitchens laughed either. Not at Jesus. Hitchens tended to favor the spurious argument that Jesus never even existed.

I read in Larry Taunton's book about Hitchens, *The Faith of Christopher Hitchens* (a gift from my dad a couple years before he passed away), that the song "Higher Love" by Steve Winwood was played at Hitchens's memorial service.[10] Taunton's son, who accompanied him, mentioned to his father that he knew this to be one of Hitchens's favorite songs. I was shocked and amused. I'd expected something like the furious manifesto of "Dear God," by which I was riveted that day in my brother's car, to be more his style—not a practically worshipful pop tune bursting with joyful horns and lyrics about craving a love that transcends, without which life must surely be meaningless. It made me hopeful, though—hopeful that Hitchens finally, at the very end, heard too much, and not too little, in the name of Jesus and succumbed to his higher love—the only true love—at last.

Notes

Introduction: The Ambiguity of Richard Dawkins

1. Richard Dawkins, "Religion's Misguided Missiles," *The Guardian*, September 15, 2001, https://www.theguardian.com /world/2001/sep/15/september11.politicsphilosophyandso ciety1.

2. Tina Beattie, *The New Atheists: The Twilight of Reason and the War on Religion* (London: Darton, Longman & Todd, 2007), vii.

3. For my own response to Dawkins, see Alister E. McGrath with Joanna Collicutt McGrath, *The Dawkins Delusion? Atheist Fundamentalism and the Denial of the Divine* (London: SPCK, 2007). For my earlier assessment of Dawkins's views on science and faith, see Alister E. McGrath, *Dawkins' God: Genes, Memes, and the Meaning of Life* (Oxford: Blackwell, 2004).

4. John Gray, *Seven Types of Atheism* (London: Allen Lane, 2018), 9. Gray's own preference is for the nuanced forms of atheism associated with Joseph Conrad and Arthur Schopenhauer.

5. John Gray, "Why Humans Find It Hard to Do Away with Religion," *New Statesman*, January 20, 2016, https://www.new statesman.com/culture/2016/01/why-humans-find-it-hard-do -away-religion.

6. Gray, *Seven Types of Atheism*, 23.
7. See Gray, *Seven Types of Atheism*, 1.
8. See, e.g., John Hedley Brooke, *Science and Religion: Some Historical Perspectives* (Cambridge: Cambridge University Press, 1991), which initiated reconsideration of these issues more than a decade before the emergence of the New Atheism.
9. Richard Dawkins, *The God Delusion* (London: Bantam, 2006), 66–69.
10. See, e.g., Joshua M. Moritz, "The War That Never Was: Exploding the Myth of the Historical Conflict between Christianity and Science," *Theology and Science* 10, no. 2 (May 2012): 113–23; Jeff Hardin, Ronald L. Numbers, and Ronald A. Binzley, eds., *The Warfare between Science and Religion: The Idea That Wouldn't Die* (Baltimore: Johns Hopkins University Press, 2018); Bernard Lightman, ed., *Rethinking History, Science, and Religion: An Exploration of Conflict and the Complexity Principle* (Pittsburgh: Pittsburgh University Press, 2019).
11. Gary Wolf, "The Church of the Non-Believers," *Wired*, November 1, 2006, www.wired.com/2006/11/atheism. For a scholarly account of Wolf's point, see Christian Smith, *Atheist Overreach: What Atheism Can't Deliver* (New York: Oxford University Press, 2019), 87–104.
12. P. Z. Myers, "The Train Wreck That Was the New Atheism," *Pharyngula* (blog), *Freethoughtblogs*, January 25, 2019, https://freethoughtblogs.com/pharyngula/2019/01/25/the-train-wreck-that-was-the-new-atheism.
13. Myers, "The Train Wreck That Was the New Atheism."
14. For a highly insightful critique, see Jacob Hamburger, "What Was New Atheism? On Liberalism's Fading Faith," *Point Magazine* 18 (January 14, 2019), https://thepointmag.com/politics/what-was-new-atheism.

Chapter 1: A New Christian Meets New Atheism

1. Sy Garte, *The Works of His Hands: A Scientist's Journey from Atheism to Faith* (Grand Rapids: Kregel, 2019).
2. "The Bus Campaign: What Was the 'Atheist Bus Campaign'?," British Humanist Association, February 20, 2012, https://web .archive.org/web/20120220154544/http://www.humanis.org .uk/bus-campaign.
3. Sam Harris, *The End of Faith: Religion, Terror, and the Future of Reason* (New York: Norton, 2016).
4. Richard Dawkins, *The God Delusion* (London: Bantam, 2006).
5. Christopher Hitchens, *God Is Not Great: How Religion Poisons Everything* (New York: Twelve Books, 2007).
6. Charles Darwin, *The Descent of Man*, introduction by Richard Dawkins (London: Folio Society, 2008).
7. Richard Dawkins, *A Devil's Chaplain: Reflections on Hope, Lies, Science, and Love* (Boston: Houghton Mifflin, 2003).
8. Richard Dawkins, *The Ancestor's Tale: A Pilgrimage to the Dawn of Evolution* (Boston: Houghton Mifflin, 2004).
9. Alister McGrath and Joanna Collicutt McGrath, *The Dawkins Delusion? Atheist Fundamentalism and the Denial of the Divine* (London: SPCK, 2007).
10. Alister McGrath, *Dawkins' God: Genes, Memes, and the Meaning of Life* (Malden, MA: Wiley-Blackwell, 2004).
11. Dawkins, *The God Delusion*, 245.
12. Dawkins, *The God Delusion*, 247–50.
13. Sam Harris, "Science Can Answer Moral Questions," filmed in Long Beach, CA, February 2010, TED2010, 22:50, https:// www.ted.com/talks/sam_harris_science_can_answer_moral _questions.
14. Sy Garte, "Science and Scientism in Biology," *God and Nature*, Winter 2013, https://godandnature.asa3.org/essay-science-and -scientism-in-biology.html.

15. Harris, "Science Can Answer Moral Questions."

16. Patrick Bateson, *Behaviour, Development and Evolution* (Cambridge, UK: Open Book, 2017), 79.

17. Irma E Järvelä, "Molecular Genetics of Adult-Type Hypolactasia," *Annals of Medicine* 37, no. 3 (2005): 179–85.

18. J. C. Wang, M. Kapoor, and A. M. Goate, "The Genetics of Substance Dependence," *Annual Review of Genomics and Human Genetics* 13 (2012): 241–61.

19. Evan A. Boyle, Yang I. Li, and Jonathan K. Pritchard, "An Expanded View of Complex Traits: From Polygenic to Omnigenic," *Cell* 169, no. 7 (2017): 1177–86.

20. Remus Ilies, Richard D. Arvey, and Thomas J. Bouchard Jr., "Darwinism, Behavioral Genetics, and Organizational Behavior: A Review and Agenda for Future Research," *Journal of Organizational Behavior* 27, no. 2 (2006): 121–41.

21. Richard Dawkins, *The Selfish Gene* (Oxford: Oxford University Press, 1976), 192.

22. Jack W. Szostak, "The Narrow Road to the Deep Past: In Search of the Chemistry of the Origin of Life," *Angewandte Chemie* 56 (2017): 11037–43; John D. Sutherland, "The Origin of Life—Out of the Blue," *Angewandt Chemie* 55 (2016): 104–21; Gerald F. Joyce and J. W. Szostak, "Protocells and RNA Self-Replication," *Cold Spring Harbors Perspective in Biology* 10, no. 9 (September 4, 2018), https://doi.org/10.1101/cshperspect.a034801.

23. Martin Rees, *Just Six Numbers: The Deep Forces That Shape the Universe* (New York: Basic Books, 2001).

24. Dawkins, *The God Delusion*, 162.

25. Dawkins, *The God Delusion*, 166–67.

26. Rees, *Just Six Numbers*, 4.

27. John D. Barrow and Frank J. Tipler, *The Anthropic Cosmological Principle* (Oxford: Oxford Paperbacks, 1986), 21.

28. Charles Darwin, *On the Origin of Species* (London: John Murray, 1859).

29. Howard Fast, *Freedom Road* (New York: Routledge, 1995).

30. Louis Pauwels and Jacques Bergier, *The Morning of the Magicians*, 4th ed. (Rochester, VT: Destiny Books, 2008).

31. Nicholas Goodrick-Clarke, *The Occult Roots of Nazism* (New York: New York University Press, 1993).

32. Will Durant and Ariel Durant, *The Story of Civilization*, 10 vols. (New York: Simon & Schuster, 1935–75).

33. Will Durant, *The Story of Civilization*, vol. 4, *The Age of Faith* (New York: Simon & Schuster, 1950).

34. Harris, *End of Faith*, 106.

35. Dawkins, *The God Delusion*, 316.

36. Dawkins, *The God Delusion*, 278.

37. Ted Davis, "Galileo and the Garden of Eden: The Principle of Accommodation and the Book of Genesis," BioLogos, April 17, 2012, https://biologos.org/series/science-and-the-bible/articles/galileo-and-the-garden-of-eden-the-principle-of-accommodation-and-the-book-of-genesis.

38. Ronald L. Numbers, ed., *Galileo Goes to Jail and Other Myths about Science and Religion* (Cambridge: Harvard University Press, 2010).

39. Gary R. Habermas and Michael R. Licona, *The Case for the Resurrection of Jesus* (Grand Rapids: Kregel, 2004); Lee Strobel, *The Case for Christ: A Journalist's Personal Investigation of the Evidence for Jesus* (Grand Rapids: Zondervan, 1998).

40. Hitchens, *God Is Not Great*, 176.

41. Daniel C. Dennett, *Consciousness Explained* (Boston: Little, Brown, 1991).

42. Sam Harris, *Free Will* (New York: Free Press, 2012).

43. Harris, *End of Faith*, 22.

44. Kenneth R. Miller, *Only a Theory: Evolution and the Battle for America's Soul* (New York: Penguin, 2009).

45. Sam Harris, "Science Is in the Details" (opinion), *New York Times*, July 26, 2009.

46. Harris, *End of Faith*, 45.

47. Bertrand Russell, *History of Western Philosophy* (Abingdon, UK: Routledge, 2009), 365, quoted in Harris, *End of Faith*, 254.

48. Elaine Howard Ecklund, *Science vs. Religion: What Scientists Really Think* (Oxford: Oxford University Press, 2010).

49. Molleen Matsumura, "What Do Christians Really Believe About Evolution?" *Reports of the National Center for Science Education* 18, no. 2 (March–April 1998): 8–9.

Chapter 2: Wrestling with Life's Biggest Questions

1. Robert Boyle, *A Disquisition about the Final Causes of Natural Things: Wherein it is Inquir'd, whether, And (if at all) with what Cautions, a Naturalist should admit Them?* (1688), in *The Works of Robert Boyle*, ed. M. Hunter and E. B. Davis, 14 vols. (London: Pickering and Chatto, 2000), 11:108.

2. Robert Boyle, *The Usefulness of Natural Philosophy*, Part I, in *The Works of Robert Boyle*, ed. Hunter and Davis, 3:229.

3. Robert Hooke, *Micrographia* (London: Jo. Martyn and Ja. Allestry, 1665), preface.

4. Peter Harrison, *The Fall of Man and the Foundations of Science* (Cambridge: Cambridge University Press, 2007), 51.

5. Richard Dawkins, *The God Delusion* (London: Bantam, 2006), 80.

6. Richard Dawkins, *River Out of Eden: A Darwinian View of Life* (New York: Basic Books, 2014), 33.

7. Helga Kuhse and Peter Singer, *Should the Baby Live? The Prob-*

lem of Handicapped Infants (Oxford: Oxford University Press, 1985), 118.

8. Peter Singer, *Writings on an Ethical Life* (London: Fourth Estate, 2002), 156.

9. Dawkins, *River Out of Eden*, 133.

10. Kuhse and Singer, *Should the Baby Live?*, 189.

11. Alberto Giubilini and Francesca Minerva, "After-Birth Abortion: Why Should the Baby Live?," *Journal of Medical Ethics* 39, no. 5 (2013): 261–63. Minerva elsewhere defends "after-birth abortion," a term she prefers to infanticide because "both fetuses and newborns do not have the same moral status as actual persons."

12. Dawkins, *River Out of Eden*, 133.

13. Frank Miele, "Darwin's Dangerous Disciple: An Interview with Richard Dawkins," *Skeptic* 3, no. 4 (1995): 80–85, https://www.skeptic.com/eskeptic/10-10-27/#feature.

14. Dawkins, *The God Delusion*, 358.

Chapter 3: From Dawkins to Christ via William Lane Craig

1. Richard Dawkins, *The God Delusion* (London: Bantam, 2006), 31.

2. Dawkins, *The God Delusion*, 308; also, Richard Dawkins, *The Selfish Gene*, 2nd ed. (Oxford: Oxford University Press, 1989), 198.

3. William Lane Craig, "What Science Can't Prove: Dr. William Lane Craig Explains to Dr. Peter Atkins," October 18, 2010, https://youtu.be/BQL2YDY_LiM.

4. Richard Dawkins, "Richard Dawkins—'What If You're Wrong?,'" November 25, 2006, https://youtu.be/6mmskXXetcg. To see William Lane Craig directly respond to this clip, watch "William Lane Craig Reacts to Richard Dawkins'

Answer to Challenging Question," August 14, 2020, https://youtu.be/X-dDgJDSMv4.

5. Craig, "What Science Can't Prove."

6. William Lane Craig, "Sam Harris and Jerry Coyne: Science vs. Religion Part 2," podcast, *Reasonable Faith*, November 29, 2015, https://www.reasonablefaith.org/media/reasonable-faith -podcast/sam-harris-and-jerry-coyne-science-vs.-religion-pa rt-2.

7. For a summary of the Kalam cosmological argument, see Craig's conversation with apologist Bobby Conway, "What Is the Kalam Cosmological Argument? The One-Minute Apologist with William Lane Craig," Reasonable Faith, accessed November 16, 2022, https://www.reasonablefaith.org/videos /interviews-panels/what-is-the-kalam-cosmological-argument -bobby-conway; for an in-depth and illustrated lecture on the Kalam cosmological argument, see William Lane Craig's presentation to the University of Birmingham, UK, from 2015: https://youtu.be/Dqc42ZB24ew.

8. Dawkins, *The God Delusion*, 157. Dawkins approvingly quotes his fellow New Atheist Daniel Dennett's appraisal of his central argument (also known as "The Ultimate Boeing 747 Gambit" and "The Argument from Improbability"). Dawkins also calls his own argument "devastating" in the introduction to *The God Delusion*, 10th anniversary ed., (London: Transworld, 2016), 17.

9. Dawkins, *The God Delusion*, 157–58. These are the premises that Dawkins opens each step of his summary with. They are quoted here word for word except for the substitution of the word *explanation* whenever Dawkins used his metaphorical term *crane*. Dawkins doesn't call the argument's conclusion step 7, but that is nevertheless what it is when expressed formally.

10. "Dawkins Refuses God-Debate with William Lane Craig,"

Bethinking, accessed November 9, 2022, https://www.bethink ing.org/atheism/dawkins-refuses-god-debate-with-william -lane-craig. This includes the full text of Dawkins's email response to Dr. Peter May's invitation to debate Craig in 2007.

11. "In Defense of Theistic Arguments: Craig, Dennett & McGrath MP3 Audio," *Apologetics 315*, July 6, 2009, 46:39, https:// apologetics315.com/2009/07/in-defense-of-theistic-arguments -craig-dennett-mcgrath-mp3-audio.

12. "In Defense of Theistic Arguments," 50:05.

13. William Lane Craig and Christopher Hitchens, "Does God Exist? William Lane Craig vs. Christopher Hitchens—Full Debate [HD]," April 4, 2009, Biola University, https://youtu.be /0tYm41hb48o.

14. Christopher Hitchens, "Craig vs Hitchens Pre-Debate Press Conference," 4:11, https://youtu.be/dLP248mNRSg?t=238.

15. Luke Muelhauser, "The Craig-Hitchens Debate," *Common Sense Atheism*, April 4, 2009, https://web.archive.org/web/20 100104174635/http://commonsenseatheism.com/?p=1230.

16. "The Bus Campaign: What Was the 'Atheist Bus Campaign'?," British Humanist Association, February 20, 2012, https://web .archive.org/web/20120220154544/http://www.humanism .org.uk/bus-campaign.

17. "The Intelligence[2] Debate: Atheism Is the New Fundamentalism?," debate between Richard Dawkins, A. C. Grayling, Richard Harries, and Charles Moore, Wellington College, November 29, 2009, http://www.atheistmedia.com/2009/11.

18. "The Intelligence[2] Debate," 4:55, 5:54.

19. "Richard Dawkins Says He Won't Debate William Lane Craig," The Intelligence[2] Debate, Wellington College, November 29, 2009, 0:36, https://www.youtube.com/watch?v=JFam S4RGE_A.

20. Quentin Smith, "Kalam Cosmological Arguments for Atheism,"

in *The Cambridge Companion to Atheism*, ed. Michael Martin (Cambridge: Cambridge University Press, 2007), 183.

21. "Richard Dawkins Says He Won't Debate."

22. Dawkins, *The God Delusion*, 158.

23. "Who Designed the Designer? A response to Dawkins' The God Delusion by Dr. William Lane Craig," 100huntley.com, April 30, 2009, https://youtu.be/wcHp_LWGgGw.

24. Paul Copan and William Lane Craig, eds., *Contending with Christianity's Critics: Answering New Atheists and Other Objectors* (Nashville: Broadman & Holman), 2–5, https://www.reasonablefaith.org/writings/popular-writings/existence-nature-of-god/dawkins-delusion/.

25. Dawkins, *The God Delusion*, 149.

26. Dawkins, *The God Delusion*, 158.

27. Sir Anthony Kenny, "Knowledge, Faith and Belief," *Philosophy* 82, no. 321 (July 2007): 391.

28. For example: "Entities that are complex enough to be intelligent are products of an evolutionary process," Dawkins, *The God Delusion*, 98. Statements like these merely assert the materialism underlying Dawkins's central argument instead of attempting to justify it.

29. Thomas Nagel, "The Fear of Religion," *The New Republic* (October 22, 2006): 26, https://newrepublic.com/article/65012/the-fear-religion.

30. Scott Hahn and Benjamin Wiker, *Answering the New Atheism: Dismantling Dawkins' Case Against God* (Steubenville, OH: Emmaus Road, 2008), 63.

31. William Lane Craig, "The Resurrection of Jesus," Reasonable Faith, accessed January 9, 2023, https://www.reasonablefaith.org/writings/popular-writings/jesus-of-nazareth/the-resurrection-of-jesus.

32. "Richard Dawkins vs John Lennox | Has Science Buried God?

Debate," Oxford Museum of Natural History, October 21, 2008, 33:00, https://youtu.be/OVEuQg_Mglw?t=1980.

33. "Richard Dawkins vs John Lennox," 39:33.

34. "Richard Dawkins vs John Lennox," 34:46.

35. Sam Harris, "The God Debate II: Harris vs. Craig," University of Notre Dame, April 7, 2011, 27:42, https://youtu.be/yqa HXKLRKzg?t=1662.

36. William Lane Craig, "The God Debate II: Harris vs. Craig," University of Notre Dame, April 7, 2011, 52:25, https://youtu .be/yqaHXKLRKzg?t=3145.

37. Kevin Harris and William Lane Craig, "Richard Dawkins meets Dr. Craig," podcast, *Reasonable Faith*, January 11, 2011, https://www.reasonablefaith.org/media/reasonable-faith-pod cast/richard-dawkins-meets-dr.-craig, recording at http://con tent.blubrry.com/reasonable_faith/Richard_Dawkins_Meets _Dr_Craig.mp3.

38. Tim Ross, "Richard Dawkins Accused of Cowardice for Refusing to Debate Existence of God," *The Telegraph*, May 14, 2011, https://www.telegraph.co.uk/news/religion/8511931/Richard -Dawkins-accused-of-cowardice-for-refusing-to-debate-exis tence-of-God.html.

39. Richard Dawkins, online forum comment, Richard Dawkins Foundation for Reason and Science, May 28, 2011, part of a thread of comments beginning from post #631683. The forum has since been closed, but screenshot documentation of these comments exists in "British Humanists (Toynbee, Dawkins & Grayling) Run from William Lane Craig," 1:55, https://www .youtube.com/watch?v=0mioJYqRVDE&t=113s.

40. William Lane Craig, "Is God a Delusion?," lecture at the University of Oxford, October 25, 2011, https://youtu.be/fP9CwDTR oOE.

41. "The Case for Christian Theism: The Reasonable Faith UK

Tour," Reasonable Faith, posted July 15, 2019, https://youtu.be
/vCa9WQBrARc.

42. Anthony Kenny, "Dialogue with Richard Dawkins, Rowan
Williams and Anthony Kenny," Oxford University, February
23, 2012, 1:14:47, https://youtu.be/bow4nnh1Wv0?t=4487.

43. Richard Dawkins, "Dialogue with Richard Dawkins, Rowan
Williams and Anthony Kenny," Oxford University, February
23, 2012, 1:14:47, https://www.youtube.com/watch?v=bow4nn
h1Wv0&t=4487s.

44. Richard Dawkins, "Q&A: Pell vs Dawkins—April 9, Easter
Monday Night," Richard Dawkins Foundation for Reason and
Science online forum, discussion thread, April 10, 2012, post
#933553. The forum has since been closed, but screenshot docu-
mentation of this post exists in these videos: 1:05, https://youtu
.be/O5mlMJXJ_nQ?t=65 and 0:33, https://youtu.be/015sSV
svVg8?t=33.

45. *The Unbelievers*, JJC Films & Primordial Productions, 2013,
14:23.

46. The specific type of biblical counseling I received was modeled
on the principles of the Christian Counseling and Education
Foundation (CCEF). Biblical Counselling UK is the name of
the movement that is working to make this approach more
widespread and available in the United Kingdom.

Chapter 4: A Winding Path Through New Atheism to Faith

1. Richard Dawkins, *The God Delusion* (London: Transworld,
2006), 15, 56, 83.

2. Hannah Furness, "Richard Dawkins: Churchgoers Enable Fundamentalists by Being 'Nice,'" *The Daily Telegraph*, August
13, 2014.

3. Christopher Hitchens, *God Is Not Great: How Religion Poisons Everything* (New York: Twelve Books, 2007).

4. Christopher Hitchens, "Why Women Aren't Funny," *Vanity Fair* (January 2007), https://www.vanityfair.com/culture/2007/01/hitchens200701.

5. Dawkins, *The God Delusion*, 43.

Chapter 5: Hearing God Through an Enchantment with Nature

1. Members of the order Passeriformes, or "perching birds." The order contains more than half of all bird species in the world, which in total may range from ten thousand to twenty thousand, depending on how a species is defined; see G. F. Barrowclough, J. Cracraft, J. Klicka, and R. M. Zink, "How Many Kinds of Birds Are There and Why Does It Matter?" *PLoS ONE* 11 (November 2016): e0166307, https://doi.org/10.1371/journal.pone.0166307.

2. C. T. Downs, R. J. van Dyk, and P. Iji, "Wax Digestion by the Lesser Honeyguide *Indicator minor*," *Comparative Biochemistry and Physiology Part A: Molecular & Integrative Physiology* 133, no. 1 (Sept. 2002): 125–34.

3. L. L. Short and J. F. M. Horne, "Family *Indicatoridae* (Honeyguides)," in *Handbook of Birds of the World*, vol. 7, *Jacamars to Woodpeckers*, ed. J. del Hoyo, A. Elliott, and J. Sargatal (Barcelona: Lynx Edicions, 2002), 274–95.

4. K. A. Dogantzis et al., "Thrice out of Asia and the Adaptive Radiation of the Western Honey Bee," *Science Advances* 7, no. 49 (Dec. 2021), https://www.science.org/doi/10.1126/sciadv.abj2151.

5. Short and Horne, "Family *Indicatoridae* (Honeyguides)," 275.

6. Developed through the early twentieth century, the "neo-Darwinian" model linked Charles Darwin's theory of evolution by natural selection with the new science of genetics. Lacking knowledge of the biochemistry of inheritance or genetic change, the neo-Darwinists assumed that genetic change arose spontaneously as random mutation.

7. No published theory of the emergence of *Homo sapiens* acknowledges the part inevitably played by other species in the dynamic narrative of negotiation and renegotiation with nature that was human evolution: nature in dialogue with Adam.

8. A long-running debate over whether greater honeyguides might guide honey badgers (*Mellivora capensis*) suggests that they probably follow them rather than lead and that individuals experienced with human honey hunters might attempt to lead honey badgers by giving the "leading" calls, but there is no evidence that they succeed. See J. E. Fincham, R. Peek, and M. B. Markus, "The Greater Honeyguide: Reciprocal Signalling and Innate Recognition of a Honey Badger," *Biodiversity Observations* 8, no. 12 (March 2017): 1–6.

9. I am indebted to Claire Spottiswoode for many honeyguide details.

10. This relationship is unique also because no other wild bird species in the world shows such a specific interdependence with humans. See Dominic L. Cram et al., "The Ecology and Evolution of Human-Wildlife Cooperation," *People & Nature* 4, no. 4 (June 2022): 841–55.

11. Hussein Adan Isack, "The Biology of the Greater Honeyguide *Indicator indicator*, with Emphasis on the Guiding Behaviour" (PhD thesis, University of Oxford, 1987).

12. See Hussein A. Isack, "The Role of Culture, Traditions and Local Knowledge in Co-Operative Honey-Hunting between Man and Honeyguide: A Case Study of Boran Community of Northern Kenya," in *Proceedings of the 22nd International Ornithological Congress held in Durban, South Africa, 1998*, ed. N. J. Adams and R. H. Slotow (Johannesburg: BirdLife South Africa, 1999), 1351–57.

13. Such desecration of sacred space reminds us of Isaiah 1:12, "this trampling of my courts." See also "Everest Clean-Up Campaign

Aims to Airlift 100 Tonnes of Waste," BBC News, March 17, 2018, https://www.bbc.co.uk/news/world-asia-43443196.

14. Julian Huxley, *Evolution: The Modern Synthesis* (London: Allen & Unwin, 1942).

15. See, e.g., Denis Noble, *The Music of Life: Biology beyond Genes* (Oxford: Oxford University Press, 2006).

16. Richard Dawkins, *The Selfish Gene* (Oxford: Oxford University Press, 1976).

17. Andrew G. Gosler, "Surprise and the Value of Life," in *True Scientists, True Faith: Some of the World's Leading Scientists Reveal the Harmony between Their Science and Their Faith*, ed. R. J. Berry (Oxford: Monarch Books, 2014), 176–95.

18. Isaiah 1:12–17 gives instruction that the nature of right religious action is founded on love and the kindness that comes from that; Romans 8:28 expresses this sense of mutual dependency as all things working together for the good of those who love God.

19. Noble, *The Music of Life*; Denis Noble, *Dance to the Tune of Life: Biological Relativity* (Cambridge: Cambridge University Press, 2017).

20. S. T. Emlen and P. H. Wrege, "The Role of Kinship in Helping Decisions among White-Fronted Bee-Eaters," *Behavioral Ecology and Sociobiology* 23, no. 5 (1988): 305–15.

21. James Shapiro, *Evolution: A View from the 21st Century* (Upper Saddle River, NJ: FT Press Science, 2011); Noble, *The Music of Life*; Noble, *Dance to the Tune of Life*.

22. I shall explore this rich territory elsewhere.

23. Note that the Greek word *krisis* means "judgment."

24. A description offered by my poet wife, Dr. Caroline Jackson-Houlston, when I first described this perception of time to her.

25. James Lovelock, *Gaia: A New Look at Life on Earth* (Oxford: Oxford University Press, 2000).

26. Richard Dawkins, *The Extended Phenotype: The Long Reach of the Gene* (Oxford: Oxford University Press, 1982), 209–10.

27. Saint Francis, who eight hundred years after his birth was to become the patron saint of ecology, was baptized in the cathedral church of San Rufino in Assisi. This church was built on the site of a Roman temple dedicated to the earth goddess, Gaia. Our beloved Francis wrote in the "Canticle of the Creatures": "Be praised my Lord for sister, our mother earth, who sustains and governs us and produces diverse fruits and coloured flowers and grass." Society of Saint Francis, *The Daily Office SSF* (London: Bloomsbury Continuum, 2010), 530–33. All things, both in time and space, are connected in the mind of God.

28. Short and Horne, "Family *Indicatoridae* (Honeyguides)," 282.

29. Short and Horne, "Family *Indicatoridae* (Honeyguides)," 286.

30. Great tit sexes differ in bill size and shape, adapting them subtly to different ecological niches.

31. Sonia Tidemann and Andrew Gosler, *Ethno-ornithology: Birds, Indigenous People, Culture and Society* (London: Earthscan, 2010).

32. J. Ruka, *Huia Come Home* (Auckland: Oati, 2017).

Chapter 6: An Afrikaner's Faith Pilgrimage

1. Although see chapter 8 for an exception.

2. Aldous Huxley, *Ends and Means: An Enquiry into the Nature of Ideals* (New York: Harper & Brothers, 1937), 270, 273.

3. "The Bus Campaign: What Was the 'Atheist Bus Campaign'?," British Humanist Association, February 20, 2012, https://web.archive.org/web/20120220154544/http://www.humanism.org.uk/bus-campaign.

4. Laurence J. Peter, comp. and ed., *Peter's Quotations: Ideas for Our Times* (New York: HarperCollins, 1977), 44.

5. Peter Boghossian, *A Manual for Creating Atheists* (Durham,

NC: Pitchstone, 2013), 79. For a more concise summary, see "Street Epistemology: The Basics," Street Epistemology International, accessed January 10, 2023, https://streetepistemology .com/blog/street-epistemology-the-basics.

6. N. T. Wright's book *The Resurrection of the Son of God* (Minneapolis: Fortress Press, 2003) is a monumental work. It is 850-odd pages of serious scholarship by probably the most prominent theologian of the last few years. For most, myself included, it can be too much. Perhaps a more digestible suggestion is to skip to pages 585–616 and 683–738, which focus more on the historicity of the resurrection accounts.

7. I recommend *The Bible Project* podcast as well. Tim Mackie, who is the main contributor, has wonderful biblical themes that he unpacks in the episodes. N. T. Wright as a Bible commentator makes the Bible come alive in ways I didn't think possible. See https//bibleproject.com/podcasts/the-bible-project-podcast.

8. C. S. Lewis, "Is Theology Poetry?," in *They Asked For a Paper: Papers and Addresses* (London: Geoffrey Bles, 1962), 164–65.

9. Matthew Parris, "As an Atheist, I Truly Believe Africa Needs God," *London Times*, December 27, 2008, https://www.thetimes .co.uk/article/as-an-atheist-i-truly-believe-africa-needs-god-3x j9bm80h8m.

10. Boghossian, *Manual for Creating Atheists*, 31

11. Tom Holland, *Dominion: How the Christian Revolution Remade the World* (New York: Basic Books, 2019), 13.

12. Robert Barron, *Seeds of the Word: Finding God in the Culture* (Skokie, IL: Word on Fire, 2015), 84–87.

13. Lesslie Newbigin, *Honest Religion for Secular Man* (London: SCM, 1966), 76.

14. See Andrew Sullivan, "America's New Religions," *Intelligencer*, December 7, 2018, https://nymag.com/intelligencer/2018/12 /andrew-sullivan-americas-new-religions.html.

15. Francis Fukuyama, *Identity: Contemporary Identity Politics and the Struggle for Recognition* (London: Profile Books, 2018), 97–98.

16. Aleksandr Solzhenitsyn, *The Gulag Archipelago: 1918–1956* (New York: Harper & Row, 1974), 312.

17. Miroslav Volf, *Exclusion and Embrace: A Theological Exploration of Identity, Otherness, and Reconciliation* (Nashville: Abingdon, 2019), 68.

18. See John McWhorter, "The Virtue Signalers Won't Change the World," *The Atlantic*, December 23, 2018, https://www.the atlantic.com/ideas/archive/2018/12/why-third-wave-anti-rac ism-dead-end/578764.

19. Thomas Cahill, *Desire of the Everlasting Hills: The World Before and After Jesus* (New York: Random House, 1999), 141.

20. Of this statement, the Society of G. K. Chesterton says, "This story has been repeated so often about Chesterton that we suspect it is true. Also, it seems it is never told about anyone other than Chesterton. What we have not found, however, is any documentary evidence for it. It may indeed be from *The Times*, as the story is usually told, but no one has taken the trouble to go through the back issues and find a copy of the actual letter." "What's Wrong with the World," Society of G. K. Chesterton, April 29, 2012, http://chesterton.org/wrong-with-world.

21. Greg Lukianoff and Jonathan Haidt, *The Coddling of the American Mind: How Good Intentions and Bad Ideas Are Setting Up a Generation for Failure* (New York: Penguin, 2018), 47–48.

22. *Collateral*, directed by Michael Mann, written by Stuart Beattie (Los Angeles, CA: Dreamworks Pictures and Paramount Pictures, 2004).

23. *Fargo*, season 1, episode 2, "The Rooster Prince," directed by Adam Bernstein, written by Noah Hawley, April 22, 2014, on FX.

24. "More People Drawn to Religion after Disasters," Radio New

Zealand, December 9, 2012, https://www.rnz.co.nz/news/canter bury-earthquake/122972/more-people-drawn-to-religion -after-disasters.

25. Van der Post argues that distance between the occurrence of an original political injustice and the remembering subject often leads to an intensification of feelings of resentment. This can be ascribed to, among other things, the power of the imagination. Laurens van der Post, *Venture to the Interior* (Middlesex: Penguin, 1957), 26.

Chapter 7: Coming to Faith via The God Delusion

1. "Why There Almost Certainly Is No God" is the title of chapter 4 in *The God Delusion*.
2. Richard Dawkins, *The God Delusion* (London: Black Swan, 2006), 151.
3. Dawkins, *The God Delusion*, 100–101.
4. Quoted in Dawkins, *The God Delusion*, 7.
5. Dawkins, *The God Delusion*, 137–39.
6. Dawkins, *The God Delusion*, 251.
7. Dawkins, *The God Delusion*, 147–48, 150.
8. John Lennox, "The Monkey Machine," in *God's Undertaker: Has Science Buried God?* (London: Lion Books, 2007), 163–73.
9. Dawkins, *The God Delusion*, 283.
10. Dawkins, *The God Delusion*, 283.
11. Dawkins, *The God Delusion*, 299.

Chapter 8: The God Delusion and Probability

1. Huck Gutman, "Walt Whitman's *Song of Myself*," in *The Oxford Encyclopedia of American Literature*, vol. 4, ed. Jay Parini (Oxford: Oxford University Press, 2004), 696.
2. Fred Hoyle, *The Intelligent Universe* (London: Michael Joseph Limited, 1983), 19.

3. Fred Hoyle, "The Universe: Past and Present Reflections," *Engineering and Science* 45, no. 2 (November 1981): 8–12.

4. Richard Dawkins, *The Blind Watchmaker* (Harlow: Longman, 1986), 11.

5. Richard Dawkins, *The God Delusion* (London: Bantam Books, 2006), 114.

6. Dawkins, *The God Delusion*, 153.

7. Leonard Mlodinow, *The Drunkard's Walk: How Randomness Rules Our Lives* (London: Allen Lane, 2008), 23.

8. Daniel Dennett, quoted in Dawkins, *The God Delusion*, 157.

9. Daniel Dennett, *Darwin's Dangerous Idea* (New York: Simon & Schuster, 1995), 155.

10. Dawkins, *The Blind Watchmaker*, 13.

11. Dawkins, *The Blind Watchmaker*, 13.

12. Dawkins, *The Blind Watchmaker*, 13.

13. *Microsoft Encarta*, Standard Version (CD-ROM, 2006), s.v., "Natural Selection."

14. Dawkins, *The God Delusion*, 138.

15. A. J. Ayer, *Probability and Evidence* (London: MacMillan, 1972), 40–41.

16. Gilbert Ryle, *The Concept of Mind* (Abingdon, UK: Routledge, 2009), 11.

17. Dawkins, *The God Delusion*, 83.

18. Brandon Carter, "Large Number Coincidences and the Anthropic Principle in Cosmology," *Symposium—International Astronomical Union* 63 (1974): 291–98, quoted in Dawkins, *The God Delusion*, 83.

Chapter 9: My Egyptian Journey to Faith

1. Dawkins makes a similar point in *The God Delusion* (London: Bantam Press, 2006), 77.

2. "Does God Exist? William Lane Craig vs. Christopher Hitch-

ens—Full Debate [HD]," April 4, 2009, 51:36, https://www
.youtube.com/watch?v=0tYm41hb48o.

3. See "God Is Not Great by Christopher Hitchens," Unfebuck-
inglievable, April 19, 2012, https://unfebuckinglievable.word
press.com/2012/04/19/god-is-not-great-by-christopher-hitchens.

4. Gary R. Habermas and Michael R. Licona, *The Case for the
Resurrection of Jesus* (Grand Rapids: Kregel, 2004).

Chapter 10: From Lukewarm Theism to Committed Faith

1. Richard Dawkins, *The God Delusion* (New York: Houghton
Mifflin, 2006).

2. Pope Benedict XVI, Joseph Ratzinger, *Jesus of Nazareth: From
the Baptism in the Jordan to the Transfiguration*, trans. Adrian
J. Walker (New York: Doubleday, 2007).

3. Plato, "Euthyphro" in *Five Dialogues: Euthyphro, Apology,
Crito, Meno, Phaedo*, 2nd ed., trans. G. M. A. Grube, rev. John
M. Cooper (Indianapolis: Hackett, 2002), 8.

4. Dawkins, *The God Delusion*, 159.

5. G. K. Chesterton, *The Catholic Church and Conversion* (San
Francisco: Ignatius, 2006), chap. 2, Kindle.

6. Dawkins, *The God Delusion*, 58.

7. Dawkins, *The God Delusion*, 116.

8. Dawkins, *The God Delusion*, 116.

9. Author summary of Dawkins's points from Dawkins, *The God
Delusion*, 187–88.

10. Dawkins, *The God Delusion*, 165.

11. Dawkins, *The God Delusion*, 153.

12. Pope Benedict XVI, *Jesus of Nazareth*, xxii.

13. Pope Benedict XVI, *Jesus of Nazareth*, 43.

14. Pope Benedict XVI, *Jesus of Nazareth*, 36.

15. Pope Benedict XVI, *Jesus of Nazareth*, 193.

16. Chesterton, *Catholic Church and Conversion*, chap. 3.

17. Fulton J. Sheen, quoted in Mason Beecroft, "The Evangelical Ministry of Fulton Sheen," Alcuin Institute for Catholic Culture, May 12, 2022, https://alcuininstitute.org/writings/essays/god -loves-you-the-evangelical-ministry-of-the-venerable-fulton-sheen.
18. Chesterton, *Catholic Church and Conversion*, chap. 4.
19. Chesterton, *Catholic Church and Conversion*, chap. 4.
20. Chesterton, *Catholic Church and Conversion*, chap. 4.

Chapter 11: From Religion to Agnosticism to Faith in Christ via Dawkins

1. Tiaan Gildenhuys, *Maak Skoon Jou Huis* (Pretoria, South Africa: Groep 7 Drukkers en Uitgewers, 2006).
2. Thomas Paine, *The Age of Reason* (New York: Dover, 2004).
3. One documentary expounding the view that Jesus was a mythical person that I found compelling at the time was *The God Who Wasn't There*, directed by Brian Flemming (Beyond Belief Media, 2005).
4. *The Blind Watchmaker*, produced by Jeremy Taylor and Richard Dawkins (London: BBC, 1987); *The Genius of Charles Darwin*, presented by Richard Dawkins (London: IWC Media, 2008).
5. *The Root of All Evil?*, directed by Russell Barnes, written by Richard Dawkins (London: Channel 4, 2006).
6. Some of the more impactful debates that I watched during that time include: William Lane Craig and Christopher Hitchens, "Does God Exist? William Lane Craig vs. Christopher Hitchens—Full Debate [HD]," 2009, Biola University, https://youtu .be /0tYm41hb48o; *The God Delusion Debate*, Richard Dawkins vs. John Lennox, disc 1 (Birmingham, AL: Fixed Point Foundation, 2007), DVD; "The God Debate II: Harris vs. Craig," University of Notre Dame, 2011, https://www.you tube.com/watch?v=yqaHXKLRKzg; "Does God Exist? (Frank Turek vs Christopher Hitchens)," 2008, https://www.youtube

.com/watch?v=S7WBEJJlYWU; "Poison or Cure? Religious Belief in the Modern World (with Christopher Hitchens and Alister McGrath)," Georgetown University, 2007, https://www.youtube.com/watch?v=Xc0kbM4tBYE; "Debate: Richard Carrier vs. Mike Licona," 2010, https://www.youtube.com/watch?v=0IpKHdVLZb4.

7. See William Lane Craig, *On Guard: Defending Your Faith with Reason and Precision* (Colorado Springs: David C Cook, 2010); Alister McGrath, *Why God Won't Go Away: Engaging with the New Atheism* (London: SPCK, 2011); James Porter Moreland, *The God Question* (Eugene, OR: Harvest House, 2009).

8. Doug Powell, *Holman Quicksource Guide to Christian Apologetics* (Nashville: Holman Reference, 2006); Lee Strobel, *The Case for Christ: A Journalist's Personal Investigation of the Evidence for Jesus* (Grand Rapids: Zondervan, 2001).

Chapter 12: Seeking the Truth via New Atheism and Psychedelic Drugs

1. Christopher Hitchens, *God Is Not Great: How Religion Poisons Everything* (New York: Hachette, 2007), 120.

2. Hitchens, *God Is Not Great*, 111.

3. Hitchens, *God Is Not Great*, 13.

4. Horatio Spafford and Philip Bliss, "It Is Well with My Soul," 1876, public domain.

5. Gotthold Lessing, *Anti-Goeze* (1778), quoted in Hitchens in *God Is Not Great*, 277.

6. Hitchens, *God Is Not Great*, 278.

7. C. S. Lewis, *The Great Divorce: A Dream* (New York: Simon & Schuster, 2001), 39–41.

8. Christopher Hitchens, "God Bless Me, It's a Best-Seller!," *Vanity Fair*, August 15, 2007, https://www.vanityfair.com/news/2007/09/hitchens200709.

9. Frederick Buechner, *Secrets in the Dark: A Life in Sermons* (New York: HarperCollins, 2007), 28.

10. Larry Taunton, *The Faith of Christopher Hitchens: The Restless Soul of the World's Most Notorious Atheist* (Nashville: Thomas Nelson, 2016), 4.

About the Contributors

The Editors

Dr. Denis Alexander is the cofounder of The Faraday Institute for Science and Religion in Cambridge (www.faraday.cam.ac.uk), where he is Emeritus Fellow of St. Edmund's College. He is a past chair of the Molecular Immunology Programme and Head of the Laboratory of Lymphocyte Signalling and Development at The Babraham Institute in Cambridge. Alexander was previously at the Imperial Cancer Research Laboratories in London (now Cancer Research UK). From 1992 to 2013 he was Editor of the journal *Science and Christian Belief.* Alexander's latest books are *Is There Purpose in Biology?* and *Are We Slaves to Our Genes?*

Professor Alister McGrath studied Chemistry at Oxford University before gaining his doctorate in Molecular Biophysics under the supervision of Professor Sir George Radda, while at the same time studying theology. A former atheist, McGrath has a particular interest in the relation of science and faith and has been heavily involved in debates with the leading representatives (including Richard Dawkins) and ideas of New Atheism. He has served in several senior academic roles at Oxford, including Andreas Idreos Professor of Science and Religion. He is the author of the international bestseller *The*

Dawkins Delusion? but is probably most known for his best-selling textbook *Christian Theology: An Introduction.*

The Authors

Sy (Seymour) Garte has a PhD in Biochemistry and is the author of the award-winning book *The Works of His Hands: A Scientist's Journey from Atheism to Faith.* He has been a tenured professor at three major US universities and held leadership positions at the National Institutes of Health (NIH) and the Uniformed Services University. Garte has published more than two hundred peer-reviewed scientific papers and five books, as well as articles on science and Christian faith. He is a fellow of the American Scientific Affiliation (ASA) and serves as the editor in chief of the ASA's quarterly online magazine *God and Nature.*

Dr. Sarah Irving-Stonebraker is Associate Professor of History and Western Civilization at Australian Catholic University. She received her BA with First-Class Honours and the University Medal from the University of Sydney in 2003, followed by a PhD in history from Cambridge University (2007), where she was a Commonwealth Scholar at King's College. Irving-Stonebraker was later a Junior Research Fellow at Wolfson College, Oxford University, and then Assistant Professor at Florida State University. Her book entitled *Natural Science and the Origins of the British Empire* was awarded the Royal Society of Literature and Jerwood Foundation Award for Non-Fiction.

Peter Byrom grew up in the United Kingdom loving art, films, and acting; attended the Year Out Drama company in Stratford-upon-Avon (where he was awarded Best Hamlet Soliloquy by Christopher Nolan's uncle); and studied Drama and Theater at the University of Kent. It was there that exposure to Christian apologetics awoke his left brain to combine these passions with analytic philosophy. Byrom has gone on to support apologetics through media production, publishing, and administration. He is a champion of the Getting Things Done® "stress-free productivity" methodology, loves wildlife (swans especially), and lives in the United Kingdom with his wife, Helen, and their two children.

Anikó Albert grew up in Budapest, Hungary, in the latter years of the socialist era and is a graduate of Eötvös Loránd University. A serial migrant, she taught English as a foreign language in Budapest; high school Spanish in Kingston, Jamaica; and English and various other subjects in Alameda, California. She is currently managing editor of *God and Nature*, an online magazine published by the American Scientific Affiliation, and executive director of Rockville Help, an interfaith emergency-assistance charitable organization in Rockville, Maryland. She is the mother of two adult children.

Reverend Professor Andrew G. Gosler is Professor of Ethno-ornithology at the University of Oxford, a joint position between the Edward Grey Institute of Field Ornithology (in biology) and Institute of Human Sciences (in anthropology). He is also Fellow in Human Sciences at Mansfield College, teaching courses in ecology, evolution, ethnobiology, and conservation, and is research director of the Ethno-ornithology World Atlas project (www.ewatlas.net), cofounded with BirdLife International. A childhood fascination with birds led both to a career in ornithology and to faith. A third order Franciscan, he has been an ordained minister in the Church of England since 2018.

Johan Erasmus has degrees in philosophy and theology and is currently doing his PhD at the North-West University in South Africa on the subject of race and reconciliation. He pastors a small multi-cultural church in Pretoria called Dialogue Community and is also involved with the Betereinders movement focusing on social development and reconciliation. He is married to Loraine, a film lecturer, and they have two boys, Louw and Eben.

Nick Berryman is an Engineering Manager for a cutting-edge technology company, a role that provides the opportunity to solve challenging technical problems. He is married to Ruth, and they have two preschool boys. Berryman is currently serving as a lay elder at Above Bar Church in Southampton in the United Kingdom. Balancing the responsibilities of those roles—home, church, and work—is the perennial challenge, requiring wisdom and grace for each day. His passions include running and camping, and he is attempting to coax his sons into the latter.

Louise Mabille is a Nietzsche scholar, holding a PhD on Nietzsche's theory of justice and a PhD in English on John Milton's parrhesia; her research examined the Protestant tradition of speaking truth to power. She is the author of, among others, *The Rage of Caliban: Nietzsche and Wilde Contra Modernity* and *Nietzsche and the Anglo-Saxon Tradition*. More recent publications include academic essays on Marx, Darwin, and D. F. Strauss, and *The Morality Wars*, coedited with Henk Stoker and featuring essays by Sam Harris, William Lane Craig, John Lennox, Michael Ruse, Paul Copan, Jonathan Haidt, Richard Howe, and the late Steven Weinberg.

Rafik Samuel grew up in Alexandria, Egypt, and currently lives in Cairo. He is a graduate of the American University in Cairo. Samuel studied Philosophy and Political Science, with a deep yearning to find answers to life's biggest questions: Does God exist? What is a life worth living? What is an ideal society? These are the questions that have animated most of his life. He currently works as a researcher at Egypt's Ministry of International Cooperation. Previously a skeptic regarding religious belief, he now loves Jesus and is passionate about serving in his church's youth group and engaging in deep conversations with others.

Judith R. Babarsky graduated from the International School of Bangkok in Thailand during the height of the Vietnam War, an experience that taught her to appreciate many different cultures and belief systems. She went on to Wellesley College and Virginia Tech in the United States, earning a BS in Sociology. She earned an MS in Clinical Psychology at Radford University and an MA in Theology from Holy Apostles College and Seminary. She is a licensed professional counselor (LPC) and has engaged in private practice for twenty-five years. She and her husband live near Washington, DC. They have five grown children and six grandchildren.

Waldo Swart grew up in Pretoria, South Africa. He completed a BA in Information Design at the University of Pretoria and is now a graphic designer and website developer. He is married to Isabella, an English lecturer. They have two awesome dogs, Tashi and Raven. Swart enjoys reading popular science and philosophy, and he dabbles in theology and apologetics from time to time. He is involved at Dialogue Community, an apologetics-focused church. He enjoys hiking and playing board games. He still enjoys the metal music he discovered in his childhood.

Ashley Lande is an American writer and artist. Her writing has been published in *Fathom* and *Ekstasis* magazines, and her artwork has been shown in galleries in London, New York, Los Angeles, and Melbourne. She is writing a memoir to be published by Lexham Press about her journey from seeking transcendence through psychedelic drugs to becoming a follower of Jesus Christ. She lives in rural Kansas with her husband and three children.

GOOD FAITH AND GOOD SCIENCE SHOULDN'T BE ENEMIES

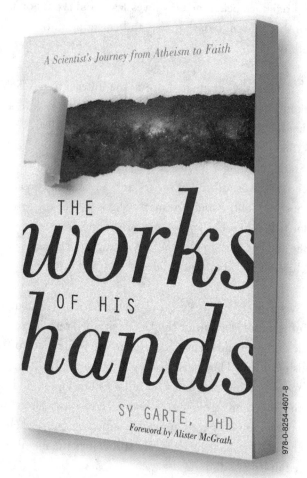

A Scientist's Journey from Atheism to Faith

THE
works
OF HIS
hands

SY GARTE, PHD
Foreword by *Alister McGrath*

978-0-8254-4607-8

"Garte's insights, offered in narrative and creative storytelling, provide a road map for reconciling science and faith, both for spiritual seekers peeking over the fence from the yard of agnosticism and for worried believers gazing out the chapel window at the so-called challenges of modern science."
—STEPHEN O. MOSHIER, professor of geology at Wheaton College

KREGEL
PUBLICATIONS